Narrative and History

Alun Munslow

palgrave
macmillan

First published 2007 by
PALGRAVE MACMILLAN
Houndmills, Basingstoke, Hampshire RG21 6XS and
175 Fifth Avenue, New York, N.Y. 10010
Companies and representatives throughout the world

PALGRAVE MACMILLAN is the global academic imprint of the Palgrave
Macmillan division of St. Martin's Press, LLC and of Palgrave Macmillan Ltd.
Macmillan® is a registered trademark in the United States, United Kingdom
and other countries. Palgrave is a registered trademark in the European
Union and other countries.

ISBN-13: 978–1–4039–8728–0
ISBN-10: 1–4039–8728–9

This book is printed on paper suitable for recycling and made from fully
managed and sustained forest sources. Logging, pulping and manufacturing
processes are expected to conform to the environmental regulations of the
country of origin.

A catalogue record for this book is available from the British Library.

A catalog record for this book is available from the Library of Congress.

10   9   8   7   6   5   4   3   2   1
16   15   14   13   12   11   10   09   08   07

Printed in China

As always, for Jane

Contents

Conclusion   123

Acknowledgements

The completion of any book is an opportunity to thank those who have been a part of its creation. My thanks, therefore, to Robert A. Rosenstone, Keith Jenkins and Beverley Southgate, who gave me the benefit of their thoughts on earlier drafts of this book. I also thank them for showing me, in their different ways, how it is possible to rethink history. More recently I have benefited from working with David Harlan as the US co-editor of *Rethinking History: The Journal of Theory and Practice*. There are also many other friends and colleagues with whom, for over 30 years of teaching, I shared the academic grind. My thanks to them all. However, I wish particularly to acknowledge the collegiality and the friendship of Owen R. Ashton.

Introduction

The aim of this book is very simple. It is to explain how historians make, and specifically, *write* **history**. By that I mean what 'rules', 'procedures', 'figurative' and 'compositional techniques' do historians follow and what decisions do they make in **order** to turn 'the past' into that **narrative** about it we choose to call 'history'? It follows from what I have just said that the basic assumption behind the book is that history is a form of narrative written by historians. Professional historians are generally well aware of the construction of historical **explanation**s – especially the basics of hunting out the **sources** and the most appropriate ways to work out what they mean. Indeed, many historians have written at length about the techniques of source analysis and **inference**. However, discussions of the nature of history *as a narrative-making* exercise have primarily been left to a few philosophers of history who have an interest in what seem to be matters largely irrelevant to practitioners who actually do the job. Because of this deficiency, I offer in this book an introduction to the nature of the history narrative. That requires that I outline the rules of, and functional relationships that exist in, the actual writing of history as a narrative form. I will be illustrating this mainly from twentieth-century historiography.

Clearly, there are many kinds of written as well as non-written narratives. There are novels, films, comics, digital games, university lectures, church windows, ballet, dramatic play, annual reports of accounts and, of course, histories. It is because history is a species of narrative that it is useful to examine how it is created and how it relates to the claims usually made that history explains and offers **meaning**ful interpretations about the past. When we have a general guide to the writing of history, we are better placed to understand how individual histories work and can assess their claims to understanding the nature of the past.

Precisely because history is a form of literature the rules of historical writing or, to be precise, historical authorship are derived from the nature, production and operation of narrative. Though occasionally modified according to the peculiarities of the discipline, the history narrative – as with all narratives – is concerned with the general process of **representation**. While, no doubt, a few historians remain blissfully unaware of the status of historical writing as a mode of representation,

happily most understand that their fundamental task is the construction of a narrative *about* the past. It is for this reason that all students of history should have access to a primer that describes that activity. Though this book is necessarily brief, my approach is holistic because I address the theory and practice of historical authorship and historical representation within which the **empirical**, the analytical and all other aspects of historical study are encompassed.

As you will probably be aware, most 'what is history?' texts still tend to begin with how historians find out what happened in the past according to the sources. They then explain why events occurred as they did and, most important of all, interpret 'what it all means' with the 'results' or 'findings' of this complex activity – the explanation and meaning – then being put into a prose narrative.[1] In other words, this simple mechanism is said to reproduce the 'coherent **reality**' of the past, which is then rendered with analytical **objectivity** as a historical narrative that conveys the most likely **truth** of the past. This is why in such texts we have the strong sense of ' . . . here is the true **story** of . . . '.

Most if not all historians write history to correct what they view as the shortcomings of previous generations to open up hitherto neglected facets of the past. Moreover, they acknowledge that certain aspects of the past such as race, class, gender and women's experiences are often silent in terms of sources, and this requires the application of fresh conceptualisation and theorisation.[2] It is clear that most historians have a highly developed sense of what constitutes their disciplinary theory and practice. Nevertheless, because they continue to regard the notion of **reference** as absolutely fundamental, most tend to ignore the significance to generating explanation and meaning of their 'poetic' or 'writerly' processes. So, while historians understand what they mean by sources, events, reference, the nature of explanation, objectivity, meaning and so on, there is still a tendency to be less clear on concepts like authorship, story, expression, **voice**, **focalisation** and, most importantly, the nature of narrative itself.

This is indicated by the debates within mainstream historical thought. Until the so called **postmodern** revolution in historical thinking and practice of the past 15–20 years or so, the conventional view of history was often summarised in the debate between E.H. Carr and Geoffrey Elton over the nature of history.[3] Carr described the essence of history as causal analysis stiffened with substantial doses of theory as judged appropriate by the historian. This is a classic view of history as a faithful construction of the past. Carr claims that the study of history is a study of causes. His advice, when faced with past events (data) and the need to explain them is to initially apportion several possible causes and then work out a hierarchy that suggests a set of causal relationships. Only once the historian determines long- and short-term causes can the next stage – interpretation – present its self. Rather than a construction (though it is faithful to the data), for Geoffrey Elton this Carr 'data-theory' approach places the historian too centrally in the process of

working out the meaning of the past. Preferring to view history as a reconstruction (rather than a construction), Elton favours **empiricism** over the 'probable' history theorising of constructionism.

For Elton, Carr's approach was too theoretical and because theory came from the mind of the historian, this meant the history thus produced was liable to be too much of a **subjective** rather than an objective interpretation. Elton was suspicious that theory was probably just an excuse for idleness in the archive and, anyway, invariably begged too many questions of the evidence. However, as Keith Jenkins has pointed out – and why he is justifiably regarded as a major contributor to the debates over the nature of history – both Carr and Elton were asking the wrong questions and debating irrelevant issues. For Jenkins no history – whether it is a Carr construction or an intended Elton reconstruction – is innocent. No historical interpretation springs forth either 'objectively' or 'subjectively'. For Jenkins, who was writing then in the early to mid-1990s, history was plainly a textualised **discourse** that was unavoidably 'positioned'. I endorse this judgement today. It is never possible to empty 'history' of the **author-historian** and/or his or her theories, attitudes, values, arguments, ideologies and so forth. But in this book I am going to explain how history is an authored narrative. Consequently, I argue that this moves us even further away from the misguided Carr–Elton debate in the disputes over the nature of history.

Now, despite the intervention of Jenkins and the many other theorists that we will come across, the majority of historians also assume that telling *the* truth about the past (even if it cannot be fully realised) requires the *re*-telling of *the* most likely story of the action and events of the past as accurately as possible by deploying *both* theory (Carr) and empiricism (Elton). This conflation of theory and empiricism means, *in effect*, the past and history can become one. But this will not work in practice. Even the most scientific of social science histories are still a form of 'telling'. This has long been summarised as 'this happened, then that, because . . . '. As the philosopher of history William Gallie said,

> . . . the exercise of the capacity to follow a story, where the story is known to be based on evidence and is put forward as a sincere effort to get at *the* story so far as the evidence and the writer's general knowledge and intelligence allow. (italics added)[4]

Since Gallie said this, over 40 years ago, what is called the **narrative turn** in history has posed two fundamental questions. First, does *the* story of the past actually exist to be 'found'?[5] And second, does the *order of priority* of (1) reference, (2) explanation, (3) meaning and (4) prose narrative presentation tell us all we need to know about 'doing history'?[6]

Before getting to those two basic questions it is worth noting that the concept of narrative is in itself nothing new to historians. Narrative, however, has generally been defined as the presentation of 'a story' about the past. Even occasionally described as 'a narrative history', there are still examples about today, like George B. Tindall's *America: A Narrative History*.[7] But from the eighteenth through to the present century, histories were and still are often regarded as *the* story about a particular past. Thus one well-known contemporary US history text describes the efforts of Hiawatha to restore peace among his own tribe and the outcome of his meeting with the holy man Deganawidah which facilitated it, as '*the* (my italics) story of Hiawatha and Deganawidah . . . '.[8] This might be just a slip of the mind by the authors of this text or it might not. But the point is that the concept of a history as a narrative form is known, if not always well understood. Although the matter of narrative as a philosophical question was acknowledged in the 1960s when it first began to be distinguished from just telling 'a story', even today the conflation of 'history' with 'a narrative of the past' remains common especially in 'popular histories' and survey texts.[9]

Yet, before we can address the two questions noted above, we have to be clear not just about the difference between 'a story' and 'narrative', but 'a story' and its 'narration' (the act of creating a narrative). Essentially a story is the recounting of a sequence of events. This is what is told. Narration, on the other hand, refers to the manner in which a story is told. It is in not recognising this distinction that one can be led to the belief that the historian does not really do anything other than carefully recount the given story of the past (remember '*the* story of Hiawatha and Deganawidah . . . '). But, because the process of 'telling' or narrating constitutes a complex system of representation, *how* a history is told is as important as *what* is being told. To put this in the context of Carr and Elton, it is not just a matter of theory and/or empiricism.

Though it passed Carr and Elton by, since the early 1960s when Gallie was writing, this distinction between story and its representation has been at the centre of a major debate over how historians view historical thinking and practice.[10] Given that history is the representation of something in the past (it might be the Crusades or US Second World War Japanese internment camps), what is represented (told) as history is the historian's choice. For clearly, if there is no given story to discover in the sources that relate to past events, then there is no 'natural' or unmediated connection between 'the chosen past' of the historian and the historical narrative she or he writes about it. So it follows that while the past existed in the time of the past (hi)stories only happen when they are told.

While historians 'refer' to the past through the evidence of change over time (temporal change), because this is done in a narrative constructed by the historian, then historical meaning is as much the result of the act of narrative making as it is of anything else. As Linda Hutcheon famously noted, whether it is in 'fictional' or 'historical' literature, the notion of a story with a beginning, middle and end ' . . . implies a structuring process that imparts meaning as well as order'.[11] So, while the past defined as a period of time during which many things happened is not invented, history, on the other hand, is a constructed narrative representation (a narration) *of* it or, to be more precise, *about* it.

I will summarise what I have said so far. First, I have been suggesting that the history narrative is a totalising (bringing together) procedure of representation. Second, this makes problematic the notion of discovering 'the story back there'. And third, the central organising factor in representing the past is the historian as the author who narrates the history. Indeed, as the French philosopher of history and literature Paul Ricoeur has argued, we can only engage with what he calls 'temporality' (specifically the past in our case but also the present and future) in the form of an authored narrative. This is recognition of the fundamental state of our existence as narrative making creatures or what the theorist of time, history and literature Elizabeth Ermarth calls our 'discursive condition'.[12] Ricoeur's and Ermarth's arguments have liberated many historians to now 'speak' for themselves as much as the past, and to become less constrained by the customs of conventional objective non-partisanship that only a belief in recovering *the* story can produce.[13]

Now, while the notion of history as a representation may not exactly be new, many historians continue to dispute and debate the significance of its implications. The comment made by the French literary theorist Gérard Genette about literature is pertinent to history. He said that like any other activity of the mind, literature (think history) is based on conventions of which, with some exceptions, it is not aware.[14] To be sure relatively few historians today remain preoccupied with discovering *the* story existing back there (as 'found' in the data or made up for its absence in some other way); most historians acknowledge that they present *a* story. Yet this story is one that is always primarily – and for some it will always be solely – the product of the sources (or the lack of them). But, the distinction between story and narrative raises the problem of how the sources can be *made* to speak in a narrative. Indeed, as we shall see, many influential history theorists do not believe narrative is actually built to access reality, even though it refers to it in terms of **facts**.

Undoubtedly the foremost advocates of history viewed as a narrative represent-ation are Roland Barthes, Hayden White and Paul Ricoeur. Heavily influenced by Barthes, White specifically has examined what he calls the metahistorical struc-ture of history, but all, during the past 40 years, have explained in substantial detail the nature of literary and historical writing and have explored the struc-ture of narrative as a vehicle that can represent the past.[15] Barthes' (followed by White) famous insight is that the similarities between history and other forms of non-realist narration are manifested in the figurative nature of both discourses. As Barthes asked over 40 years ago, is there actually any real difference between factual and imaginary narrative? What, if any, **linguistic** aspect distinguishes the two modes?

Those who have challenged the Barthes–White analysis in particular claim their comparison of historical narratives with 'fictional' ones obliterates the differences between them because they are said to share the same literary form.[16] This is a misunderstanding especially of White as he has great respect for the data and never claims history is a fictional literature. The point is that 'history' cannot be equated with **'fiction'** once it is understood that history is a narrative representation that pays its dues to the agreed facts of the past. The point White is making is very straightforward. It is that history is history and fiction is fiction, but that both are narratives, which are as much written by the reader as the author (history narratives are in this sense 'writerly'). Hence history *and* fiction, as well as writing and reception, are imaginatively organised. In this sense both sets of activities are **fictive** because both are authored. By acknowledging this as well as the relationship between narration and story – in effect **form and content** – we can move on in understanding the nature of history.

For, although historians are aware that they create narratives there still remains a need to explain how they use literary techniques in so doing.[17] This field of study, called 'historiographic narratology' by Dorrit Cohn, is now well established. Cohn's view, however, is that of the 'physicalist' who operates, as does Ricoeur, on the history and fiction distinction. Cohn argues that historical and fictional narratives work according to different rules about our understanding of physical reality, and that this produces a difference of kind rather than degree in distinguishing the two literatures of history and fiction.[18] Cohn maintains the writer of fiction is entirely in control (omniscient) whereas the historian is in a state of ignorance (nescience).[19] In other words, fiction is an emancipated discourse, unlike history that is always in thrall to 'what happened'. Ricoeur agrees that what distinguishes history from fiction is the former's referential and documentary dimension (its physicality), and also agrees with Cohn that it deals more with groups and structures than with individuals. The Cohn position (and Ricoeur's on this) seems to still place too much emphasis upon the claims of empiricism and inference, which, in effect, hold that the historical narrative is ultimately an interpretative report of what happened.

Historians today still generally accept that empiricism and analysis are the two key strategies of explanation. However, among the many other concepts we come across in creating the history narrative is that of **story space** (a notion only a few empirical historians actually ever entertain as we shall see). This is the authored model of what, how, when, why and to whom things happened in the past, which the reader/consumer enters into when they read, view or 'experience' the past, constituted as history. Naturally, every story space possesses authorial premises and hypotheses as well as data. Historians constantly re-work, overhaul and amend their story spaces (often as 'revised' editions of books) so it is important to understand story space creation in order to grasp history's constructedness and its ability to absorb consumers and engage them with the past in a meaningful way. Recognising history as a story space permits historians not only to understand how narrative is instrumental in creating meaning and truth; it also disabuses us of the notion that the historian is a cipher (the 'historian as midwife') in the sense which Cohn suggests. Rather we need to see historians as what they are – authors – and thus central to the history narrative making process.

Because of its story space character, the historical narrative is not a recording instrument for knowledge derived by non-narrative means. For this reason I do not endorse the Cohn view of history. While Cohn has made a significant contribution to debates, his analysis remains essentially a retread of the 'classic empirical-analytical model' as provided by most 'what is history texts'. But, *as a narrative*, history *cannot be* a report of 'findings', that is, explanations and meanings discovered *in* the archival sources that have enabled us to sniff out *the real story* – only authors tell stories in narrative forms.[20]

In this text, to more fully understand history as a narrative making activity I will deploy the thinking of several narrative history theorists starting with Gérard Genette. I shall begin (in Chapter 1) by noting what he has described as the triad of *story*, *narrative* and *narration*. He also recognises the 'how' or the *expression* that the story and its telling takes through the intervention of the historian-author. Thanks primarily to the work of Genette, in most analyses of the structure of narrative and narration the '*what* happened' is referred to as the story told, and '*how* it is narrated' is referred to as the discourse. As will become plain, this story–discourse duality is central to an understanding of history as a narrative form of knowledge.

It is also necessary to explain a range of other concepts that clarify the nature of the connection between story, narrating and narration/narrative in creating history. Some of these ideas were noted many years ago by the French history thinker Michel de Certeau when he argued in his *The Writing of History* that the *writing of* history is not outside the conception and composition of history. He was saying that the past (the 'what happened') is not translated but is transformed (or turned) into a narrative construction and only through that 'narrative turning' can the past be explained and given meaning.[21]

Since de Certeau wrote, the 'narrative turn' in historical studies has been facilitated by a number of significant developments in continental philosophy, mainly **structuralism** and **poststructuralism.** This is reflected in several new kinds of history that usually carry the prefix 'post': post-Marxist, postcolonial, postmodern, postfeminist and so on. This 'postist' narrative turn has often been summarised, largely incorrectly, as a battle between **postmodernism** and classic empiricist history.[22] But this is misleading because it suggests that there is an 'alternative' and a 'conventional' history. This is a false distinction because history has *always* been a narrative making activity.

As with all forms of narrative, a key feature of history is its interpretative nature, which means there is always a constant deferral of meaning and closure.[23] If we fail to acknowledge that language and narrative are 'empty' signifiers until 'filled' with a meaning through their construction, we misunderstand the nature of history.[24] What this means is that because history is a narrative making activity, the four principles of (1) reference, (2) explanation, (3) meaning and (4) prose narrative presentation presumed to work in a particular epistemological way (**epistemology** is the theory and study of knowing and knowledge) are now being fundamentally rethought.[25]

The various 'turns' that started with the narrative and the post structuralist inspired **linguistic turn**, then, have challenged the foundational epistemological arrangement of reference, explanation and meaning. It is now widely acknowledged they are not insulated from the role of narrative, language and the historian as an author who possesses a voice. This has, nevertheless, generated the most intense arguments and produced a variety of other 'turns' such as the '**ethical turn**', '**aesthetic turn**' and 'cultural turn' as historians have acknowledged the challenge to epistemology.

We must note, however, that very recently there has been a counterblast, which might be called the 'empiricist re-turn' or the '**new empiricism**'. This re-emphasises the belief that while language and, therefore, the discourse (a.k.a. the narrative) we call history mediates the past as a narrative representation of it, it is still possible to engage meaningfully, truthfully and objectively with the true (or most likely) story of the past. Of course this attempt to harmonise what for a few historians are still two separate approaches (empirical-analytical and narrative-linguistic) is complicated by the fact that every act of empiricism and analysis is, by its nature, a narrative-linguistic (a literary) **performance**. It is, in other words, not a matter of determining how history and narrative differ in terms of text types (fiction or fictive, or narrative and non-narrative) but how history looks when considered only as a narrative making activity (though it includes empirical-analytical elements). What also distinguishes new empiricists is a seeming confusion in their minds over the distinctions of story and narrative.

Whatever the peculiarities of these turns and re-turns, understandings and misunderstandings, the debates have always ended up with the same 'big question'. That is, can we really tell the truth about the past when we can only 'know' it as a constructed history narrative (see Chapter 7, pp. 111–122)? Many of these debates might disappear if we were to forget the word 'history' in favour of, say, '**the-past-*as*-history**'. At least this would remind us that the past exists now only as a form of a created (written, physically built, filmed or whatever) phenomenon. As we shall see, the notion of 'as' is central to understanding the narrative nature of history.

In *Telling the Truth About History* three American historians noted that history, as an organised mechanism for truthful and objective knowing, had ' . . . been shaken right down to its scientific and cultural foundations . . . at the very time that those foundations themselves are being contested'.[26] As the authors said, there was much uncertainty about the creation of historical knowledge, and specifically the ability of being able to 'turn' our knowledge of the past into an objective written representation. The implication the authors were circling around was that reference, explanation and meaning might not actually precede the narrative.

To use the noun 'history' as a synonym for 'the past', as the authors of *Telling the Truth About History* did in the title of their book, both illustrates and perpetuates the problem I have been exploring. So, we are required to ask not how we can render the past empirical world *into its own* historical narrative, which corresponds to it, but what happens if we become convinced we cannot? To accept that *the* story does not exist back there or, if it does, that it remains unknowable to us because of the problem of turning data into narrative actually revolutionises our understanding of the nature and practice of history.

▶ The past and history/the-past-*as*-history

In everything I have said so far it is important to understand that 'the past' and 'history' are separate entities or categories. The past is what once was, is no more and has gone for good. History, on the other hand, is a corpus of narrative discourses *about* the once reality of the past produced and fashioned by historians. While it may seem odd to stress this, we do need to realise three important implications. First, that the past is a category of *content* (real events); second, that the significance of how it is told is crucial (the issue of discourse or narration of a *story*); and third, that history is a category of *expression* (varieties of narrative representation) has to be stressed. These 'implications' are central to the understanding of history as argued for in this text.

In writing a history for the past we create a semiotic representation that encompasses reference *to* it, an explanation *of* it and a meaning *for* it. So we have a situation whereby because of the absence of the past (for that is by definition a phenomenon which is inaccessible), as the historian David D. Roberts has argued, we have 'nothing but history'.[27] And this, plainly, is a textual or other form of substitution – the 'as' – as already noted. For, even though this references what happened and can demonstrate according to the rules of comparison and verification that certain things very probably occurred, its meaning is created as we narrate (and express) our history. In other words, as Paul Ricoeur has argued, the past can only meaningfully exist *in* the narrative we write about it.

It is, therefore, pertinent to note here what the French cultural theorist Roland Barthes noted as the referential illusion in which he analysed the error of ascribing to one category (call it history) a feature or features that are really only attributable to another (call it the past).[28] Unfortunately those (admittedly now very few) historians who believe history is the past rebuilt have been committing what philosophers identify as a 'category mistake'. Barthes' point is that historians who commit this error collapse that which is signified (representation) into its referent to create an invalid signifier–referent association. Barthes summarises this category error by claiming that in the so-called 'objective history' the 'real' is never more than a nebulous signified, hiding behind the all-powerful referent.

Only by making this category error could a historian say that 'according to the available evidence *the* meaning of the French Revolution was . . . ' or ' . . . *the* cause of the American Civil War was . . . '. There is, as most historians acknowledge, no *one* history of anything if by that we mean 'the true story of it'. Nevertheless, we must ask why some historians do still claim that a narrative representation is close to being the thing to which it refers? After all, a narrative description of the Eiffel Tower is not the Eiffel Tower no matter how detailed is our description of its dimensions and structure. This category mistake leads to the referential illusion if we believe that a history narrative and the past can correspond at any level *beyond* simple sentence length statements that refer to the available evidence.

Though history can contain the element of reference, its nature does not flow from that alone. Moreover, as we shall see, there are many different ways the category of history can be expressed. Consequently, more and more historians recognise that there are competing approaches to the-past-*as*-history. This can be seen in the existence of three such approaches that encourage a variety of legitimate **modes of expression** and forms of narration. These three approaches to the past may be considered to be 'genres' of history as they work in a very similar fashion to their literary counterparts. The three genres are **reconstructionist history, constructionist history** and **deconstructionist history**.[29] Essentially they reflect the enduring epistemological debate over the relationship between empiricism, analysis and narrative.

▶ Three genres of history

Epistemology is about understanding the theory and fundamentals of knowledge acquisition. Historians in the West, as the progeny of the seventeenth-century Cartesian Revolution and the subsequent Enlightenment, have traditionally held to a view of history derived from analytical philosophy. This suggests that historical knowledge is acquired through an essentially scientific and rational process that employs an evidence-based method. This reflects the realist demand that historical statements will correspond (see the **correspondence theory** of knowledge) to evidence that is independent of mind and culture.

According to this theory, historians arrive at their conclusions in terms of arguments that best fit the data. Evidence of real experience, plus reason (inference or inductive argument) will generate true knowledge of reality. So influential has this theory of knowledge become that it has actually hijacked the general term for the study of knowledge acquisition – epistemology. However, in the twentieth century this definition of epistemology was challenged as *the* way to engage with the real. This challenge has been translated in the world of history in the variety of 'turns' (noted above) which have moved historians away from the supremacy of epistemology. This move against epistemology has produced the three genres I have mentioned as different approaches to the past.

Why are these three genres in conflict given my argument that there is only one kind of history defined in terms of being a narrative making activity? Well, first, we need to understand that historians make epistemological choices. They choose how to gain knowledge about the past. The epistemological choice historians make can be detected – basically – in how they view the role of narrative making in what they do, and how the history narrative is constituted as a form of knowledge through the relationship between reference, explanation and the creation of meaning.[30] There is a clear difference in this relationship within each genre.[31]

As an epistemological choice, reconstructionist historians believe they gain true knowledge through the primacy of **referentiality** and delivering its inherent story as *the* true narrative.[32] The issue of history as a mode and structure of representation does not arise. Reconstructionists hold two basic beliefs. First, they reject the idea that there is *a* choice in thinking about and doing history. Second, they believe history exists outside the here and now, which means it should not be any way subject to the **ontological** demands and pressures of the present. In other words, it must not be **historicist**.

Apart from referentiality, which is defined as the single factual statement of **justified belief**, the touchstone of reconstructionism is inference and the accurate demonstration of the historical agent's actions (**agency**) (see constructionist history below).[33] This means that the past can be 'located' by well-informed historians who suspend their personal judgements and any personal desire to 'tell the story' in ways that deviate from what they read it to be in 'the sources'. This is despite the long-standing argument, as we shall see, that the reader is as important as what they read in creating meaning. The ultimate basis of the reconstructionist realist-referential epistemology that permits 'fair descriptions' of the past is the correspondence theory of knowledge and the objectivity (the 'thereness') of historical data.[34]

This 'realist' position depends on the twin beliefs that the historian's mind can engage (largely unproblematically) with knowable reality and that that engagement can be transcribed without too much difficulty onto the page (for reconstructionists it is still primarily the printed page). Only through this practice can historical knowledge be emancipated from the hazards of **subjectivity** if not entirely freed of cultural bias. Proper knowledge that is fair and even-handed thus depends on the reality of a knowable world that is independent of both our minds and our narrative making. Hence, the concept of a story or, more accurately, an **emplotment** is rejected. In other words, it means that truthful statements are what they are because of how things were in the world.[35]

This naive **realism** wins over very few historians these days. Nevertheless, the reverse seems also to be unconvincing – that all we can know about the past is what we learn through our *a priori* best guesses, or our biases, our private onto-logical beliefs and our constructed narratives. Most historians try to steer clear of these two apparent extremes. Most accept the 'common-sense' or practical realist position that there is a reality beyond us, and, fortunately, we possess a capacity to satisfactorily represent (re-present) it. Hence we can produce truthful historical statements because they match or correspond to the facts of known reality.

What this means for reconstructionist historians like Arthur Marwick, Geoffrey Roberts, David Loades, Edward Royle and Gertrude Himmelfarb (a few selected at random from the ever-diminishing tiny group) is that narrative is the end result of their description of events and their analysis. They would certainly not accept that their narrative is the *medium* through which their *historical* knowledge is fashioned. Reconstructionists view narrative like a wire that transmits the current of meaning from the past to the history page. As Geoffrey Roberts says, (my italics) '. . . telling *the* story, explaining *the* action, and *reconstructing the* experience of people in *the* past . . . ' is what historians do, and it is no more (or less) complex than that.[36] The trick is simply to recognise that *the* story exists in *the* action of the human actors, and then to describe it acknowledging cause and effect. In this way description equals history and history equals the past.

Indeed, the British social historian Arthur Marwick insists that historians do not reconstruct the past. He says, ' . . . it is knowledge . . . about the past that historians produce'.[37] Despite saying this, the Marwickian makes the epistemological assump-tion that there is a direct correspondence between reference and representation which is ultimately located in (the writing up of) the narrative. So triumphant has this 'common-sense' **realist-representationalist** position become that the history-consuming general public and amateur historians alike see it as the only way to engage with the past and its knowable truth. Indeed, the reconstructionist approach has become the culturally acceptable way of producing past reality (how many TV history programmes either explicitly or implicitly offer the 'real story of . . . '?). But even in Marwick's definition you will note that he uses the verb 'produce'. He also acknowledges the product is 'about' the past. As you can tell, it is actually very difficult to be an unreconstructed reconstructionist.[38] This is because while the historian's narrative will always be constrained by what happened in the past, it is also going to be subject to their preferred ways of connecting the individual historical agent to the larger structures that created change in the past.

Indeed, as the historians Donald N. MacRaild and Avram Taylor have explained, the data always come loaded with theories, concepts and ideologies.[39] Although most historians would never reject the referential bedrock of empiricism, the majority do acknowledge that there is more to history than just finding out what happened. Hence, a second kind of history shifts us dramatically beyond the limited reconstructionist approach. The constructionist genre of historical knowing is a highly complex conceptual and theory-laden social science approach which, while it is empirical, nevertheless acknowledges that explanation demands 'a body of knowledge that is usually referred to as 'theory'.[40] History is not just empirical – it is also analytical and deploys *a priori* thinking.

Basically this means hypothesising about the causes of regularities in the past and explaining them, rather than operating at the level of individual historical actors.[41] Biography, for example, is not a constructionist exercise in this sense. Of course biographers acknowledge that structures and powers beyond their control (class, race, gender, imperialism, technology, nationalism, war, etc.) 'influence' individuals. The overt use of theory, while it is claimed to substantially enhance explanation, is still intended by its constructionist practitioners to maintain a firm and direct contact with past reality.

But the level of sophistication of constructionist history is such that the vast majority of historians working today fall into this broad category. Two British constructionist historians John Belchem and Neville Kirk explained in the late 1990s the central tenet of realism to which they as historians both adhere. It is that ' . . . aspects of culture, such as words, consciousness, and norms and values, coexist and interact with political, economic, social and other structures and processes which come into being . . . ' 'out there'.[42] In other words, past reality demands a ' . . . dialogue between concept and evidence, and . . . due attention to context and chronology . . . especially along the lines of race, gender and class . . . '.[43] Other hard-core materialists like Bryan D. Palmer declare anything other than a thoroughgoing realist epistemology (influenced by, in his case, a humanist Marxist *a priori* constructionism) are simply a 'descent into discourse'.[44]

Belchem and Kirk were prodded into their defence of constructionism by the dangers, as they saw them, of the so-called postmodern historians. As they said, ' . . . epistemological and methodological credentials and procedures [are] diametrically opposed to those employed by postmodernists who see nothing beyond subjectivity, no lurking or hidden external material and other structures and interests beyond what is captured by self-referential and more or less autonomous languages and discourses'.[45] Clearly, they are endorsing an epistemological approach to knowledge prompted by the fear that 'postmodernists' not only dissolve the 'link' between 'representation' and the 'real' and between 'language' and the 'social world', but the 'real' becomes merely a 'representation'.[46] While this is a parody of 'postmodernist' views, the constructionist position remains an intellectual advance on the naivety of reconstructionism.

However, because of their belief in the correspondence theory (of truth), the majority of constructionists still think that they can access *the* story, *the* pattern of (race, gender, imperialism and class?) structures *in* (behind and determining) the events of the past. Narrative making is not really on their radar either, even though they are very much aware that they are intervening in the past on behalf of some present constituency or another. As I just noted, constructionist history is the most popular form of history practised today, ranging from biography to (one or more of many varieties of) cultural and economic history. Its practitioners are constantly innovating and assembling novel ways of explaining the empirical by resort to theorising about its assumed and often 'apparently hidden' structures.[47] Sophisticated constructionists are keen to explain not just why individuals did what they did or how they exercised their powers of agency, but how their decisions were influenced by the deeper structures that controlled their lives. Addressing race, class, imperialism and gender has, in fact, become a major historical industry. Indeed, it often seems that 'new approaches' to the past are now as important as 'the past'.

The third epistemological choice is that of deconstructionist historians. Essentially, the deconstructionist historians hold that past events are explained and acquire their meaning as much by their representation as by their 'knowable actuality' derived by conventional (empirical-analytical) epistemological means. Their history is different for five reasons.

- First, deconstructionist history rejects the fundamental(ist) epistemological belief in the correspondence between literary word and empirical world that is claimed to create meaning.
- Second, deconstructionist history acknowledges the poststructuralist rejection of essentialism that holds that knowledge is 'out there' rather than created.
- Third, given the first two reasons, the history narrative is the only site available for the construction of historical knowledge and, for those reasons, such history makes different kinds of truth claims.
- Fourth, deconstructionist historians are willing to work with and explore the notion that all knowledge in the arts and humanities is in some degree relativist (see **relativism**).
- And fifth, this rethinking encourages the possibility of radical and **experimental history** practice (see pp. 103–109).

One general consequence of these five assumptions is the acknowledgement of the authored nature of historical knowledge. This immediately casts doubts on the notion of the discovery of *the* story in favour of understanding the nature of the past through the logic of their own narrative making and all that which goes with it. Indeed, the way we achieve understanding is part of the nature of understanding. This also generates questions concerning what Linda Hutcheon has called 'postmodernist representation'.

Briefly, as a representation of the past, history is not capable of knowing the thing-in-itself and, moreover, as a discourse, it can be expressed in many different modes or forms (see **mode of expression**). This is not really a major claim given that it follows much accepted thinking on realism by many philosophers. So, while a deconstructionist would claim all we have is history, to be more precise, all we really have is representation with all its attendant problems. And not least among these is what happens to questions of truth. Indeed, for each epistemological choice there is, as we shall see, a different definition of what is truth in history. Those deconstructionist historians who wish to continue to accommodate a notion of truth do so by addressing the ontological situation of the historian as an author. As the German philosopher Hans-Georg Gadamer has suggested, the connection between the historian (subject) and the past (object) has to be understood not as an obstacle to truth but as an element in its creation (see Chapter 7).[48]

The deconstructionist investment in recognising the authorial function of the historian means doubting the epistemological belief that separates the knowing subject from the observed object. From an epistemological position (both reconstructionist and constructionist) 'subjective knowledge' or 'textually constructed knowledge' is not just undesirable, it is dangerous. But, as Gadamer suggests, this is precisely what you get with historical knowledge. It cannot be any other way. The historian either goes into denial or gets on with it by acknowledging history is not 'the real thing'. Not least, the process of the acquisition of knowledge about the past implies and acknowledges the determining role of the historian as a creator – and author – of history. To put this as plainly as I can, the deconstructionist historian writes history through the acknowledgement that its logic derives from the way she or he creates a narrative representation.

▶ Conclusion

In this chapter, I have introduced the relationship between narrative, history and the past. This has meant confronting the nature of epistemology and meeting head-on the epistemological belief that history can be made to correspond with the past even though the past no longer exists. I have suggested that because history is not the same as the past, the notion of correspondence has to be replaced with the logic of narrative representation. I explained how we get to this position through a consideration of the three primary epistemological orientations available today: reconstructionism, constructionism and their challenger deconstructionism. I will now move to the consequences of our narrative epistemological decision by starting the task of outlining the basic choices all historians make in creating a narrative about the past.

1 Narrating the Past

► Representation

Human beings are **story** tellers who exist **ontologically** in a universe of **narrative** making.[1] Narrativist thinkers like Jerome Bruner hold that narrative making is wired into the human brain as the key mechanism for representing **reality** (i.e., not added on after we have analysed, explained and produced **meaning**). For Bruner, narrative is the *a priori* concept through which we apprehend reality.[2] This suggests narrative is *the* mode of cognition. Moreover, in acknowledging this we are forced to consider Hayden White's famous **metahistorical** argument concerning the functioning of the **trope**, which is the metaphorical (linguistic) turning of one thing into another in **order** to create meaning. As Bruner suggests, narrative is a form of cognition (knowing), one that is particularly applicable to story telling disciplines like **history**.

Moreover, as the Dutch philosopher of history Frank Ankersmit maintains, history is not and never can be simply a report of events even though it contains **empiricism** supported by **inference**. This is because, as Paul Ricoeur also pointed out, history is the representation of change over time, and as a form of narrative it enables temporal creatures like us to create meaning. Not to accept this would be to embrace the rather odd **epistemological** belief that **reference** somehow insulates the historian against his or her own existence as temporal and narrative-making creatures. It is important, therefore, to understand how the data is always embedded within and accessed as a representation of human actions rather than the other way around.

As Ankersmit suggests, then, taking history seriously requires that we confront the epistemological view of it as a 're-presentation'. This means asking (along with anti-representationalist philosophers like Richard Rorty and even the more epistemologically conservative Donald Davidson) if there really is some kind of **tertium quid** (or 'third thing') that connects the word and the world.[3] Normally, for epistemologically inclined historians this *tertium quid* is an accurate and unprob-lematic device that by its nature allows us to discover *the* story. Unfortunately, the idea of adequate representation can only work when it is confused with description. Description is defined as a 'subject term/reference' plus the 'predicate term' that is asserted about it. This definition underpins the notion that the past can be described (re-presented) thereby delivering its given meaning. However, representation is entirely different to description. Representation is a picturing process categorically different to the notion of subject and predicate.

So what I am supporting is a position of **narrative constructivism**. Although there are different forms of narrative constructivism, it is my contention that history is a narrative representation of past reality that specifically recognises the sequential and temporal relationships that exist in and between 'the real', 'the story' and 'its telling'. This, of course, also allows for self-conscious, insightful and shrewd history making. Such history, as we shall see, may be **experimental** in its form as the historian explores, for example, the turning of 'real time' into 'story time'. In this way **explanation** and meaning can also be proposed within history. History does not, in other words, just re-tell stories about the past; it is itself a storied form of knowledge. This is the situation *even* though it contains statements of **justified belief** based on **sources** and evidence.[4] Historians always have a duty of care (to themselves and their readers) not to lie about the evidence and to make reasoned and balanced judgements. But in itself that is simply not enough. We need to know how and why we construct our narratives.

There are philosophers of history, of course, who have a profound interest in narrative but who may be described as being anti-narrativist. Such philosophers believe that history narratives tend only to replicate large-scale belief narratives – sometimes called **discourses** – such as neo-conservatism, liberalism, fascism, religion and Marxism.[5] Of course most of the theorists and historians who are critical of the **narrative turn** endorse epistemology first, last and always. For them any story *imposed* on the past means it must be at least anachronistic or, worse, just a fiction. The irony here of course is that constructionists can be and are accused by reconstructionists of anachronistically imposing 'theory and concept' on the past. Perhaps the greatest irony is the reconstructionist belief that 'the past' imposes itself on 'history'. In their rush to empiricism, the **fictive** and the discursive nature of history is ignored.

In other words, being a deconstructionist historian does not mean regarding as unimportant our ability to provide, in the words of the leading realist philosopher of history C.B. McCullagh, ' . . . credible, intelligible and fair history'.[6] But what it does mean, again to quote McCullagh, is that it is ' . . . incumbent upon serious students of history, to know how they should justify their conclusions'.[7] To be even-handed in responding to this entreaty I think we must understand the narrative logic of history. This is because it is only as we *narrate a story* that we justify our conclusions.

▶ Story, narrating and narration

Given its status as a narrative representation, the notion of history as an **aesthetic** undertaking requires us to modify the epistemological hierarchy of reference, explanation, meaning and narrative.[8] I will start by considering the concept of **story space** (which I have already mentioned briefly a couple of times) in more detail. The argument goes like this. Every **author-historian** has to imagine, as White suggests, that part of the past with which they wish to engage. The story space is the world of the once real past (or not as the case may be in some experimental history) as imagined (i.e., fictively constructed) by the historian and which the history consumer is invited to visit through the history. The story space clearly references a part of the once real world, but in that reference the historian chooses to invoke who *said* what, who *did* what, assumes there are mechanisms which will explain to us *why* they did it, what *agencies* and *structures* operate(d), what events were *significant* and which were not, and which theories and arguments will be applied to explaining the meaning of it all. Moreover, new information can be added and old information reconsidered.

The historian's story space is a universal space. History can only be presented 'in' it. It is the only means through which we project the past. How and why we do it depends ultimately on our epistemological choices. For the reconstructionist, for example, it will tend to be a catalogue of events within a time sequence the story of which speaks for itself. Indeed, the very concept of a story space as an intellectual building site where elements of the past are situated to create 'a history' will be anathema to such a historian. They will reject the very concept because it smacks of heavy-duty narrative constructivism. Thus, the notion that historians construct the past (as, say, David W. Noble constructed 'the Progressive Mind, 1890–1917'[9]) is claimed to be an error because of the logic of the discovery of *the* story. Unfortunately this ignores the situation that all **facts** are constructed (as is this one).[10]

But one reason why there are so few reconstructionists around is that the vast majority of historians acknowledge that they never just reconstruct chunks of time together with their 'contents'. Most historians are constructionists (though not narrative constructivists) because their historical story spaces are as much the ethical, emotional and intellectual products of themselves, their agendas and their theories as they are reflections of and on 'what happened'. Indeed historians generally acknowledge that 'what happened', though important, is no more important than any other feature of the story space. The constructionist's story space is a rich intellectual as well as a referential environment in which social theory and concept are freely used to assemble (though the aim may be to re-assemble) the past. There will remain a strong belief that the story space reflects *upon* the actuality of the past while acknowledging the intellectual commitments of the author-historian to their particular story space vision *for* the past.

For the deconstructionist, though, the history story space is the site of all kinds of possibilities and imaginaries. First and foremost they will be concerned with the way in which historians can create story spaces, also why, for what purposes (practical, ethical or whatever), for whom and, most importantly, how they can change it to meet the demands of different modes of expression. They will view their own self-consciously made story space for what it is – an invention, a tool for doing things with the past that impacts back upon how we think about it and what we want out of it. There will probably be a desire to know useful things about the past but, equally, perhaps also the wish to experiment.

By definition there are as many story spaces as there are histories and re-visions. Indeed, story spaces are often re-constituted by the same historian (think of Claude Monet and the dozens of painting he did of haystacks, though for historians it is likely to be new editions of books). By way of illustration, take the constructionist historian who wishes to provide a history of the American Left. Because there is no given or inherent story of the American Left as might be provided by an Ideal Chronicler who knows everything as it really was, a story space has to be created. The historian John Patrick Diggins created a story space that he turned into a book called *The Rise and Fall of the American Left*.[11] But he actually created two story spaces: one for the first and another for the second edition of the book.

The second story space (edition) was changed to add new topics and, as he says, the ' . . . story has now been brought up to 1990'. In this fresh New Left story space Diggins pursues the notion that the American Left, having been defeated in the factories and the fields, is now continued (up to 1990) by carrying the fight for cultural hegemony into the classroom.[12] The artifice of this story space is well illustrated by Diggins who expanded the time frame and extended the concept of cultural hegemony given, as he says, that his history was the product of his being politically 'to the left of the right and to the right of the left'. None of this has anything to do with the events of the past *per se*, but everything to do with the decisions that went into creating a fresh story space within which the past can be put to new uses.

Apart from being brought up to 1990, Diggins' second story space is also constructed out of three elements the author refers to as 'theory'. This is devoted to the historical background and theory issues, and the lack of an American proletariat. Second, there is a 'history' that deals with the Lyrical Left, the Old Left and the New Left. And the third is constructed around the idea of 'anomaly', which addresses the vestigial remains of the Left in academe. By definition neither of the two story spaces *existed* in the past. Of course all the details are honestly researched according to the available evidence, but the past has never been fitted into this particular story space before.

Take another example, this time of Christopher Lasch's *The Agony of the American Left*.[13] This story space was created out of several smaller story spaces of previously published journal articles brought together intending, presumably, to provide a coherent but different story of the American Left. For Lasch, however, the time period is slightly different to that of Diggins as are the topics covered. Not surprisingly, the theoretical and ideological compulsions behind his story space also differ. Is this the same New Left past? What we have now are two competing story spaces using roughly the same body of data (primarily relating to the New Left). However, the function of each story space is to give a form to and a meaning for the past for reasons that have little to do with the past itself, but everything to do with history as an authored narrative creation for current, political reasons. So, these two story spaces, though labelled 'New Left', inevitably contain different meanings because two different historians build the story space with selective reference to **agency**/action, character and setting, and not simply to the whole universe of past events, decisions, beliefs, intentions and structures.[14] It is an inadequate understanding of what is going on here to simply say they are different or revised interpretations.

Our rethinking of history as story space using the examples of Diggins and Lasch makes it easier to acknowledge what flows from the critical distinction, noted briefly in the Introduction, between the content, the story of the past, its *expression* and the process of *narration*. Though the distinction will be discussed in much greater detail in Chapters 2, 3 and 4, it is important to understand how the difference between content, story, narration and expression is central to the narrative making logic of history. Through examining these differences we can more clearly identify and locate the author-historian's role in the process of constructing history 'story space' representations. To understand how this works, we need to begin with a brief introduction to the theory of narrative.

The text *Narrative Discourse* by Gérard Genette and his response to criticisms of the book in his 1983 (published in English in 1990) *Narrative Discourse Revisited* provides us with what is the best-known and still the most comprehensive and systematic theory of narrative available. Derived from the analyses of Genette but also drawing on Seymour Chatman's commentary, we can loosely combine the two to consider the theory of narrative in terms of the story (what is to be told) and discourse (how it is told) distinction already noted.[15] Some line diagrams may be useful in the exposition that follows.

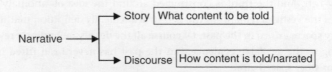

The story consists of content which refer to 'things' called *existents* such as historical agents/characters/physical location/context/setting and *events* brought about by the actions of characters. Usually this turns out to be, as one might expect, a simple, graphic summary of the reality of human existence – things happened to people at certain times in certain places. So, the story – essentially a chronology of happenings in time and place – looks something like this:

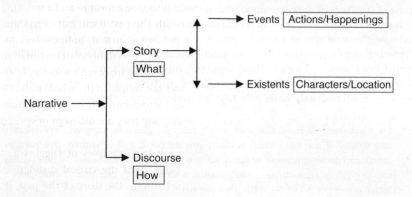

Turning now to discourse, here we find this encompasses a variety of aspects or elements of the narration or communication of the story by the narrator. These narrational devices are essential to the telling of the story and giving it a meaning.

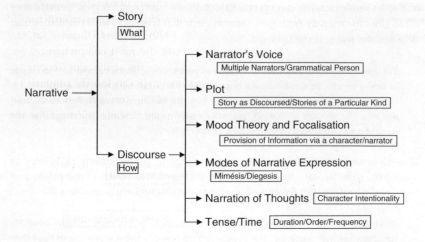

According to Genette and Chatman, narrative theory discourse consists of the six elements sketched in the diagram above. These shape our insight into, and understanding of, a/the story of what happened. I will examine these elements in subsequent chapters though they will be, as we shall see, modified to meet the specific needs of history narrative making. Plot, for example, will be removed entirely from discourse and re-located in the new **content/story** element (see pp. 29–43). For the moment, however, it is only necessary to understand the general structure of narrative upon which the logic of history relies.

Now, it follows that the history narrative is built in conformity to this logic because the structure of prose narrative is universal. It is universal in that, as Genette suggests, there are three fundamentals common to all narratives including realist ones such as history. These common fundamentals are, of course, *story*, *narrating* and *narration*.[16] Genette's comments on these are worth quoting in full because he immediately notes how they all work together. He says,

> I will not return to the distinctions, which today are generally accepted, between *story* (the totality of narrated events), *narrative* (the discourse, oral or written, that narrates them), and *narrating* (the real or fictive act that produces that discourse – in other words the very fact of recounting) . . . conceptually, it seems to me that [the] . . . triad gives a better account of the whole of the narrative fact.[17]

Note that Genette uses an alternative term for discourse; namely 'narrative'. However, for him the three key elements in every realist or fictional narrative remain *story*, *narrating* and *narration*. But, also note, he uses the term 'fictive' too. It is these elements and their fictive organisation we need to recognise to grasp the essential logic of history thinking and practice for, as we shall see in Chapters 2, 3 and 4, no single element can operate in isolation from the other two. Genette goes on to gloss the triad by noting a common error that has to do with the distinction between the real and the fictional.

> The greatest defect of that triad is its order of presentation, which corresponds to no real or fictive genesis. In a non-fictional (for example, historical) narrative, the actual order is obviously *story* (the completed events), *narrating* (the narrative act of the historian), [and] *narrative* (the product of that act, potentially or virtually capable of surviving it in the form of a written text, a recording, or a human memory).'[18]

Here Genette is describing the usual chronological understanding of history as story first, then its narrating and, finally, the narrative, which is the product of story and narrating. But he immediately and very significantly qualifies this:

> As a matter of fact . . . Narrative in its earliest occurrence – oral or even written – is wholly simultaneous with narrating, and the distinction between them is less one of time than of aspect: *narrative* designates the spoken discourse (syntactic and semantic aspect . . .) and *narrating* the situation *within* which it is uttered (pragmatic aspect). In fiction, the real narrative situation is pretended to – and this pretense, or *simulation* (which is perhaps

the best translation of the Greek *mimésis*) is precisely what defines the work of fiction. But the true order is instead something like

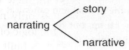

with the narrative [narrating] act initiating (inventing) *both* the story and its narrative, which are then completely indissociable. But has a pure fiction existed? And a pure non-fiction?[19]

I will unpack what Genette is saying here. He is suggesting that regardless of whether the narrative is fictional or non-fictional, while both seem to start with the story to be told, this is never the case because it is impossible to have *any* kind of narrative without the three elements combined together (though they have to be separated out for reasons of explanation). But more than this, for Genette the narrating element initiates (note Genette says 'inventing') both the story and its narrative, and then the three become irretrievably mixed (indissociable).

Consequently, in history, he says, the narrative is supposed to begin with the story of the 'real events', while in fiction there is only the pretence that it starts with the 'real story'. Obviously we all know the story (in fiction) originates with the author, which is the fulfilment of the narrating function. But once done, the three components cannot be separated out. Genette concludes by asking what happens to this model once we face the fact that no pure fiction or non-fiction has existed – the effect of the indissoluble nature of the triad. This is an important point given the epistemological status of history as a 'literature of fact' that is then supposed to be 'written up'.

Genette concludes that there never has been a pure fiction or non-fiction. He does this in the context of Marcel Proust's 1934 *A la recherche du temps perdu* (*Remembrance of Things Past*) and which is the subject of Genette's book *Narrative Discourse*. He says,

> The answer in both cases [pure fiction or pure non-fiction] is obviously negative, and the semi-autobiographical text of the *Recherche* illustrates fairly well the mixture that forms the standard fare of our narratives, literary or not. Nonetheless the two pure types can be conceived of; and literary narratology has confined itself a little too blindly to the study of fictional narrative, as if as a matter of course, every literary narrative would always be pure fiction. We will return to this question, which at times is very definitely apposite. For instance, the typically modal query 'How does the author know that?' does not have

the same meaning in fiction as in non-fiction. In non-fiction the historian must provide evidence and documents, the auto-biographer must allege memories or secrets confided. In fiction, the novelist, the storyteller, the epic poet could often reply, off-fiction, as it were, 'I know it because I'm making it up'. I say off-fiction as we say off-mike because in his fiction, or at least in the normal and canonical system of fiction... an author is not supposed to be making [it] up, but reporting. Once again, fiction consists of that simulation that Aristotle called *mimésis*.[20]

Genette is pointing here to the fact that history appears to be a matter of a report of the findings and not an invention (making it up). Even today historians occasionally refer to the 'findings' in the archive in their narratives, but virtually never to how the narrating activity goes all the way through the process – the important point to which Genette alerts us. This raises the issue not of 'discovering history' but 'making history'. It is never a wasted effort to know about the research dead ends, errors, **subjective** decisions, permanent prejudices, hindsights, publisher and editor pressures, figurative choices and so on that go into making a history. But what is still all too rarely explained is how the triad of *story*, *narrating* and *narration* incorporates *every* aspect of the history production process. Narrative is, as we know, conventionally viewed as the end product after all the referential and inferential ingredients have been blended. But history does not work that way in practice, as the concept of story space hopefully makes clear.[21]

For, plainly, apart from the referential element, everything in the story space creation process is a simulation based upon the notion of *mimésis*, where art imitates (note: not corresponds to) reality. The concept of *mimésis* is significant in any understanding of the narrative making logic of history. As we shall see, Paul Ricoeur's analysis of *mimésis* is that it is more than simple imitation of an appearance; more substantially, it constitutes a representation of an action in the past precisely and exclusively in the form of a history narrative. (In the next chapter, I will argue this becomes the essence of the historian's **emplotment** of the past).

Meanwhile, Genette is suggesting that only through realist convention do we assume the content of events cast as a story begins the narrative making process which then 'reflects' the data. In practice no historian works in the 'hit and miss' way that generates the 'discovery' of where they end up. Archival research can be 'hit or miss', but 'history' is narrative artifice all the way through from the initial figuring of the past to the finished history. No historian, for example, comes to the data cold without some knowledge of a pre-existing narrative in their minds. All historians start with the texts of other historians. They can, and they often do, come across fresh data, but it is always processed within a pre-existing narrative understanding (just as the eventual history is) – though the data may indeed suggest there are alternative stories to be created.

Genette next goes on to address the nature of narrating (narratology). This is the manner in which the story is told in different media (film, comic strip and photographic magazine). I will henceforth refer to this media choice as a history **mode(s) of expression**. Genette recognises this when he suggests that the specific nature of narrative

> ...lies in its mode and not its content, which can equally well accommodate itself to a 'representation' that is dramatic, graphic, or other. In fact, there are no 'narrative contents'. There are chains of actions or events amenable to any mode of representation – the story of Oedipus, which Aristotle more or less credited with the same tragic quality in narrative form as in dramatic form – and we call them narrative only because we encounter them in a narrative representation.[22]

The important point here is that there is nothing in narrative's essential form that can be deployed theoretically to differentiate stories. The practical difference lies in the functions each is expected to perform. This is very important when considering the history narrative because in addition to the elements of *content*, *story*, *narrating* and *narrative* there are these varieties of modes of expression available to historians. The history narrative is expressed in many different modes and forms – text, visual, graphic, digital, **performative**, experiential, ideational and cultural. The history narrative is at once a memorial and a remembrance, but it is also anticipatory and emancipatory. All histories have very practical present, and future-orientated dimensions are always situated in its mode of its expression. It is because of this that the triad of *story*, *narrating* and *narrative* requires modification to take this into account. The modification is the addition of the new category of *expression*.

For even if one gives the factual or the referential elements primacy it cannot disguise the fact that the explanatory structure of history is fundamentally that of *story*, *narrating*, *narrative* plus an *expression*. In a history we expect referentially based **truth**, while in fiction we do not. It is indisputable that there is reference to the real in the one and not the other. But this has nothing to do with 'meaning creation', which is entirely the product of the narrative that connects *story*, *narrating*, *narrative* and *expression*. In so far as truth is claimed to be central to history (at least some sort of empirical truth) I will examine that claim in more detail in Chapter 7 (see pp. 111–122). And as we shall see, truth (as well as reality, **objectivity** and meaning) must be considered as part – a function – of the narrative making exercise.

Despite that (and using Genette's terminology as appropriate), historians still tend to view the logic of history as being, you will recall, something like this:

reference to events ⟶ historian's explanation/meaning ⟶ the history
(usually
textual)

However, by viewing history as a narrative representation (of the past) it becomes

story (reference to events) ⟶
 narrating (historian's explanation/meaning)
  ⟶ *narrative* (the history)
   ⟶ *expression* (form/s of
   representation)

This means that through Genette's analysis of narrative we have learned four things and reached an important conclusion about history. The first thing we have learned is that the history narrative shares the same three fundamental elements as fictional narrative – they are, after all, universals. Second, in fictional narrative the order is something like this:

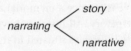

Third, the above three elements cannot be disassociated from each other. Fourth, it is more realistic to view the relationship of these elements in both fiction *and* history as one of over-determination. This is despite the apparently determining role of documentary attested data in history.[23] And the conclusion is that history is a complex narrative making discipline that incorporates **referentiality** but it is not controlled by it in the sense that it works according to epistemological notions of **correspondence**.

By understanding the over-determining relationships between the narrative elements of content, story, narrating, narration and expression, we are alerted to history defined now as the story space relationship existing between

- Past events – the content of the past explained as a story, and which I will conflate and call *content/story*.
- The author-historian's act of *narrating* (in which I will henceforth include the concept of *narration*).
- The past represented as a 'history narrative' of a particular kind – the *mode of expression* as a kind of history narrative – textual, film, performance, comic strip and so on.

Thus, I suggest that the relationship between narrative and history construed as a mutually determining narrative making exercise can be graphically represented now as

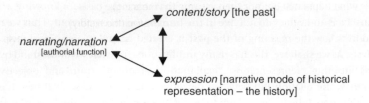

Note the directions of the arrows. Now, there are three further things to note about how this model of narrative has now been turned into a mechanism for explaining the logic of history. Given that history deals with the reality of the past it is necessary to explore the way in which the historian establishes the content/story of the past primarily through the function of plot (the historian's act of emplotment). Following the works of Hayden White and Paul Ricoeur, rather than being a function of discourse, the plot decisions of the historian are now re-located as part of the construction of the content/story. In history, the 'story/how' and 'discourse/what' distinction is much less clear-cut than in non-history. So, we need to acknowledge how historians transform a set of historical events (the chronicle of 'what happened') into a sequence organised through the structure of the four primary plot typologies, which, White [and literary theorists] maintains, are romance, tragedy, comedy, satire. What I am saying is that organising the data of the content of the past can only be accommodated as a storied narrative act.

In summary:

- First, the past has to be storied, but the story (emplotment) does not pre-exist in the content of past events. The content/story element is the location for the creation of beginnings, middles and ends, moral statements, the empirical reference and inference/analysis.
- Second, the nature and functioning of the historian, as a narrator (the authorial **voice**) probably requires a far more detailed analysis than it has hitherto received. Though a highly self-conscious group of people, historians are not generally aware of the functioning of the elements of discourse such as voice but also, as we shall see, the narrative concepts of **tense/time**, mood and **focalisation**.
- Third, the fact that history can be expressed in many different modes (verbal, textual, filmic, digital, performative, etc.) requires a basic understanding of how each mode is at once constrained by and, in turn, influences the epistemological

status of the history produced. In other words, the story space is governed by its mode of expression.

What I am suggesting, then, is that to understand the nature of history we need to know what happened but not then assume that this is the basis for knowing *what* it means: facts and values do not live in the form of logical entailment. Thus we need to address *how* the meaning of the past is created *beyond* the empirical facts and analysis. As we shall see, this has many implications for what we understand by the terms 'meaning', 'representation', 'explanation', '**realism**', 'truth' and 'objectivity'. Of course, the relationship between narrative and history described here has no more (but hopefully no less) claim to being 'the way to look at the logic of history' than any other rational approach. What it does do, however, is accept that history is a narrative making exercise rather than solely an empirical-analytical one.

▶ Conclusion

In this chapter, I began by confronting the reconstructionist and constructionist belief that reference, explanation and meaning are merely re-presented in the form of a narrative. I argued that as a representation – as a story space – history is categorically different from the past and there can be no translation between the two by the methods of empiricism. While empiricism is a significant element in history, it should not obscure what happens in the 'telling' process. Thus, I have argued that the story space, as the site of the historian's narration, is the location for her or his various strategies for narrating. For this reason, if for no other, we ought never to assume that reference equates with truthful meaning.

My analysis so far has been indebted primarily to Gérard Genette, Seymour Chatman, Hayden White and Paul Ricoeur. I have construed history as a mode of explanation and meaning that results from the relationship between *content/story* (the past), *narrating/narration* (historian as author) and the *mode of expression* medium (of representation). Rather than the narrative being merely a medium of report, it is the organising principle for the aesthetic turning of the past into what it patently is: the-past-*as*-history. It is now necessary to turn to a more detailed analysis of content/story, narrating/narration and history as a mode of expression. I begin in the next chapter with content/story.

2 History as Content/Story

Plainly, while it aims to be an accurate **representation**, **history** is not a replication of that which is past and gone. The implication is that for the notion of replication to make any sense we would have to assume that the historian could pass through the textual veil of historiography and be able to get back to 'historical **reality**'.[1] As noted, this is not feasible and, hence, history remains a **fictive**ly determined attempt at recovering (whether it is reconstructing, constructing or deconstructing) the past in the only way possible – through the creation of a **narrative** about it.

Given its fictive, 'substituting' nature, then, as Frank R. Ankersmit argues (and I agree), history is never as good as the original it represents.[2] We should not forget that **epistemology** works on the principle that 'things' (reality) and 'words' (cognitive language) can be tied together via a *tertium quid*. But a **representation** connects the represented (a thing) only to its representation (another thing). This is, by definition, only ever connect things to things. Thus a representation of President Ronald Reagan can only be compared to another representation of Ronald Reagan. Consequently, we cannot cross-reference our narratives as representations with past reality, but only against other narratives or, to use Ankersmit's term, other 'narrative substances'.[3] Remember that while our historical narratives may be overflowing with factual sentences, these do not of themselves entail **meanings.** In spite of empirical-analytical arguments, the *history text* cannot provide a knowable reality that is *independent of the history text*.[4]

You will recall that I said in the Introduction that we could define history as that set of relationships that exists between a **discourse**/narrative and the real events it recounts/explains. I did this by invoking the Genette model of **story**, narrating and narration. I also noted how, given the peculiar needs of history as a realist literary discourse, we must take into account what it is that historians actually do beyond gathering data and inferring what it most likely means. Using Genette's narrative model I argued that history is a **story space** which, informed by its content, constitutes the structure of a storied (*histoire*) sequence of events and actions. This conception is rooted in Gallie's as well as Genette's notion of story. The narrative theorist Seymour Chatman also suggests that the process of narrating has substantial consequences for the expressive medium chosen for the narration, and the medium itself 'reflects' back on, or resonates with, the process of narrating according to the demands it makes for **explanation** and meaning creation.[5] So historians are recognising that both history's storied content (as well as its reception by the reader/viewer) and its **mode of expression** are authored activities working together.[6]

Now, before explaining more fully what comprises the past defined in terms of content and story, authorial functioning (the narrating process) and expression (the narrative medium of **representation**) I should explain the assumptions I have made about history and its production so that we can proceed on this basis. The seven assumptions I have made are

(1) Like all human made objects, history is always subject to the question 'how was it made?' and such questions are normally answered through an explanation of its formal structure.

(2) In the case of the historical narrative, I have assumed that we need to distinguish the content of the past (that story which is to be narrated) from the ways in which it is expressed (its narrative form).

(3) This narrativism now allows us to construct **the-past-*as*-history**. Here its logic is not that of detection and discovery (although detection and discovery probably has a role in scouring the archive), but the logic of story space.

(4) Any model of the narrative logic of history must be functional in that it must have an explicit and **order**ly arrangement of discrete elements – what I will call **narrative choices**. These are found in all history texts. At the same time we have to acknowledge the boundless diversity of ways in which narrative choices can be meaningfully arranged. So, while all histories work within a common (and formal) functional narrative structure, their meanings will always be different.

(5) Any narrative model of history must acknowledge the question of authorship (the authorial function). 'How was it made?' must always sit alongside 'what does it tell us about past reality?' Without this, history remains just an exercise in data gathering plus **inference**.

(6) No history model (narrative or otherwise) can ignore values and ideology. This means our judgement of the 'worth', 'utility', 'value' or 'quality' of a history should be concerned not just with the question of 'how it was written or constructed?', but also why. In other words, what 'persuasive message' does it carry?

(7) If the work of history is to be defined adequately as an authored **referential** literature, its **aesthetic** shaping must be considered as prior to its empirical authority vis-à-vis the meaning of a history at the level of the **fact**.

What follows from these assumptions is that the three elements of content/story, narrative/narration and expression constitute the historian's key narrative choices. The notion of a narrative choice is derived from a variety of theorists including Roman Jakobson, Vladimir Propp, Roland Barthes, Gérard Genette, A.J. Greimas and Tzvetan Todorov, as well as history theorists like Louis Mink and Paul Ricoeur.[7] Vladimir Propp, for example, noted over 30 narrative functions in his analysis of the Russian folktale. He argued they were required to make sense of the story (at a simple level the 'hero leaving home' is a story function that comes before 'their return'). Clearly Propp's narrative functions were intended to make explicit the orderly and plausible development of the story of the content.

As we shall see, the narrative model of content/story, narrative/narration and expression provides a vocabulary of concepts for understanding how a history narrative 'realises' the past. As we know, the arrangement, priority and operation of the narrative choices are dependent upon the individual historian's epistemological preferences (**reconstructionist, constructionist, deconstructionist** or even postist or anti-history). How the historian displays their awareness of and deploys their narrative choices allows us to determine the nature of their epistemological judgements. Thus, for example, Eric Hobsbawm's and Charles More's understanding of the British 'industrial revolution' differ dramatically in terms of their respective epistemological choices as reflected in both data selection and level of theorisation (and not forgetting their radically divergent ideological positions). But neither reflects on the issue of representation nor on the nature of the story they are creating.[8] And this is central to the interpretation/creation of meaning.

▶ Following a story

As you will recall, Gallie said that a history is a sequence of the actions of people, which provides the content of the story.[9] Thus, to follow a story as a form of historical explanation is to understand the content of the past as a series of successive actions and thoughts that seem to possess 'directedness' that pulls us forward to 'the conclusion'. This is the narrative function of **followability**. This is why every history story space must possess both content *and* story. Seymour Chatman agrees that the 'what' of narrative is content 'storied' as a chain of events, actions and happenings.[10] A story is a sequence of events based on the mechanism of 'this happened, then that ... ' as opposed to chronicle – a mere listing of events.[11]

Moreover, as the narrative theorist Jerome Bruner argues, only by considering action itself *as* a text can we understand history or, indeed, action itself. Paul Ricoeur concurs understanding action demands telling a story. Without the story's 'telling' the content of the past remains just things that happened in time and space and literally has no meaning. What is required is something beyond sequence – a way of constituting meaning through an explanation of the story (assumed to exist?) in the content of events.[12] For Ricoeur this constitution of meaning emerges from knowledge of the historical agent's intentions (**agency**). For Frank Ankersmit, however, meaning emerges from the historian's construction of a story (of which agent **intentionality** is only one feature).

It is probably worth emphasising at this point that facts *in themselves* are not relevant to the process of *following* a story. By this I mean that individual events carry no inherent followability. This is because events function as narrative units akin to Propp's narrative units (a birth, a death, a discovery, a victory, a decision, a mistake, good then bad weather in the English Channel . . .). This is most obvious in the manner in which some historians prefer a thematic approach to the past as with Charles More's industrial revolution (which is a different industrial revolution to that of any other historian). In other words, events are subsumed within a class, and the classification creates the meaning.

But this logic means that the 'ending' of the history, in effect, 'writes' the 'beginning' and 'middle' of the **emplotment**. Compare More's thematic story with Eric Hobsbawm's who emplots British economic development chronologically taking events as they occurred. Another useful recent example is *Women in Italy, 1350–1650: Ideals and Realities* by Mary Rogers and Paola Tinagli.[13] Subtitled 'a **source**book' the authors' narrative is cast as 'the other **voice**', which is a thematic device that attempts to recapture the experiences of Italian women from the fourteenth to the seventeenth century. Collecting together a range of **sources** to 'illuminate' the civic and courtly culture of Renaissance Italy ' . . . as it affected women' is their forming of such a story in order to make it followable.[14] Indeed, even the sources are collected thematically – nature of women, life cycles and the variety of women's roles.

Clearly, the concept of the story space requires that we must understand the nature of content/story.[15] So what explanatory strategies organise a history's content/story? There are six key narrative functions or authorial decisions that constitute the content/story element of all history. From what I have already said, it should be no surprise that the first on the list is that of the historian's epistemological choice. But the full list is as follows:

- epistemological choice(s)
- aesthetic/figurative/**tropic** predispositions
- emplotment inclinations
- mode of cognition and analytical argument
- ethical preferences
- selection of factual references to events that took place and what happened to the historical agent.

Prior to explaining each of these decisions, we need to note that they impact on each other in a reciprocal (over-determining) fashion and also that they operate differentially as between historians. Thus, the historian's narrative choices create the explanatory coherence that we sense in each history (or lack of it in 'poor' histories). An example would be when the historian makes an ethical or ideological judgement about the decision of an agent in the past and this 'leads' the historian to make a choice about the priority of agency over structure. This may then influence further decisions about how they choose to narrate, and eventually their preferred mode of expression. In this way every historian establishes a unique 'signature' of narrative choices as they work within their chosen epistemological tradition.

But because the historian's decisions are personal they are always subject to priorities and preferences. As White has pointed out in his model of the historical imagination, there are always 'elective affinities' between narrative choices, which in his case are generated not by epistemological preferences but tropic/figurative choices. Whether epistemological or figurative (maybe they are the same?), the narrative choices of reference and emplotment, for example, will generate a different explanatory coherence for a reconstructionist than for a deconstruc-tionist. I will now turn to the individual functional decisions. The first of the six, as noted, is the historian's epistemological choice.

▶ Epistemological choice

Epistemology is that area of philosophy that explores the foundations, theory, nature, possibilities, conditions and limits of knowledge. Today, philosophers of history ask three epistemological questions:

- What is the proper structure of historical explanation?
- Can the study of the past be **objective** and **truth**ful?
- What is the function of narrative in communicating historical knowledge?[16]

The lack of an agreed answer to each question reflects the fundamentally uncer-tain nature of history as a way of knowing. As children of the Enlightenment, reconstructionist and constructionist historians have answered the first question by endorsing an empirical-analytical epistemology. They have collectively said 'yes' to the second question (with certain reservations), and to the third generally maintain that it is a matter of reporting their inferences.

As should be clear by now, historians do not universally agree on the most suitable methods to be employed in the pursuit of the-past-*as*-history given their epistemological choices. Before making an epistemological choice all historians face two questions. First, how does the notion of reference connect to *the* narrative that is assumed to have existed in the past? And second, if they have a mech-anism in mind that explains that connection (usually called 'a theory of historical change'), how then can they then claim the data *tells its own story*? In other words, what mechanism is there that automatically connects knowing what happened with what it means as a true story? So, what third element or *tertium quid* exists that permits the faithful translation of the facts of the past into 'the true' meaningful history? What is it that makes the 'past world' and the 'present historical world' correspond to each other? Why do most historians believe that their general interpretative conclusions are true, defined as what they *must* mean, as opposed to being merely references to happenings?

While every history text is an instance of this, the inventions associated with gender history are particularly illustrative. John Tosh's *Manliness and Masculinities in Nineteenth Century Britain* (2005) is a self-acknowledged (constructionist) case in point.[17] The author begins by saying the making of manhood ' . . . suggests something new and challenging', and he hopes ' . . . to show that the history of masculinities is just that'.[18] As a constructionist historian, Tosh makes his history in order to constitute a new historian's consensus (as a particular story space), but the important epistemological point is that it is a creation intended to provide a meaning for the past. Epistemologically, Tosh has made his decision to create what he believes is a new (hi)story founded on the *tertium quid* of a particular theorisation of masculinity.

In pursuit of the matter of epistemological choice we should also note that much Western continental philosophy in the past 50 years has turned away from empirical-analytical philosophy. The challenge to, and occasionally the outright rejection of, **empiricism**, inference, objectivity, truth and representation (as understood at the relatively uncomplex level of most epistemologists) produces what is for some an anti-realist and for others an anti-representational intellectual stance. The broad elements associated with these positions vary: from a willingness to accept the collapse of the distinctions of epistemology (the nature of knowing) and **ontology** (the nature of being), or of reversing them, or of overturning the priority of content over form, or of acknowledging the practical fusion of observer and observed, and/or happily accepting the auteur (author) theory of history. This is a situation that has generated much angst among reconstructionists and only a little less among constructionists.[19] Reconstructionist's high anxiety has not been dampened by the philosopher Frank R. Ankersmit's effort to persuade them to end their fixation with epistemology in favour of the ontology of the historical narrative as the locus of historical knowledge.[20] However, the most radical step appeared to have been taken by Hayden White and his emphasis upon the determining role of figurative choice.

▶ Aesthetics/figuration/trope

There is no doubt that the model of the historical imagination offered in the early 1970s by Hayden White (building on the insights of Roland Barthes) remains the significant point of departure for all debates on the narrative logic of history.

Certainly his work provides an original analysis of the essential functions that organise content/story. White's own epistemological choice is to adopt a deconstructionist position in as much as he argues that the ultimate determining narrative choice (though 'narrative choice' is not a term he uses) is vested in the historian's aesthetic preferences – specifically in the power of figuration.

White insists (as does Ricoeur) that all historians unavoidably aestheticise the past. What this means is that the historian's vision of the past is always cast in categories that derive their meaning ultimately from the process of narration (see also the functioning of voice, Chapter 3) – or in White's case specifically the process of troping.[21] So when a historian characterises world-wide consumerism in terms of 'the global city' this is an aesthetic decision (as much if not more than it is referential because it establishes a metonymic or **correspondence** notion).[22]

Troping is a basic human intellectual faculty through which we ascribe meaning to events (past and present) in terms of similarity or difference. Substituting constituent parts for the whole or the other way around often accomplishes this. Thus for 'US domestic/foreign policy' a historian may substitute 'the (Western) frontier' with the one part representing the essence of the other, usually connected in some way through the *tertium quid* of 'democracy'. As just noted with 'the global city' this is, in its effect, the creation of a complex metonymy. Metonymy is, unsurprisingly, the most favoured **trope** of historians as it establishes a (figurative) relationship between entities based on similarity and contiguity suggesting cause and effect. This is the figurative basis of the correspondence theory.[23]

White, specifically, is saying that tropes (the basic kinds are metonymy, metaphor, synecdoche and irony) are essential for understanding how the content of the past is 'prefiguratively grasped' by the historian, that they are, in effect, preparatory to the organisation of our content/story. By virtue of being human, historians cannot 'turn off' this prefigurative act though they do have a choice (whether consciously or unconsciously is never going to be clear) of the trope (to create a mental-visual figuration) in which they predominantly wish to cast content/story as history. Glossing White, Ricoeur believes that what is important about metaphors is that they are the mechanism that forces us to interpret reality. Ricoeur claims metaphor is that aspect of language which allows historians to undertake their **hermeneutic** activities. Indeed, it is with and through metaphor that reality meets meaning and truth.

The philosopher Stephen Pepper's analysis of what he calls 'root metaphors' is that all hypotheses about the nature of the real world (and in this sense, historical proposals are always hypotheses) emerge through the process of analogy.[24] What this means is that equivalence, resemblance and difference is the linguistic mechanism for explanation and meaning. History owes its very nature to the fact that language is an incredibly rich medium for describing and explaining the meaning of objects in the world. In metaphor, for example, the analogical process takes the form of transfer (either as similarity or as difference) to create meaning often as an extended simile. This is most obvious in history book titles though they are embedded in full-scale historical narratives.

Thus, while many book titles are bland and intended to be simply descriptive of their contents such as *Gender and American History Since 1890* or *A History of the British Isles*, others do tend to be analogical from the outset.[25] Examples would include *The Many-Headed Hydra* subtitled *The Hidden History of the Revolutionary Atlantic*, or *Jumpin' Jim Crow* subtitled *Southern Politics from Civil War to Civil Rights*.[26] But even in blandly entitled histories, authors cannot escape their analogical thinking. In Barbara Melosh's edited *Gender and American History Since 1890*, biological conceptions of 'difference' are rejected and the cultural determination of sex difference explored from a variety of competing figurative perspectives.[27] Gender history is invariably cast as an exploration centred upon the tensions between metaphor, metonymy and synecdoche as 'gender difference' is configured in terms of distinct conceptions of 'the other' and 'othering' though these terms are not necessarily deployed.

Beyond epistemological choice and figuration, it is the view of both White and Ricoeur that a further choice for the historian is the constitution of 'a story of a particular kind' about the past. As should be clear by now, it is a fundamental of historical explanation and meaning creation that a story is being told to the reader/viewer/listener. This is an explanation through another aesthetic choice – specifically that of emplotment. What is crucial is that it does not matter to their construction whether the stories are fictional or non-fictional. Bracketing off reference to past reality for the moment, the inner workings of stories are universal. While reconstructionist **author-historians** in evidencing 'past reality' will claim that there cannot be any 'story invention' on their part, the logic of the story demonstrates that the choice of emplotment is also a major element in creating historical meaning.

▶ Emplotment/story

Emplotment works by endowing events with the structure of one of the four archetypal emplotment types.[28] This is a belief held by most narrative theorists, even realists like Paul Ricoeur.[29] He notes '... that history imitates in its own writing the types of emplotment handed down by our literary tradition'.[30] To be honest, the reason for the particular choice of the historian is not always very clear. But, as I noted in the last chapter, Paul Ricoeur's analysis of *mimésis* is significant and helpful. Taking his cue from Aristotle, Ricoeur makes the crucial connection between figuration (specifically metaphor), *mimésis* and human action. Defining metaphor as 'seeing-as' (seeing one thing *as* another in the sense of substitution) leads Ricoeur to defining *mimésis* as an imitative substitution of human action through the mechanism of an emplotment/story.

In other words, Ricoeur believes that in order to make past action meaningful history works as a substitute for past action through the process of emplotment. Thus, *mimésis* translates as the emplotment of it (defined as the narrative organisation of human action) and not just an imitation of the past (as data). Hence Ricoeur's argument is that history is the figurative (in this case metaphoric) imitation of human action. This is a judgement supported by a substantial range of literary and historical theorists – Vladimir Propp, A.J. Greimas, Northrop Frye, Tzvetan Todorov, Gérard Genette, Louis Mink, Hayden White, Keith Jenkins, and others.[31]

Historians have 'heroes' (a person, class, race, nation, idea, political orientation, etc.) and the **characterisation** of a story of events and actions into a mode of emplotment is normally defined by what happens to the 'hero'.[32] So, 'the English king died. His consort went on holiday. She met a foreign prince. She subsequently married him' is just a series of events. But if we said 'the English king died and then his consort went on holiday because she was so happy where she met a foreign prince who exploited her state of mind in order to woo and marry her', this is an emplotment (of which kind you decide). In other words, to penetrate cause and effect (assuming we can do that) the historian will call upon what are the four basic forms as a way or organising the otherwise dissonant events in the past. These are tragedy, romance, satire or comedy. For example, in *The American Radical*, a collection of mini-biographies of 46 dissenting radicals in American history, the authors tend to navigate between the poles of romance and tragedy.[33]

Neither realist nor non-realist narratives are simply a listing of events. This is because both work by establishing causal connections. The key differences between history and non-histories are two. First, there is the nature of emplotment. It is not merely that in history the events are real, but in (conventional) history the author-historian does not create the ordering of events (they are given as they occurred according to the data stream) unlike the writer of fiction. And second, in a non-history the writer is not trying to spell out why one explanation is better than another. However, what both modes of narrative do have in common – as we shall see in the next few chapters – is that they are emplotted narratives constructed from a range of available data founded through a range of competing epistemological assumptions and expressed in a variety of different modes. The significant difference between realist and non-realist narrative is, as Ankersmit insists, the balance between the compulsions of the real and the fictive.

While in the history story we can fairly assume that 'what happened' actually did happen, the process of explanation and meaning through emplotment is an aesthetic and **mimetic** artifice all the way through.[34] The reason is very simple and we have already come across it. It is founded on the authoring of a beginning, middle and end to the story (though as we shall see, in **experimental history** or as Jean-Luc Godard said famously about film, they do not necessarily have to be in that order).[35] White rejects the notion that the historian 'finds' or 'identifies' emplotments in 'this happened, then that' adding '... because...'. White is unconcerned about the extent of 'invention' in the historian's operations observing how the same event can provide for different purposes in different stories depending on whether it is located as a beginning, middle or end (or noted briefly only to henceforth omit it). The corollary to this is that the meaning of the past does not lie in the absolute significance of a single event but how that event is fitted into an appropriate story narrative.[36] So, if a history is emplotted as a tragedy it is 'explained' as a tragedy. Often events are said to be 'crucial', 'pivotal', 'determining' or 'central'. But they only become so when fitted into a story of a particular kind.

It would be irresponsible to insist that an emplotment is always a free choice for the historian. History, as a referential literature, works under the impress of past reality (and often it can make sense to view it in a mimetic way) (see Chapter 3, pp. 44–63) – as well as being a narrative construction and the product of dominant metanarratives (usually ideological or ethical, or both). Thus a narrative that connects religion with the rise of capitalism will have to emplot reference to Puritanism into it in some way or another.[37] Of course, every historian is obliged to weave a variety of emplotments within their history in one overall or archetypal story form assuming that they wish to generate a dominant meaning in their history (of a set of events). As we shall see, experimental history is often provocative because it may not do this.

Of course the (non-experimental) historian can experiment with different emplotments to examine the process of the creation of historical meaning itself. Thus, Donald McCoy in his *Coming of Age: The United States During the 1920s and 1930s* offered a history deploying the notion of continuity and change that is associated with a youth emerging into adulthood.[38] Offering a history of an event from different perspectives – and with, perhaps, different heroes and villains – is always a possibility for historians.[39] In spite of their unavoidable emplotment activities, any vagueness among historians about the narrative functionality of emplotment is almost invariably the result of their conventional epistemological investment in what is usually called 'argument' and almost as often 'analysis' or 'explanation'. So, what is the role of argument, analysis and explanation in organising content/story?

▶ Argument/analysis/explanation

Historians, particularly constructionists, use hypothetical models (hypotheses about the likely meanings of the past) that are imagined and then tested in the evidence. This is known, technically, as the hypothetico-deductive method. When the evidence does not fit, the hypothesis is modified while, at the same time, more evidence is sought. The logic is 'theory → evidence → modified theory → more evidence → theory → evidence . . . '. In this way it is assumed the pursuit of 'true knowledge' is edged forward. If intuitively you feel that history is not quite so scientific in its practice as this description suggests (after all, at what point does this process produce 'true knowledge'? When the historian decides enough is enough or the book contract deadline approaches?), there are many hard-core constructionist historians who would disagree. Nevertheless, given the chronological nature of events, it seems the past has to be explained in terms of 'this happened, then that, *because* . . . (. . . insert the appropriately theorised referent at this point)'.

This demonstrates why narrative is the essential mode of historical explanation for it is only within a narrative that cause and effect can be grasped, let alone demonstrated. Remember what William Gallie said, that to explain the meaning of the past is to discover *the* story or, as White has it, offer one that is plausible (according to the available evidence). Hence, Tosh's concept of 'manliness' as a mechanism through which to examine the history of men is as much invented as it is found. Similarly, in the case of John Y. Simon and Michael E. Stevens' brave attempt at sorting out the myths from the realities of the American Civil War, while they can clarify the data, they cannot do it without creating new stories, new arguments and fresh explanations.[40]

Of course, none of this impairs the historian's effort to demonstrate that something happened/did not happen, much less their ability to infer what it probably signifies (means). As a constructionist (though with heavy reconstructionist leanings) the historian Richard Evans says, historians ' . . . have always been obliged to get their hands dirty' in the archives before they can draw appropriate inferences.[41] Deconstructionists would probably agree not only with Evans, but also with history theorists Louis Mink and Hayden White. Deconstructionists maintain that while all past actions, processes and events have to be located in time and space according to the evidence, they must then be rendered (narrated) into a story, and that telling such stories is itself a cognitive act.

While this does not do away with the need for empiricism and analysis, only a doctrinaire and dogmatic belief in objectivity would be the reason for not addressing the narrativist nature of argument and analysis. This, by the way, has nothing to do with, for example, 'telling lies about Hitler', which is entirely a matter of false data and spurious inferences. That anti-deconstructionists occasionally imply otherwise has much to do with their equating knowing the actuality of the data stream with a 'proper' moral position. That this is an invalid belief demands we examine the narrative function of ethical, political and ideological choice.

► Ethical/political/ideological choices

Historical representations always have moral/ethical and political/ideological dimensions. Moreover, the matters of **subjectivity** and **relativism** demand important decisions by the historian. But we do not simply want to understand what moral assumption(s) historians bring to their study of the past. More important is why some historians still imagine they can be morally neutral/objective? Most historians do, of course, accept that they are influenced by their ethical and/or ideological affinities. Of course they may not think immediately in terms of what Martin Kreiswirth calls 'storied knowledge', which is particularly effective in packaging ideology, especially in telling the narratives of marginalised groups (gender, race, class, etc.).[42] However, for most historians the notion of an overtly ideological (and for some a 'moral') history remains a worrying notion especially when associated – as it has to be – with the idea of an 'authorial voice' (see Chapter 3, pp. 44–63). This is because it seems to drive a wedge between the idea of the knowing and honest historian, and truthful and objective history. This can readily be witnessed in the debates of some 30 or so years ago over the economic efficiency of American chattel slavery, as historians then debated the balance of economic efficiency and morality.

While this issue of morality in history will arise again, for now we need only to note that historians always consider the ideological, ethical and moral dimension of what they do. Indeed, the history theorist Beverley Southgate goes so far as to suggest that historians have to make moral choices about what they want to see their history leading to in the future. For Southgate, history is unavoidably an ethical activity.[43] In arriving at a judgement on the determining power of ideology, ethics and moral choice in explaining the meaning of the past, there are two issues of which all historians are aware. First, how reasonable is it to argue that the ideological and ethical narrative choices historians make can be 'set aside' and subordinated to their experience of the archive? And second, what is the relationship between ideology, ethics and aesthetics?

The first issue can be dealt with very briefly if you think it odd that we can separate our life from being a historian. Airline pilots may be able to do because, presumably, they are not making moral judgements when they land a plane in a crosswind. Further, would it not be serious waste of time to pursue the argument that the recognition of the historian's ethical choice(s) may weigh to some extent *against* scholarship? The historian of biography and autobiography Jeremy D. Popkin's belief that an academic's ideological choice does not necessarily discredit scholarship also misses the point though in a different way.[44] What is missed by both arguments is the spurious nature of the belief (a) that we can separate 'the self' from 'the historian', and (b) that some historians can do a better job of it than others can and, as a result, they will be 'more objective'.

As for the second issue, while a few historians will narrate history that is very obviously self- and/or cause-serving, the point is *all* history is situated, positioned and *for* some thing or someone. By merely writing a story we are destined to make ethical decisions. 'The other', 'the forgotten' and 'the institutions for funding research' are always lurking either in or behind the history narrative. In this sense, history is a liminal activity. It is always on the edge of something else. Feminist history, for example, aims to bring the object of study (for feminists it is the female) into view.[45] Equally, doing 'experimental history' has a purpose, as does nationalist or racial history. Even not doing history has a purpose. Indeed, invoking one set of data rather than another has an ethical purpose. So, what is the role of the data in producing a history narrative?

▶ Reference/sources

Empiricism holds that the ultimate compulsion in history is reference to the past. Normally this wisdom is anthropomorphised in the self-effacing empirical **sceptic**. Many historians agree that we may start by doubting what our sources tell us, but not accepting that eventually we will be forced to believe in demonstrable truth is dangerous. Deconstructionists – as epistemological sceptics – might call this the 'empiricism effect'. The pursuit of the humility that accompanies the empiricism effect also creates the image of the historian as a humble toiler – a kind of empirical gleaner.[46]

Concomitant with all this is the notion of evidence being subject to certain 'craft principles' similar to those rules of evidence in a civil court of law with the case 'proved' according to the balance of probabilities though never beyond reasonable doubt as in a criminal court. The way historians use evidence, as we shall see, also hinges on the issues of contextualisation and comparison. To reject these two principles would substantially redefine, as one historian claimed recently,

> ... the relationship between the historical account and the actual past in a manner that made reality (understood as objective entity) either minimally or not at all accessible to any inquirer.[47]

Most historians would accept, then, that evidence can be 'converted into facts' thanks to the use of 'critical methods and rules'.[48] The problem with this emerges when it is used to bolster the bigger epistemological argument that this enables a correspondence of 'consciousness to reality' that gives 'the facts' the central functional role in historical inquiry.[49] This is, of course, the primary claim of reconstructionist historians.

The constructionist would agree that the accumulation of data yield a 'greater approximation to the truth by revealing the structures and forces at work' in the past as facts.[50] Hence, Arthur Marwick, the British social historian and author of a best-selling defence of empiricism, while generally agreeing with these sentiments, puts his emphasis upon sources. He argues that facts ' . . . come from the traces that have been left by past societies, that is, the primary sources'.[51] He rejects what he calls 'the **postmodern** fantasy' of '*the* facts' offering instead the notion of knowledge derived by inference.[52] Only such knowledge can guarantee objectivity because it is built-in to the empirical and analytical equation. Marwick makes this explicit in his 1980 book on class when he examines the representation of class in films and then explicitly returns to ' . . . the *realities* of class'.[53]

As the self-proclaimed voice of empiricist sanity, Marwick argues that while sources alone do not make history, without them 'there is no history'.[54] For Marwick only continuous archival research will remove the historian's misconceptions, which will in turn foster more convincing interpretations (meanings). So, for Marwick the reconstructionist the history equation would seem to be like a wheel with reference the hub. But it is important to note that while Marwick sees a constant interrogation between reference, explanation and meaning, the narrative representation of such interrogations is ignored. The reconstructionist assumption remains that the narrative is essentially a self-regulating report of empirical findings extrinsic to it.[55]

This is reinforced with Marwick's evaluation of what he calls 'the communication of historical knowledge'.[56] For Marwick, historical knowledge is presented largely outside language. Even though he notes the complexities of dealing with past language use, he has no sense of the nature of history as a totality that is empirical-analytical *and* narrative-linguistic. And Marwick is not alone. Kevin Passmore's recent defence of empiricism and analysis uses Marwickian logic by which use he (thinks) he sees off a clutch of poststructuralist historians or fellow travellers. These include Hayden White, Patrick Joyce, Joan W. Scott, Keith Jenkins, Simon Schama, Robert Berkhofer, Robin Bisha, Jacques Derrida and Michel Foucault because such people clearly do not exercise any empirical self-control.[57]

Despite Passmore's and Marwick's arguments, what an understanding of history as a narrative making activity addresses is not reference itself, but the belief that it is *the* fundamental regulator of historical explanation and meaning. What viewing history as a narrative representation does is correct Marwickian epistemological myopia – the failure to see reference as only *one* element within the structure of history.

▶ Conclusion

In this chapter, I began by stating seven assumptions about the narrative representational nature of the historical enterprise. Following on from this, and based on Genette's analysis of narrative, I pursued the notion that content/story is one of three key elements in historical thinking and practice. I suggested that the element of content/story is composed of several narrative decisions the historian must make to explain what happened in the past as a story and what it means as history. I suggested that for the content/story, narrative decisions initially comprise the historian's preferred epistemological orientation, which is then followed by the aesthetics of figuration, the creation of an emplotment, the role of argument/analysis, ethical/ideological choice and the role of **referentiality**. Most importantly, what follows from this analysis is that the notion of what happened in the past must be placed on the same level as its telling. I will now examine how that telling can be undertaken because, as should be coming clear, for every content/story there is an author-historian speaking to us.

3 Narrating and Narration

Key to any understanding of the authorial act of narrating and narration is the analyses of Gérard Genette in his *Narrative Discourse* and *Narrative Discourse Revisited*.[1] Genette, with the **narrative** theorists Roland Barthes and Michel Foucault, has identified several categories through which we can understand what authors are doing when they narrate.[2] Whereas Genette evaluates the speaking function in narratives, Barthes asks us to consider the prior question of 'who is speaking', claiming that we cannot ever be sure given the nature of writing and language. This led him to his (in)famous announcement of the 'death of the author' suggesting that there is an unavoidable pluralism in the **meaning** of every text beyond the 'fixing' of the author. Hence reading **history** is not about trying to set *the* meaning (*the* interpretation or *the* story of *the* past) of the author; rather the act of reading itself (the destination or consumption of the text, film or museum display) becomes the centre of meaning creation.[3]

Foucault's contribution is, however, to ask if it matters who is the speaker? Foucault says 'yes', but only if we ask *that* question. More important for Foucault is what is the consequence of the 'disappearance of the author'. For Foucault the concept of an author suggests they are the origin of meaning. This applies to history where it is the function of the **author-historian** to create a **story space** even though they are/become self-effaced. While this is not so in every case, generally history is assumed to provide us with the security of the omniscient and impersonal 'news from nowhere' narration of the past. However, as Foucault pointed out and as we shall see, while the historian's **voice** may appear to be impersonal, it remains ubiquitous. Like an absent God, the historian, through their non-appearance, becomes the originator of meaning and **explanation**. For Foucault the author is not dead but just like the historian, is hiding.

While I will return to Barthes and Foucault later, first I need to ask how meaning and explanation provided through the authorial functioning of the historian are derived from Genette's analysis of voice and **focalisation**. I also need to examine Ricoeur on the connection between **time** and narrative. As I will demonstrate, the following structure of (the act of) narrating and narration seems universal in history:

- The Historian as Author.
- Voice and Focalisation.
- **Tense/Time** (Order, **Duration, Frequency**).
- **Intentionality**, Action and **Agency**.

When taken together, these four elements provide an analysis of the historian's narrating and narration function.

▶ The historian as author

Historians make numerous narrational decisions about the **representation** of the-past-*as*-history although most remain a little queasy about being regarded as an author because of the **subjectivity** such a description is supposed to entail.[4] Thus, in *The Soviet Century* the author Moshe Lewin makes no overt appearance in what he calls 'the immutable **reality** that cannot be altered by successive interpretations . . . ' of Soviet Russia.[5] This is, presumably, because of his **epistemological** intention to be realistic and let the **sources** tell their own true story of 'Soviet Russia'.[6] In this sense Lewin is making a claim to being a 'reliable narrator' who can offer an authoritative account 'according to the sources'. Indeed, all 'realist' historians make this claim though usually less explicitly than Lewin.

Conversely, in his *Mirror in the Shrine* about the early American 'opening up' of Japan, Robert A. Rosenstone has created a story space in which he explores the kind of history he has written and why.[7] This is presumably because of his belief in the essential discontinuity between life and art. Similarly Richard Price in his *Alabi's World* offers multiple voices.[8] The lack of realist fundamentalism in the work of Rosenstone and Price contrasts starkly with that of Lewin. This does not necessarily make Rosenstone an 'unreliable narrator' (and, therefore, quite unlike Lewin). Unreliable narrators have strictly limited knowledge, may be ethically suspect and may be personally involved, though not in Rosenstone terms but, rather, in terms of ideological axes to grind.

This brief introduction does not exhaust the nature of history authorship. It is also necessary to acknowledge the role of the 'implied author'.[9] Every history story space is produced through a set of narrating decisions (the history's tacit and often 'unspoken' norms) that create the text as it turns out to be. Implied authorship is increasingly less implied and more apparent, as history becomes a kind of 'instrument of policy' with an overt purpose. Thus, in her editor's introduction to *Haunted by Empire* (2006) Ann Laura Stoler is clear that her collection is intended to '. . . carve out a common ground of conversation between United States history and postcolonial studies'.[10] As she acknowledges, Abu Ghraib and Guantanamo Bay 'haunt the edges of these pages'.[11]

So, to be clear, what is an 'implied author'? For the literary theorist Wayne Booth, the 'implied author' is the governing consciousness that directs the work as a whole. While the author is a flesh and blood person open to all the inconsistencies of being human, the implied author is a fixed, coherent and consistent directing force. So the historian is not simply the anthropomorphisation of the 'implied' author who is 'behind' the ideational structure of the history text. Thus, for example, the name E.P. Thompson may refer to a person subject to all human vicissitudes, whereas the implied author behind his texts is primarily a constructionist humanist Marxist worldview. The name Keith Jenkins implies a 'postist' epistemological ethical orientation. The name Patrick Joyce could imply a left-liberal **deconstructionist** position.

But more than this, it is important to note that the implied author encompasses not just a world-view but also produces the design of the text. Inevitably it becomes even more complex than this once we acknowledge the arguments of Barthes and Foucault. It is complicated further by the author-historian should they attempt to divorce themselves from the concept of authorship: here they may (like all 'realist' historians) deny 'implied authorship' in favour of **objectivity** or **realism**. But texts are never absolutely coherent or synchronous as any detailed reading can reveal. Derrida is famous for his **poststructuralist** theory of deconstruction, which is mindful of the innate impermanence of and contradictions within all written texts. The implication is that meaning is always constructed again and again, as we read, re-read and re-write in our own minds the writing (what Derrida calls *écriture*, which is the French for 'writing'). Clearly this undercuts the ideal of **truth** as the equation of word and world.

The fond hope of truth, objectivity and realism apart, the **narrative choices** of the 'implied' author are normally directed towards a 'narratee' who is the agent, person or audience for whom the narrative is intended.[12] This 'implied reader' (the narratee/addressee) is the reading counterpart of the implied author. For narrative theorists like Gerald Prince the narrator/narratee relation is highly structured.[13] But, conscious of the Barthes–Foucault argument, poststructuralists and many deconstructionist historians are doubtful. This strict communication model has the unfortunate consequence of separating out the **ontological** distinction (the 'separate being-ness') of historian and narratee. The reason for their concern is that such a model simplifies what is a highly complex process of writerly meaning creation and reception – the reader in effect creating/re-creating the text's meaning as it is re-written in their own minds.

Most deconstructionist historians argue that the reception of the text in terms of what it means has much to do with the **intertextual** nature of the exchange.

The foundational belief that history is a report (though be it interpretative) has the consequence of ignoring the reciprocity between history text and its reader. By its nature as a virtual representation there must be a degree of freedom for the reader to interpret the (already interpretative) text. The notion of a 'readerly realist' text even at the simple level of statements of **justified belief** is not to be dismissed. Reading realist texts is always an uncertain activity not only because of the nature of language as a mode of meaning creation, but also because the author-function is connected to the 'institutional system' that encompasses the **discourse** that supervenes (exerts a control over) the text.[14]

When the historian Moshe Lewin shows us the immutable reality of his subject in his realist text, he is endorsing a belief in events utterly constraining *the* story. Rosenstone, on the other hand, tells us about *his* role in creating *a* story. Lewin is, consequently, an example of an **extradiegetic narrator** (who exists essentially outside the story *and* its telling), and Rosenstone an **intradiegetic** one (a part of both the story *and* its telling). Rosenstone constructs his story space this way presumably because he believes his presence directly affects how the narrative is produced and that it is important to acknowledge it especially in a universe where history is writerly as well as readerly.

Using this text as an example, I am an intradiegetic author-narrator. This is because I openly wish to encourage you to rethink your ideas about the nature of history and, given my particular arguments (about writerly texts at this point), I want to acknowledge your power over my intervention. Having said all this, it seems reasonable to ask why any historian should assume an extradiegetic position. Why do so many historians still prefer not to acknowledge *in the text* their existence as the author of the history and also the power of the reader? As we shall see, it is because of the epistemological hold of the concept of **mimésis** (see pp. 51–59). Such anonymity even stretches to the single sentences of justified belief that, as Jenkins says, are always derived, selected and written *into* evidence by the author-historian. As we shall see, rather than distance and non-engagement, it is authorial interventionism that is crucial to understanding the nature of history. This, consequently, necessitates an understanding of the two fundamental narrational concepts of voice and focalisation.

▶ Voice and focalisation

Voice is concerned with the audibility of the historian-author 'who tells the story' and which is sometimes called 'point of view'. The historian has a particular voice or point of view, which is made explicit *in and through* their narrative choices.[15] The US women's historian Jacquelyn Dowd Hall has called on women's history to develop 'a historical practice that turns on partiality, that is self-conscious about perspective, that releases multiple voices rather than competing orthodoxies . . . '.[16] As this comment implies, voice cannot be considered in the history text without **reference** to the concept of focalisation. In Hall's analysis the voice is that of the historian while the agent of focalisation, as determined by the historian (as a focaliser herself), is the discourse of the historical female. Clearly, given Hall's comment, the history narrative is a megaphone for a moral commitment for the focaliser in much the same way as any other narrative. Historians of gender can choose, for example, to voice the discourse of inclusion, exclusion, complaisance or resistance.

Specifically, focalisation refers to the author's choice, regulation and organisation of information in the story space in terms of 'seeing' events and existents from someone's point of view, usually a historical agent, narrator or one through the other, and in so doing establishing a focal point for the history. If voice deals with 'who speaks' (the subject of the history narration, i.e., the narrator), focalisation is concerned with 'who sees' (the subject of focalisation/the focaliser as an agent/character/gender/class/race) within the story space. As the narrative theorist, Mieke Bal reminds us, it is important to understand that the focaliser is also a narrator.[17]

Historians do not have a choice in this. They must adopt a perspective or point of view (which is not at all the same as either a pre-formed or referentially uninformed opinion) in order to see the past as a whole. Who it is that sees is, therefore, a fundamental choice for the historian and it is possible to distinguish three focalisation types – internal, external and zero. In other words, the historian as narrator focalises by choosing a point of view through a particular historical agent, but the agent then becomes the/a focaliser. The historian is thus both the voice and the focaliser of the discourse (who works through the historical agent).

The historian thus establishes a communication with the narratee by determining *how* to tell and from what focal perspective. Despite the variety of thinkers from Bakhtin to Genette, there is common agreement on the existence of four basic kinds of narrating voice. They are as follows:

1 A character/historical agent may tell their story in the first person (first-person or homodiegetic narrator with internal focalisation as with an autobiography).
2 A character/historical agent can tell a story they observed but still in the first person (first-person observer who is also a homodiegetic narrator with internal focalisation as with a witness).
3 The author-historian can tell what happens without exploring the minds of the characters/agents and not offering any commentary (author-as-observer or limited heterodiegetic narrator with external focalisation).
4 The author-historian can tell the reader what happened, explore the minds of the characters/agents and provide explanations/commentary/analysis

(omniscient author narrator or unlimited heterodiegetic narrator with zero focalisation).

Obviously these are not sealed from each other and there can be mixed modes (especially in **experimental history**), but type 4 above exemplifies what has been the conventional **reconstructionist** but now challenged view of the audibility of the voice of the historian.

Briefly, a homodiegetic narrator is one of the characters/agents in the story and a heterodiegetic narrator is a narrator who is not. These voices are not to be confused with an extradiegetic narrator and an intradiegetic one. In conventional histories the historian is always a heterodiegetic narrator. This appears to limit the historian's voice to types 3 and 4. Internal focalisation refers to the presentation of events from the perspective of a focal character/agent in the story (this is a choice of the historian). External focalisation refers to the presentation of events as perceived by an observer who knows less than the focalised character/agent knows. This would also appear to further foreclose on type 3 as a likely form of focalisation for the historian who, we would assume, knows everything. Zero focalisation refers to the heterodiegetic narrator who does not limit him or her to the 'real-life' and 'at the time' restricted points of view and knowledges of the agents. The zero focaliser is omniscient. Theorists as diverse as Louis Mink, Hayden White, Paul Ricoeur and Seymour Chatman all agree that historians can only construct the past by deploying mechanisms such as voice and focalisation.[18] What should by now be becoming clearer is the parallel between historical/factual and fictional narratives in terms of how they are created rather than the nature of their content.[19]

Reacting against reconstructionist conventions, Paul Ricoeur opposes the idea that events can tell themselves without the *effective* intervention of both voice and focalisation decisions. Ricoeur asks, can past events

> ... whether real or imaginary, be presented without any intervention of the speaker of the narrative? Can the events simply appear on the horizon of the story without anyone speaking in any way? Does not the absence of a narrator from historical narrative result from a strategy by means of which the narrator *makes* [my italics] himself absent from the narrative?[20]

Frank R. Ankersmit has also noted the significance of focalisation, offering the insight that it is its apparent absence that conventionally distinguishes history from the novel.[21] By implication, voice and focalisation are primary mechanisms through which historians apprehend past reality rather than only or simply through scientific-like hypothesis testing.[22] This can most readily be seen (literally seen) when we express history on film, as we see shifts in focalisation from the zero focalisation of the narrator (narrator-focaliser) to an internal focaliser via the perception of a character in the **content/story** (character-focaliser). Initially we see from a perspective that floats above the scene in its entirety. Then the perspective changes to focus on an agent with the camera offering the agent's acuity and awareness of situation (as they run or hide, smile or frown, or die or live while holding the flag of revolution). The camera readily changes our audience perspective from zero to internal focalisation (when the agent becomes the focaliser). Thus, focalisation changes meaning, understanding and explanation. The same effect is achieved in textual (verbal) narratives with the 'historical overview' focussing down to individual elements.

This technique is most obvious in history texts where quotation is used. In the following quotation the historian-author Richard J. Carwardine shifts from a position of zero focalisation to internal focalisation for explanation and interpretation purposes. Thus Carwardine says,

> Lincoln's rhetoric galvanised republicans ... the young stenographer Robert Hitt, judged the Alton speech Lincoln's greatest: its moral clarity captivated this son of a Protestant minister. He was not alone in pointing to the effect on Lincoln's audiences at Alton and elsewhere of his 'melting pathos'.[23]

Is this simply an **inference** by the historian backed up by evidence? While it may embody an inference, the shift in focalisation from zero to internal is as important to meaning production and explanation as is the quotation offered 'in evidence'. I do not know if Carwardine realised that he was shifting focalisation. In a way it does not really matter. The point is that history works in this respect like any other kind of literature – **fact**ual or non-realist. The omniscient narrator (Carwardine) can not only narrate outside the story, but also (and invariably does) invoke and adopt the limited point of view of one historical agent/character (Robert Hitt in this example). Most importantly, focalisation works in the loop of 'theory → evidence → modified theory → more evidence → theory → evidence ... ' with which we are familiar. That Lincoln was an able rhetorician is deemed by Carwardine to be significant in Lincoln's life. Obviously Carwardine will have reached this conclusion by examining the theory and the data, but the meaning of that process is only facilitated when Carwardine constructs his narrative – in this example shifting focalisation.[24]

This leads us to a further and extremely important dimension of historical narration. This is the way in which the historian constitutes and constructs time. The above short extract was taken from that part of the biography of Abraham Lincoln covering the period of Lincoln's life from 1854 to 1858. Not only did the extract provide a straightforward example of shift in focalisation but, as we shall see, it was also an element in the larger process of the author-historian's organising of tense/time within the text.

▶ Tense/time: Mimésis, order, duration and frequency

The function of tense/timing in ordinary language is to organise the temporal locations of situations and events in the content/story.[25] According to Suzanne Fleischman, narration is the linguistic representation of experience viewed from a retrospective vantage point. Experience is, by definition, 'past' whether it occurred 'in reality' or 'in fiction'. Hence history does not have exclusive possession of 'the past tense' because the prototypical tense of narration as a mode of reporting information is 'the past' (the preterite expressing a past action or state).[26] Historians, by and large, still tend to ignore the question of tense/timing in what they do.

This is surprising given that Paul Ricoeur has explained at great length that what he calls the unavoidable 'interweaving of history and fiction' results from the similarities of their aims through the appropriation of time. Ricoeur argues that history 'reinscribes the time of narrative within the time of the universe'.[27] Without doubt the 'temporal turn' is central to historical narrative thinking and practice.[28] Given that the past cannot be re-lived as it actually was (because it no longer exists), all the historian can do is 'manage' recorded memories of it by putting them into a narrative and regulating 'real time' in the process. This can be done in many different ways with the same general topic. Take the issue of black identity in American slave history and compare the approaches of Lawrence W. Levine and Eugene D. Genovese.[29] While both their story spaces reference similar empirical material, the histories produced are entirely different in respect of their 'time signatures'. Levine thus tends to ignore time as an organising concept using themes (about song and oral cultural development). On the other hand, Genovese deploys a much stronger sense of change over time because of his (Marxist-inspired) insistence on slavery as a form of class control which evolved inexorably over time.

For Ricoeur (and, earlier on, for Dilthey) the work of the historian centres (as a comparison of Levine and Genovese demonstrate) on the temporal turn from 'real time' as it is culturally understood and 'narrated history time' which is manufactured for purposes of explanation and meaning creation. Though normally conceived of in terms of centuries, decades, years, seasons and days, real time is also perceived to be both cyclical (weeks, seasons, genealogical) and also linear as with a life, a presidency, a Royal House or a dictatorship. Historians do not only have to do justice to the **referential** nature of the past chronologically, but (primarily in the West) also re-organise real time in terms of order, duration, frequency and tempo in order to create meaning.[30] In this respect the history narrative is a story space (and what Dilthey called 'a nexus') in which all that constituted the past is made to connect by the historian.[31]

So, just how do historians deploy order, duration and frequency to 'time' the past? We need to start with Seymour Chatman and Paul Ricoeur. Agreeing with

Ricoeur, Chatman maintains the temporal turn suffuses every aspect of writing, noting the **timing** in **emplotment** (with which we are already familiar), of a beginning, a middle and an end.[32] Though, he says, this works very well in fiction it cannot usefully organise reality – even past reality – because 'the real' can never know where it is or was between beginning, middle and end. As Chatman says, beginning, middle and end

> ... apply to the narrative, to story-events as imitated rather than to real actions them-
> selves, simply because such terms are meaningless in the real world. No end in reality is
> ever final the way 'The End' of a novel or film is. . . . such a term marks out plot, the story-
> as-discoursed. It is strictly an artifact of composition, not a function of raw story-material
> (whatever its source, real or invented).[33]

When the (author-historian) Carwardine says, 'Thus Lincoln, through his life and death, bequeathed an enhanced and ambitious nationalism to his successors'; according to conventional empirical-analytical history logic, he is simply offering an attested and, therefore, an informed, fair and balanced interpretation of the meaning of the life of Lincoln. But, in terms of creating a history, the author-historian has provided an interpretation that is founded on a 'classic realist' (though) constructed metonymic (**mimetic**) continuity or contiguity between the real and its representation. In this case it is in terms of a beginning, a middle and an end to the life and meaning of Lincoln.[34]

This is an example of the classic realist notion (of contiguity) where we move from event to event, and the narrative replicates this realistic progression. Metonymy functions in such a way that some 'thing' stands in for another 'thing' as with 'Lincoln' and 'ambitious nationalism'. The problem is that in this example we cannot know if this is the actuality of the meaning of Lincoln's life because of the uncertainty of where to locate its interpretative closure in terms of a linguistic connection between events and meaning.

Despite it being a bedrock assumption of many historians, the problem with mimésis is that it can only work linguistically (usually as a text of some kind) which ensures that language can only assert that it 'imitates' the past as a history narrative (as a mode of language use). Despite this assertion, history cannot actually be imitative (of the past) because it (is a category that) 'tells' rather than 'shows'. The best historians can hope for is an illusion of mimésis through the use of direct speech representation (the quotation bolstered by the 'knowledge power' of the reference).

While recognising the problem of mimésis, following Chatman, Ricoeur offers a detailed and complex analysis of the temporal turning of the past (as spatial human action) into our (historical) appreciation and understanding of it through his own definition of mimésis. Following the meditations of St. Augustine on time,

Ricoeur accepts the paradox that we cannot know the past, present or future. The past is gone and unknowable, the present is 'now' but is instantaneous so we can never 'know' the 'now', and the future is unknowable because it is the future. So, now following Heidegger, Ricoeur argues the human mind experiences time mediated by memory (of things past) and expectations (of things to come) within an imagined continuous now. This is Ricoeur's notion of 'distension' and it is the essence of his thinking about our timed condition of existence. So, our human understanding of time is a product of the mind rather than 'reality' (which, as indicated, is unknowable except as memory or expectation – as mental states).

To 'know' time we would have to step outside it into eternity. But we cannot do that so we human beings have to live with the intention. Ricoeur summarises this process as *intentio* (intention) in *distentio* (distension of the mind seeking meaning in time). The upshot is that meaning in history (and everything else for that matter) emerges from the movement through the primary facilitation of thinking, which is language (the disclosure of words in sentences in narratives) that allows us to 'translate' time. The means Ricoeur deploys for understanding this translation of time through narrative is *mimésis*.[35]

Ricoeur talks about ' . . . the definitively aporetic character of the phenomenology of time', by which he means that our conception of time is always beyond our understanding and it is the overcoming this 'aporia' (the un-decidable decision) that Ricoeur points to that is the key function of our narrative making.[36] Ricoeur thus moves us beyond naïve **correspondence** where the past world matches the present historical word, into the more complex world of narrative making defined as the necessary abstraction of past experience and its 'real time'. He also moves us to a definition of the logic of history as being essentially analogical (denoting the past by analogue). This suggests that any coherent intelligibility we derive from the past results *only in part* from our understanding of time as a given feature of the way the universe is.

Consequently, and specifically, Ricoeur argues that the aporetic and discordant nature of time is made 'understandable' through the intervention/invention of what we already know as the emplotment (he uses the term 'plot'). Using the Lincoln example again, emplotting the President's life (emplotting action) is under-taken by turning real time into narrative time by the historian's *intentio in distentio*. Ricoeur explains the full complexity of this process through his own detailed analysis of mimésis. From the Greek *mimésis*, or 'imitation', the concept is trouble-some, as we saw in the Introduction (see pp. 10–15), if only because most historians (certainly all reconstructionists and constructionists) assume that the narrative they write imitates (mimes) past reality (which is possible thanks to empiricism and its analysis) including its 'real time'. Hence it is that 'fiction' is the term usually reserved for those narratives that do not, unlike history, purport to tell the 'real time' story. But Ricoeur argues that what fictional and historical narratives have in common is that they both stem from a more complex threefold mimetic process that he defines as mimesis$_1$, mimesis$_2$, and mimesis$_3$. What does this mean?

Well, Ricoeur defines mimesis$_1$ as that set of basic concepts we must have before we can produce a narrative. These are concepts such as 'action' (what it is 'to act' and its characterisation), agency and structure, causation and, of course, the fundamental notion of 'change over time'. We must understand these basic (so called historical) concepts so we can use them to produce a believable historical (textual) representation. For the historian then, mimesis$_1$ is the understanding she or he has of the past that must be possessed before they can progress to the creation of their history story space. Knowing these things enables the historian to move to mimesis$_2$.

Mimesis$_2$ is the stage of configuring **the-past-*as*-history** (the history story space). For Ricoeur, history works after the fashion of an analogue becoming the 'as' of the past.[37] Specifically Ricoeur is theorising the turning of past events, actions, time periods, objects and descriptions of physical locations into the emplotment of the history, which, as a mediated re-presentation, necessitates a re-timing of the past. For Ricoeur, emplotment is the essential characterising aspect of the history story space. The translation or linguistic turning of past events/actions into a story of a particular kind by means of emplotment is undertaken by the significance of their arrangement by the historian. The aim is to produce a 'followable' story constructed in time and space (hence story space) in line with the historian's belief in the translatability of human action into a verisimilitudinous narrative.

Mimesis$_3$ addresses the extent to which the reader is an elemental part of the refiguring process of meaning creation, specifically how she or he receives the truth claims that are built into the representational narrative. The reader can achieve satisfaction in 'finding out' the 'true meaning' provided by the historian. The reader can also enjoy the formal nature of the representation (the **narrative turn** and the temporal turn), or be convinced by the plausibility and persuasiveness of the argument. They can take pleasure in the range of data and be persuaded by the appeal of the figuration (the **aesthetic turn**). They can have their prejudgements and/or prejudices confirmed (the ideological turn). The intertextual nature of their reading also constitutes the meaning they derive. Equally, they can dislike the text because it does none of these and so may engender contrary emotions and beliefs. This echoes the reader reception theory with which we have become familiar. Mimesis$_3$ is the world after it has been narrated. Clearly there is a **mimetic loop** in the creation and revisioning (revising) of the-past-*as*-history.

As Ricoeur says, '. . . the world that narrative *refigures* [my italics] is a temporal world' and the aporetic nature of time (its unknowability and indeterminate nature) can only be come to terms with through the historian's narrational act. Throughout all this, reference to the real remains untouched. But the real time of the past *must* become storied time and in the process the inevitable discordances between real and narrative time have to be resolved. As a result, in history we can only have what Ricoeur calls the '**fictive** experience of time' in which '... the discordances between the temporal features of the events in the **diegesis** and the corresponding features in the narrative' are resolved.[38] Even in heavy-duty empiricist history texts, the fictive experience of time is a textual temporal 'virtual reality'. It is also a reversal of 'real time' where the 'now' anticipates the future as mediated by our knowledge (memories) of the past.

The most obvious management of time by historians is when they turn 'real' time – as measured in years, months and days – into the historical (or fictional) 'story time' and 'discourse time'. Here, Ricoeur, like Genette, explores the relationship between the time *of the narrative* and the narrated time *in the narrative*. Ricoeur calls this a 'game with time'.[39] This is the serious game all historians have to play if they want to be historians because there is no time in the history except that which is borrowed metonymically. In other words, our only access to the time of the past is through the type of timing in the narrative we write. This history analogue of 'real time' has, according to Genette, three aspects. These are *order* (when/chronology), *duration* (how long) and *frequency* (how often). Given their significance in creating history, we need to examine each in turn.

Order

While the act of narration may be intended to be an analogue – the-past-*as*-history – it is always a distortion or anachrony of 'real time'. Plainly, unlike 'real time', 'history time' (discourse time) is measured in words, pages of text or even how long it takes to read (or view or experience) it. This invariably produces a divergence between the order in which events in the past (story) happened, and the order in which they are offered in the emplotted content/story. Normally, of course, we anticipate that history will be told chronologically, but this is not the same as order. This is a crucial distinction: the actual chronology may be imitated in the discoursed story, but the concept of order requires that there are many 'anachronological' contraventions demanded to create meaning.

The most obvious characteristic of order in the history narrative is what Genette calls the 'figure of analepsis' (i.e., retrospection or narrating backwards in time). In a film this would be called a 'flashback'. Thus a historian regularly refers back to events prior to those already told. Another figure is that of prolepsis (anticipation or narrating ahead of events) or what in a film would be the 'flash forward'. Crucially, historians also anticipate events. Indeed, as Ricoeur notes, prolepses can be inserted in analepses.[40] The point of all this is not just for style or rhetorical 'effect' but to give a *meaning* to the work as a whole.

This bears out Ankersmit's insistence that historical meaning is not the result of the accretion of factual statements, but rather is that which is opened to us through our narrative understanding of time – specifically the overall anachronic (synthetic) nature of its narrative. The examples of prolepses and analepses are legion in history writing. But a typical example of analepsis is a statement by the American economic historian Louis Hacker. He says, 'movement into the public lands synchronised with upturns in the business cycle and not the reverse' in reference to the occupation of the north-west and southwest of the United States in the late eighteenth and nineteenth centuries.[41] As Ricoeur also concludes (after commenting on Genette's analysis),

> But must we not then say that what narratology takes as the pseudo-time of a narrative is composed of the set of temporal strategies placed at the service of a conception of time that, first articulated in fiction, can also constitute a paradigm for redescribing lived and lost time?[42]

Duration

Timing is also about the distortion of duration, which further serves to create historical narrative understanding (beyond the simple level of correspondence). Duration is the sum of 'real time' elapsed in the content/story and the total of discourse time (space allocated to it in the history text) taken up in presenting it. The duration techniques historians deploy are intended to either speed up or slow down the narrative in relation to the events told in order to make sense of them. Genette offers five kinds of duration that all author-historians use: ellipsis, pause, summary, scene and stretch.

- *Ellipsis* is omission (in effect deploying time as an erasure by not offering data 'in evidence'), leaving out events/agents/actions to speed up the narrative. This may be for mundane reasons like keeping to the 75,000-word book limit or emplotment, argument or reference reasons directed, as always, towards explanation and meaning creation.
- *Pauses* are points of 'natural reflection' within the text that offer opportunities for recapitulation, preparation and commentary (on an act, event or agent). Conclusions to chapters are good examples (so are comments in parentheses – like this one) of pauses for reflection and digestion.
- *Summary* is that narrative choice where real time is much greater than discourse time, hence the historian has to speed up (accelerate) the whole telling process. Survey texts are examples, but summaries can be as short as sentences (an extreme form of compression) such as 'The Thirty years War can be considered to be . . .'.
- *Scene* is the narrative choice reflected most usually in the historian's selection of and deployment of agent dialogue. It can be longer or shorter in the text

than in reality, but (by definition of it being a direct dialogue quotation) it will be approximately the same.

- *Stretch* is where content/story time (reality time) is less than discourse time. Histories are replete with examples when the historian muses over events that took only seconds or an hour or two in real time, as with agent intentions, decisions or events for example.

Now, one can obviously find an incalculable number of illustrations of each form of duration. But take summary as an example. It can be seen at work in David Hackett Fischer's treatment of the famous 18 April 1775 'midnight' ride of Paul Revere to warn the American colonists of the imminent arrival of the British. Fischer's reference to when Revere was briefly captured is illustrative. Fischer says, 'In the time that Paul Revere remained a prisoner, his message travelled rapidly across the countryside.'[43] Summary is so obviously a form of explanation as to pass unnoticed. But it is language itself that provides the necessary structure for this process.

Other examples might include Fernand Braudel, who, in his *A History of Civilizations*, moves effortlessly through Indian history of, as he says, 'yesterday and today' to create his particular realisation of the past. In a single paragraph he visits India in the 600s, 1200s and 1900s, configuring an interpretation by deploying summary, ellipsis and pause.[44] Also, the historian of sixteenth-century Europe Andrew Pettegree provides an example of summary in the first chapter of his book *Europe in the Sixteenth Century* (2002), in which he moves from theme to theme and time to time following his own particular temporal order (and dis-order).[45] F.R. Bridge and Roger Bullen's analysis of European international history between 1814 and 1914 also illustrates duration in all its forms.[46]

Frequency

The third important aspect of temporal ordering and timing is frequency. This is concerned with the concept of 'repetition'.[47] In any narrative timing of the past the notion of frequency is important and, like duration, it has several forms. Frequency is the relationship established by the historian between the number of times an event actually occurred and the number of times it appears in the discourse. Once again Genette offers a comprehensive analysis noting four kinds: singulative, repetitive, iterative and irregular.

- As the term suggests, the *singulative* tells us once (in the narration) something that happened once (in reality), or happened twice and gets told twice and so on.
- The *repetitive* re-tells the same real event several times in the narrative. Obviously this is the common form in histories of single events/decisions/actions where the event is re-told from the perspective of different agents.

- The *iterative* is the single telling in the narrative of something that happened several times (possibly *n* times) in reality. Historians would not want to bore the reader with repeated references to the tedious aspects of someone's life, or the rise and setting of the sun.[48]
- The *irregular* is the telling of something that really happened several times, but which is now told a different number of times in the narrative. Nelson's victories at sea may be an example or, more complexly, agent motivations.

Where an event or agent decision is noted only once, it is usually done to constitute or 'build up' an explanation of, say, Eisenhower's presidency under the explanation of either 'consensus' or 'conflict'. Lots of examples of the singulative mode of repetition of different single events or individual historical agent decisions are deployed to generate a critical mass of explanation in favour of, in this example, either consensus or conflict. In history it is not just an event that is constantly referred to, but what several iterations are claimed to represent in terms of explanation and meaning creation.

Again, although every history text contains countless examples of temporal control through order, duration and frequency, space here (note my management of time even in a 'theory' text limited to 75,000 words) permits addressing only one. In his 1989 book *Working Class Americanism: The Politics of Labor in a Textile City, 1914–1960*, Gary Gerstle sets about redefining the concept of 'working-class Americanism' as an explanation for the rise of industrial unionism. He does this by referring to several key concepts that resonate in several major events some of which he notes once and others a number of times. Thus the 'language of Americanism' is iterated many times but especially in the life of Belgian worker émigré Joseph Schmetz.[49] Gerstle presumably selects this historical character for reasons that are referential (and for focalisation and voice reasons) but necessary to turn the past into the time of the history. Using the example of a single life is a common timing mechanism in history texts.

But time, of course, is also related to space. A concept useful to understanding how historians organise time *and* space is that of Mikhail Bakhtin's 'chronotope' (chronos = time; topos = space).[50] The notion of time and space is plainly central to producing history. Based on Einstein's notion of the time–space continuum (that time and space are indissoluble), Bakhtin explored how time and space are *made* to interconnect in literary texts. Perhaps the most famous and enduring example is Frederick Jackson Turner's analysis of the culturally formative and nationalising power of the opening of the frontier in American history.

Bakhtin suggested (though it has to be said this is not a major insight in itself) that making time tangible in narrative is the only way to make events corporeal. Tense/timing is *the* key to constituting the reality of the past. Specifically he describes how the lives (in time and space) of real people in the past can be expressed in literary and forms other than simply the empirical, like emplotment for example. But what is especially useful in his concept of the chronotope is how it can be fashioned to express many different political, ideological and ethical world-views within the history story space. Thus, a historian can create a Whig chronotope, a Marxist chronotope or a gender chronotope. Or in F.J. Turner's case, when he said that the '... existence of an area of free land, its continuous recession and the advance of American settlement westward explain American development', a geographical chronotope.[51] The crucial point is that Bakhtin offers us another way of thinking about how we can connect past reality and present history in a fashion that is essentially Kantian (using the categories of time and space).[52]

It should be clear by now how historians create their chronotopes as they construct the content/story (within the story space) and, as we shall see in the next chapter, as they choose a particular **mode of expression**. Through epistemological choice, aesthetic preference, emplotment choice, preferred ethical orientation, selected (but never biased!) referencing, the use of voice, the different forms of focalisation, the speed inventions of order, duration and frequency, every history story space has its own chronotope. That every history makes its own peculiar connections between temporal and spatial elements can be seen in histories as divergent as those of Fernand Braudel, Tacitus, A.J.P. Taylor or Frederick Jackson Turner. So Braudel's *Mediterranean*, Tacitus's *Germania*, A.J.P. Taylor's *Origins of the Second World War* and Turner's 'Frontier' (in American History) are all chronotopes – translations of the reality of time and space into a literary form that is specifically historical – a timed story space created to explain in a desired way.

In all this, however, a further debate exists which concerns the relationship between the historical agent or character and their physical, social, economic, political, cultural, intellectual and temporal world – the relationship between agency, characterisation and structure to change over time. In its essentials this is not a debate about which is dominant (agency, character or structure) but how they relate 'in' time and space. This debate raises three very important concerns. First, how can we define the agent's power to act – action? Second, how can we determine their intentions to act – intentionality? And third, how are the intentions of agents in the past filtered and understood through the attitudes towards agency, structure and intentionality as held by individual historians?

▶ Intentionality: Text, action, agency, characterisation and the historian

According to Ricoeur, the analysis of intentionality

> ... should be combined with that of narrative voice considered as that which presents the text. The narrative voice is the bearer of the intentionality belonging to the text, which is actualized only in the intersubjective relationship that unfolds between the solicitation from the narrative voice and the response of reading.[53]

Ricoeur's point is clear, narrating and narration is a complex totality, which, by bringing us back to author, voice and focalisation, before examining intentionality, clarifies the latter. In a history narrative all those issues concerned with agent intentionality and the existents of action and agency begin with the distinction between authorial 'showing' and 'telling': in other words, every historian possesses a philosophy of action (their preferred theory of agency). In a 'showing' form of historical representation – which is essentially that imagined by reconstructionists and constructionists – there is little or no authorial voice (it is there but covert) and consequently attention is not paid to the historian's narrative choices such as focalisation or tense/timing. The reader (or a viewer or listener) is expected simply to witness the past cast in terms of discoverable rational intentions and causation.

In 'telling', on the other hand, the narrator is an overt controlling voice who self-consciously makes all the narrative choices of voice, focalisation, order, duration and frequency. The narrators also self-consciously decide *how* to present actions, describe historical characters, explore their intentions and, throughout all this, express their own views as to the nature of action and agent intentionality. All historians have their own views on intentionality. These are then 'read' by the reader (or not – by the particularly obtuse reader – as may be) as they negotiate their own meaning(s).[54]

The role of the historian in defining the significance of action and agency results from their belief in the extent to which action and agency contribute to cause and effect in human affairs.[55] For example, the French sociologist Pierre Bourdieu has tried to understand agency and structure through his concept of *habitus*. He argues that agents inhabit a social space built out of power relations and reinforced by social practices that are usually (economic) class based.[56] Any historian is free to deploy the theory of *habitus* in their history. But what complicates matters is conveying such concepts in the story space *without* the process apparently being influenced by the assumptions of the author-historian about the determining relationship between action, agent intentionality and structure.[57]

Central to understanding agent *and* historian intentionality, then, is the historian's own attitude towards one concept in particular – characterisation. Conventionally, in classic realist terms, the character/intention of the historical agent is taken to be a discoverable given. Lyndon Johnson, the thirty-sixth president of the United States, was a knee-jerk anti-communist or, perhaps, he was not, or he was at certain times but not others dependent on circumstances?[58] Surely the evidence will 'tell' us which is the most likely correct interpretation? Unhappily it will not because the data has no independent voice. Even 'explanation to the best fit' is not that much help for there is always more to the discursive construction of characters and characterisation in history – and their intentions – than the attempted reading of their nature from the evidence.

For – to continue with the Johnson example – the historian makes all the decisions as to what agents (characters) get put into the story space we call 'the history of

President Lyndon Johnson'. These decisions are not made only according to the criterion of reference. You will recall all the issues associated with focalisation. In part because of that choice, the question of what 'character functions' they will serve immediately arises. So we need to ask what decisions do historians make about the historical agents they choose to inhabit their histories? How the historian constitutes a historical character is certainly and plainly influenced by the evidence, but it is also given effect by the historian's voice, focalisation, the refiguration of time and the relative importance ascribed to agency, structure and the nature of knowable intentionality.

Because we know that histories are authored, in addition to reference what underlies the narrative choices historians make about what historical agents to include/exclude entails processes of presupposition. Presupposition happens every time one piece of evidence is preferred over another, or when one theme or topic is pursued rather than another. There is, thus, presumption when Oswalt and Neely asked the question how the native North American influenced US history. Or when E.P. Thompson said he was '. . . seeking to rescue the poor stockinger, the Luddite cropper, the "obsolete" hand-loom weaver, the "utopian" artisan, and even the deluded follower of Joanna Southcott, from the enormous condescension of posterity'.[59] These are simple examples of historians seeking out historical agents as characters so – paradoxically – they can be provided with a 'voice of their own'. There are two main models of characterisation that apply equally to history and non-history: the mimetic and non-mimetic.[60]

Mimetic historical character

The mimetic is the 'common-sense' everyday representational version with which we are all familiar. The historical character/agent was a person who existed in time and space and is represented as such. Briefly there are two forms of mimetic characterisation: semantic and cognitive. A semantic characterisation requires that a character (in accord with the available empirical evidence) is described with a name and personality in space and time. This is usually a human being but it can be a class, race, idea, gender, nation, animal or a period of time. This is deemed to be a straightforward referential description that assumes the historical agents once shared the same sort of ontological existence we do now and, therefore, they can be known in the same way as we know ourselves and other people alive today. It is a perspective that relies directly on the correspondence theory of knowledge.

The cognitive mimetic form is when the historian attributes to the character a strong (or weak) sense of their knowledge of themselves and/or their situation. This is done for explanatory reasons and often undertaken through direct quotation if available. But, dependent upon the mode of expression (such as, say, a historical encyclopaedia entry), this is not always the case. In this example, a characterisation is usually broad brush and simply stated. The variety in this form of characterisation is truly immense. Thus one historian says about John Reed, the early-twentieth-century American writer and political radical, that he was a romantic figure who ended his life as a martyr to the Russian Revolution, while another says he was generally regarded as a playboy and was politically undistinguished.[61] While it seems in history that the historical agent characterises themselves (through their own words and actions) and their co-agents (what other people said about them), in actuality the historian as narrator always does the job by blending the mimetic (in its two main forms) *with* the non-mimetic.

Non-mimetic historical character

The non-mimetic model of character is more abstract because the character though real *also* functions as a textual feature of meaning creation. Thus a historical agent can be understood as the carrier of an idea (such as strength, deceit, liberalism, conservatism, menace, etc.). Or they can be taken to represent a theme (success, failure, honour, etc.), or they can be used simply as a literary device for creating an effect (pleasure, pain, fear, hope, amusement, etc.). A real historical person can also serve as an element of emplotment (to effect success, constitute an action, generate change and be the archetypal American or be the voice of emergent nationalism) or some more or less complex blend of all these effects.

The intellectual role of John Locke in the American Revolution is just one example. There is little agreement among historians whether Locke's *Essay Concerning Human Understanding* (1690) was important to the founding of the nation. The evidence seemingly cannot resolve this interpretative question of its significance. It tends to come down to the preferences of the historian, for example, viewing Locke's *Essay* in a particular epistemological light as to how 'the character' John Locke can or should be deployed in either a mimetic or a non-mimetic fashion as the carrier of an idea of which they approve.[62] That a historical agent can be both mimetic and non-mimetic goes some way to explaining the nature and uses of characterisation in history narratives in as much as historians associate historical characters/agents with subject/dominant positions, with striving or failure, flawed genius or cretin.[63] To put this as clearly as I can, reference is never the ultimate determinant of the uses of characterisation.

▶ Conclusion

In this chapter, I have introduced and elucidated aspects of Genette's and Ricoeur's analyses of narrating and narration as the second of the three fundamental elements of the history narrative. All the narrator's choices – the nature of their authorship, 'who speaks' and 'who sees', tense/timing, the understanding of agency/action, intentionality and characterisation – are central to turning the past (and unavoidably 'de-forming' or 're-shaping' it) into a historical narrative. While insisting that **referentiality** remains a benchmark of historical work, once we venture to ask 'what does it mean?' we have passed into the realms of content/story and narration. However, to complete the explanation of this process we must now turn to the third element in the triad that constitutes the narrative logic of history. As we are now aware, a content/story and the act of narrating/narration require a mode of expression. And, of course, there is also the question of how modes of expression reflect back on to the other two elements.

4 History as Expression

History modes of expression can vary widely in their substance and function. Because they are **narratives**, they can be spoken, or written, a fixed or moving image, or a gesture, a myth, a legend, a fable, a tale, a novella, a history, an epic, a mime, a stained glass window, a film, a comic, a postcard, a **performance**, a street theatre, a conversation or a painting.[1] Because they are the result of the **content/story** and narrating/narration decisions of their author, all history modes of expression are, therefore, prefigured like any textual history. They are also subject to the **epistemological** decisions of their authors/creators.

(As expressive forms, modes of expression can both **refer** and also exemplify **meaning.** Thus, a **mode of expression** such as the painting by Frédéric Bazille of his studio *Studio in the Rue La Condamine* (1870) expresses its predicate metaphorically rather than literally. Where the painting exemplifies in its colour, brush strokes and composition (grouping and distance between figures) the working friendships between painters Bazille, Manet, Monet, Renoir and the writer Zola who are in the picture, it also expresses metaphorically their camaraderie and common concerns. The painting not only 'portrays realistically' (as much as any painting can 'portray' 'realistically') but also metaphorically.[2] This is an important feature not merely of paintings and other visual forms, but also of written texts (which also use their own kinds of colour, spacing, composition, etc.).

So, why is the textual so widely regarded as history's prime form? In Western culture and philosophy there has been a traditional emphasis upon speech as the vehicle for the knowing self to grasp meaning. This was eventually translated into the belief that writing simply reflected speech. Indeed, writing was perceived to be the ultimate mechanism for representing our engagement with **reality**. However, thanks to the impact initially of structuralism, then **poststructuralism** and eventually Derrida's deconstructionism, writing has now been rethought as a mechanism for creating meaning. Of course, the notion of transparent meaning and **correspondence** also came under attack (whether in speech or writing). The result has been to de-throne writing as the mechanism for carrying 'true meaning'.

Nevertheless, the ascendancy of textual history is still maintained because of the conventional practitioner-historian's insistence upon its apparent ability to fulfil the 'meaning function' through the mechanism of the numbered references and the justified **inference** that can be properly located in the scholarly monograph.

The theory is that textual citations, footnotes and a comprehensive bibliography allow for reference to the **sources** so, should the reader wish, they could repeat the analysis for themselves like repeating a 'scientific experiment' to test and verify the assertions of the author. While this might still seem to be the basis of proper history, its effect is now less convincing simply because it overemphasises the authority of **empiricism** and the role of citation.[3] And, of course, it reinforces the authority of the textual mode of expression. But things are changing. There is, indeed, a growing recognition that some history modes like TV can manage to convey ' . . . a whole series of often quite complex arguments without losing their audience'.[4] Such a judgement, though helpful, is still too often made grudgingly.

But this is not the argument followed by the historian Robert A. Rosenstone who has long argued in favour of breaking the textual **epistemological** straightjacket, in favour of film.[5] As Rosenstone notes, the connection between a mode of expression and the nature of **truth** and meaning raises all kinds of issues about the character and purpose of **representation.** In **order** to explore new forms of history, I will summarise the key modes of historical expression as

- written texts – books and dissertations
- film and photography
- television and radio
- graphic novels, comics, history magazines
- public histories: museums, heritage and memorials
- performance: re-enactment, 'first-person' history, games
- digitised representations.

I will briefly comment on each while addressing the important question of the epistemic relationship between **form and content**.

▶ Written texts

The mode of expression (form) selected by the historian for the representation of their history reflects their epistemological, methodological and professional orientation towards how they think they can best know the truthful meaning of the past (content). As I suggested in the previous chapter (when I had print-based history in mind), the process of narrating/narration is as important as the content/story to the history production process. However, written texts have also tended to reflect a conventional wisdom that helps bring both historians and their readers into a state of epistemological obedience which, as I have just suggested, is a function of their textual nature.

For the realist-representationalist professional academic historian (working in either the **reconstructionist** or the **constructionist** genres usually in a school, a university or a museum) the past is made flesh in 'professionally approved' ways and, primarily, in textual modes of expression. The consequence for history as a discipline is to reinforce an officially sanctioned view of what is 'proper history', the mode of expression for which is essentially the single-authored book. And, moreover, they should be published by a small number of elite university presses, or journal articles that 'do history' according to established empirical-analytical procedures and which are published in the 'leading' journals.

The history profession is complicit with this through its key institutional centres where a particular way of 'thinking about history' is systematically inculcated in undergraduate and postgraduate training. Although an illustration of Michel Foucault's definition of 'governmentality' – of a dominant discourse realised as social practice – there are variations in North America and Western Europe. However, the pattern of the taught History Master's degree and the PhD by a combination of courses and/or research strengthens reconstructionist and constructionist empirical-analytical methods and their epistemological philosophy. Despite this will to conformity, according to one recent commentator, Oliver Daddow, the discipline of history likes to depict itself as open-minded, tolerant and inclusive.[6] One manifestation of this inclusiveness is that competing interpretations reasonably exist side by side as a diversity of historians access, read and infer the meaning of the past in different ways.

As Daddow concludes, however, the fact that differing interpretations coexist is because they appear to have met the essential scholarly standards in the use of evidence: honesty, veracity, a critical reading of the data and an obligation not to misinform the reader. He then goes on to note the ideology and politics of such 'proper history' noting how the discipline is in effect a socially constructed set of rules and norms for the control of its own production.[7]

Such academic history is defined primarily, then, in terms of the heavyweight, textual monograph. This is produced in strict conformity to the basic epistemological precepts of reference, **justified belief**, incisive inference, apposite conceptualisation and lucid insight. But above all it is the result of the promotion of history as a **mimetic** (in the sense of imitation) form that is based on the correspondence theory of knowledge as opposed to the **diegetic** (narrative). In our predominately empirical-analytical historical culture the interpretative (yet also) mimetic/analogue is the most highly esteemed form of history. But also approved (for the same reasons) are postgraduate dissertations where the 'basic training' is demonstrated. Equally, journal articles are highly regarded, especially if published in professionally approved (and) epistemologically sound journals. Finally, conference papers published in 'influential journals' or part of book collections are also, generally, 'safe and sound' professionally. Of course, if the cognitive orientation of the historian is anti-realist or anti-representationalist then, clearly, the history produced will be framed in terms that are at variance with that of the 'realist' or 'representationalist' historian. As always, historians make their choice and live with the consequences in terms of professional esteem and its 'rewards'.

▶ Film and photography

As suggested, film and photography are starting to confront the epistemological-cognitive investment in approved textual representations. Of course neither comes with their references sliding across the bottom of the screen or written alongside it. Neither form is expressed as themed chapters. Neither offers a gloss on the existing historiography. Film and photography are also 'directed' and 'produced' – though we can suspend our sense of this as we gaze at them. But the important epistemological point is that film and photography are clearly creations not mimes or correspondences – in much the same way as a written text is not.[8]

But this is often forgotten – that the textual historical representation is as much invented, directed and produced as any film. There is always, for example, the textual narrational equivalent of *Mise-en-scène* or the staging of the action. But, just as importantly, film cannot, and is never intended to be, mimetic in the sense that a text is *believed* to be. What textual historians, therefore, seemingly misunderstand is that film is at once both closer and different to texts. This is because what they have in common is that filmic and textual histories are both metonymic narrative devices with the film director/producer making as many (and similar) **narrative choices** as any historian does.

With this in mind, Robert Rosenstone, the leading historian and analyst of film, has argued that 'traditional history' has now run its course in terms of textual representation and that the next step is to create a new kind of history.[9] Indeed, different modes of expression are even eschewing old notions of narrative in favour of narrative 'self-reflexivity', 'partisanship', 'self-conscious authorship', and the novelty of exploring representation rather than just assuming it. No longer for Rosenstone can film be seen as just another source (documentary visual representations of past events) rather than a legitimate mode of history in itself. He also thinks that one can explore the nature through films of history as a form of representation.

Like Rosenstone, Michel de Certeau (somewhat earlier) also effectively destroyed the epistemological argument when he used the illustration of documentary film as the analogy for traditional historiography. As he says, in both forms the social, political, economic and technological mechanism remains undiscernible to the viewer. Reflecting the views of Barthes, de Certeau suggests there is an epistemo-logical sleight of hand because the historian portrays what happened *through* the narrative functions employed. Hence it is that the past is turned into a historiography that self-consciously imagines **the-past-*as*-history**.

Photography and film as historical modes of expression are, consequently, much misunderstood. Even today there is a widespread belief that, apart from when they are 'doctored', photographs are mimetic and realist-representational. However, photographs are best regarded as a verisimilitudinous form (an artistic illusion of truth). This is because, while they generally refer through resemblance (the image of the data), they also carry with them a narrative – minimal though it may be. Indeed, photographs can be ordered to create complex narratives (photo narratives, montages, photo collage) and thus become subject to content/story, narrating/narration and mode of expression choices just like any other manufactured, cultural artefact.[10]

The historian and analyst of film and photography Siegfried Kracauer has argued that historians work from two tendencies – the *realist tendency* that prompts the pursuit of data, and the *formative tendency* that delivers an **explanation** of the material in hand. For Kracauer, the historian is both a recorder and a creator.[11] To assume that there is a priority for either one is to obscure the nature of history. There has to be 'the right balance' between the realistic and what Kracauer calls 'the formative'. He even suggested there is a fundamental analogy between historiography and the photographic media. To grasp the nature of reality as depicted in modes of expression other than print, Kracauer believed (as does Ankersmit today) that we need to understand that, like the photographer, the historian is always trying to balance the empirical with the creative with all the preconceptions and choices that involves.

Both 'camera-reality' and 'history-reality' share the hallmarks of what Kracauer calls *Lebensewelt* or 'life-world' (borrowing the term from the German philosopher Edmund Husserl [1859–1938]).[12] In effect, Kracauer was suggesting history had more in common with, and indeed, had the job of, organising our life-world – which as he says is ' . . . for long stretches inchoate, heterogeneous, obscure. Much of it is an opaque mass of facts. It is up to the historian to chart a course through these expanses. . . . [hence history is about] fact finding and exegesis . . . '.[13] The only way it can undertake these tasks, he argued, is for the historian ' . . . to tell a **story**' and it is in this process that history has much in common with film and photography.[14] History, to coin a phrase, does not come camera ready.

▶ Television and radio

The growth in TV and radio history programming has, it seems, catered for a perceived popular interest in history as a leisure activity and also to supplement the range of materials available for its more 'serious' study.[15] The popularity of the History TV Channel illustrates this development. In the United Kingdom, for example, the enormous number of programmes on the Nazis and Hitler reflects the centrality of the subject to advanced level school syllabuses as well as feeding a cultural fascination with horror presumably under the guise of 'learning from history'. But when addressing how the mode of expression resonates with the epistemological choices of historians, the question of how such content is offered becomes the significant issue. As with film and the documentary, the effort of TV and radio at historiographic analysis is unavoidably marginalised, being either cut down or just omitted in favour of maintaining the flow of the story being told. Unavoidably this generates the notion of reproduction *for* (or to create) memory.

What is of particular significance with TV and radio history is that it actually supplies what Pierre Nora in his *Les Lieux de mémoire* referred to as collective national memory (mainly through the function of memorials).[16] A recent assessment of this (though it concentrates on memory as a contrivance of a mass culture, and which is, therefore, somewhat anti-history) is Alison Landsberg's *Prosthetic Memory*.[17] Although Landsberg does not evaluate the role of TV and radio in creating 'prosthetic' or 'false' memories, her argument is important. Her analysis reminds us of the way in which different historical modes of expression function in constituting memories *as* history that are not 'natural', not the result of 'lived experience' but which result from the ' . . . engagement with a mediated representation (seeing a film, visiting a museum, watching a television miniseries)'.[18]

Providing this kind of experiential history is done most effectively in TV and radio programmes because they are visual and aural. Voiceovers reading from primary source documents or micro-exchanges between historical actors create an aura of truthfulness, especially if the TV or radio historian stitches it all together by talking directly to the camera or offering a detailed oral description with sound effects. Standing where, or close to where, the past action occurred creates a powerful truth-effect (standing on the grassy knoll by the book depository in Dallas, or on the deck of HMS Victory where Nelson fell, standing in Clay Street in San Francisco where the first cable car ran).

The audience can also identify more readily with the past through the use of **aesthetic** devices (visual metaphors and aural references) and filmic techniques (*Mise-en-scène*). This is also facilitated through an overt ideological commitment of the TV/radio historian that audiences seem eager to embrace. Popular history appears to require 'commitment' by its presenters. Emotion is no bad thing in TV and radio history, just as gloss and glamour are not either.[19] Of course, none of this addresses and certainly does not resolve the major 'issue' with TV and radio history: the assumption of *the* story and the seamless way in which *the* narrative is told. Even the self-doubts and musings to camera of Simon Schama do not break this mould.

To understand the nature and uses of TV and radio history, we, therefore, have to ask how (and why?) these expressions are constructed and for what purposes. Almost regardless of whether they are TV or radio productions (though obviously the visual nature of the one is a major difference) both modalities rely on the construction of a narrative. The intention of such is to arouse or, more likely, implant real memories (such as the *real* story of Auschwitz). TV history narration and the resulting narratives vary considerably dependent upon subject matter, production values, target audience, cost-to-profit curve, available technology, and so on. Thus, history TV programming market research acknowledges its audience cross-hatched by gender, class, age, geography, educational level and economic power.[20] TV history has to be carefully tailored to meet the needs of its ascribed consumers and the financial bottom line.[21]

Popular media history relies, like its textual counterpart, on chronology and narrational temporal choices like **order**, **duration** and **frequency** but deployed more self-consciously as 'effects'. Much favoured for such programmes is to start with an introduction that is *in medias res* (in the middle of things). Often the narration begins at a decisive point in the content/story, which is itself close to the dénouement, but does not quite give away the ending. Unlike much print history where perhaps the majority of readers have a prior idea of content/story, TV and radio (and to a lesser extent filmic) history demands a degree of 'ambiguity'. The narrative strategies adopted by TV and radio historians are to offer a set of statements about the past situation being referred to and the potential readings (stories) we can have of it. These will be linked to each other in a way akin to a decision about which explanation is most convincing. The historian offers (usually just two) competing explanatory narratives. There may be a brief note of the uncertainty among historians (though usually there is not) as to, for example, the truth of 'the life of Elizabeth I' or of 'Hitler's intentions toward European Jewry'. The unstated implication is that this TV or radio narrative will be more revealing than any other. Indeed, it may claim to provide 'the truth at last about . . . '. There is usually only a limited sense of ongoing debate.

Radio history can also take many forms, but as a mode of expression it has great utility as part of a 'nationalising' (implanted national memory) function. But whatever its aim, because radio works only by sound, history programming is constrained by three elements integral to the mode: sound effects (including music but primarily background effects), the absence of sound (silence) and dialogue (mainly the speech of a narrator or character). These constraints directly influence the construction of the content/story via the **emplotment**, argument, historical references and so on, and the nature of the narration including **voice**, **focalisation**, **timing** (with all its anachronic features), and action/**agency** issues also still apply. But because of radio's nature, aural clues abound, as do styles of speech and selected dialogue. Although the evidence has to be translated into these radio narrative elements there is a strong **fictive** and dramatic character to radio history, which is similar to that of TV and film.[22] The alternative on radio is the 'history talk' which is not that different to a history lecture (though, hopefully, more interesting).

▶ Graphic novels, comics, history magazines

As Hugo Frey and Benjamin Noys have acknowledged, the graphic novel and comics '. . . are not generally considered to be legitimate objects of cultural analyses' and yet they forcefully raise the question of what is a legitimate mode of historical analysis and meaning creation.[23] The use of the term 'graphic novel' has been an attempt at justifying itself as an expression in an academic environment that is uncongenial to such modes of representation. As Frey and Noys maintain, the graphic novel '. . . has been the site for some sustained and sophisticated engagements with the problems of representing historical events'.[24] As has often been the case the representation of specific and usually unimaginably horrific events – particularly the Holocaust – has been the focus for debates over the ability (and the right?) of historians to imaginatively figure and narrate the past in non-textual ways. However, Hayden White, the metahistorical thinker, was impressed by Art Spiegelman's graphic novel *Maus*, which represents the experiences of Spiegelman's father in the Holocaust, as an example of how aesthetics, figuration and allegory can generate historical meaning while at the same time being critically self-conscious.[25]

The vast range of graphic expressions reflects the fact that such forms of representation have been around almost since the invention of our print-based culture. So it should not be surprising that today, when that print culture is being confronted with the range of new media and the creation of new historical representations and sensibilities, historians can and will elect to use these new modes. From the invention in the nineteenth century of the 'comic strip' through to the rise of the 'comic' in the early part of the last century, up to the practices of the 'comix' (Spiegelman's term to describe the graphic novel) we now have a plurality of modes including digitised ones (see pp. 76–78). However, it seems clear that the key narrating functions that define the mode of expression remain pretty much the same despite the translation from text to image. There is, however, a greater complexity in the process of inference from comic image to meaning.

This inferential complexity arises from the existence of both textual and graphic elements in the box panels. Over 20 years ago Will Eisner detailed how the use of style and the framing of the box panels and the gap between them created voice, point of view, timing (flashback and flash forward) and so on.[26] Few people today doubt that pictures (photographs, paintings, doodles) tell stories. W.J.T. Mitchell has called this the 'pictorial turn'.[27] Pictorial or visual history is as complex in its content/story and narration as any other mode of expression. If we can discuss the nature of the pictorial in a literary narrative (emplotment, **trope**, chronotopic signature, focalisation, etc.) then, equally, we can address the nature of the narrative/narrativity in the pictorial.

Thus, as Eli Bartra and John Mraz argue, the Mexican artist Frida Kahlo's most famous painting *The Two Fridas* (1939) possesses a historical narrative that, specifically, explores the issue of identity.[28] There are two Fridas sitting holding hands, but one is in Mexican traditional attire, the other in a Victorian-era white dress. The women's hands touch but what connects them is the exposed artery that connects the healthy heart of Mexican Frida and the diseased heart of European Frida. Blood from the diseased heart drips on to the white dress. Straight-laced and exploitative Europe is bleeding authentic Mexico; a metaphor for the entwined histories of Frida Kahlo of Mexico and the developed world. Bartra and Mraz's entwined 'narrative in the visual' and the 'visual in the narrative' carry them towards their interpretation about the need for passion, social conscience and gender consciousness in the past. They are also self-conscious of the process of its translation into history.

The graphic novel, graphic histories and comics are examples of the figure/trope of metalepsis. This is the extension of reference through multiple representations towards the inference of meaning. An example is the figure of a goat wearing what appears to be Hussar's military cap taken to represent Captain Alfred Dreyfus in the graphic history *Fascism For Beginners*.[29] The representation/meaning is Dreyfus as the scapegoat for the anti-Jewish sentiments of the 1890s French establishment. Metalepsis means several leaps of imagination are required to 'get the meaning'. Textual historians use metalepsis regularly and it has the (usually unintentional and invariably unacknowledged) effect of effacing the line between the historiographically fictive and reality.

Metalepsis is particularly obvious in graphic representations, but we also need to be alert to the way in which its use has the same effect in more 'conventional' textual narratives. Thus when a historian says changes in the economic structure of Britain in the 1840s constituted 'the hungry forties' then this is a metaleptic collapse of the levels of events and their narration. The description 'Elizabethan England' is metaleptic. The fact that such a description seems highly referential and innocuously realistic should not blind us to the process of meaning creation through literary functionality in creating a sense of time and place.

The most vexed and vexing representations of the past today are to be found in popular history magazines. They seem to be neither fish nor fowl. It is not serious academic history and yet it has the aim of being trustworthy (which in itself tells us much about history). The leading UK history magazine the *BBC History Magazine* claims on its masthead that it ' . . . was established to publish authoritative history, written by leading experts, in an accessible and attractive format'. It continues, 'We seek to maintain the high journalistic standards traditionally associated with the BBC.'[30] But would any serious university student of history get past a tutor by referencing the magazine?

Magazines will, of course, claim and should encourage scholarship, but it is a mode of scholarship that always serves the epistemological *status quo*. There are few instances of a 'popular history magazine' that address issues of truth, reality, or narrative understanding from a **deconstructionist** position. **Narrative constructivism**, questions of **relativism**, revisionism and epistemology are rarely, if ever, addressed. Similarly, TV and radio programmes do not make problematising epistemological forays. 'Enjoyment' and knowledge about 'what really happened' are the hallmarks of popular magazine history. It is no surprise that such modes of expression generate their own readership both real and implied. Any defamiliarisation that challenges the epistemological *status quo* is prohibited.

▶ Public histories: Museums, heritage and memorials

Museums, heritage sites and memorials are more obviously narrative constructions than a textual or filmic history.[31] While some public history is complex, it all reflects the same process of translating what we want to believe about the past into a story: turning national mourning, for example (as with a cenotaph or commemorative plaque), into telling the story of nationalism.[32] As Roland Barthes said, narrative is there like life itself and we cannot escape it.[33] Hayden White has also argued that narrative is central to the representation of reality, specifically the 'fashioning of human experience into a form assimilable to structures of meaning'.[34] These structures of meaning are potent in direct relation to the effects they have on the lives of 'ordinary people' – as Landsberg has argued.

White has provocatively suggested that professional historians are the least qualified to police how the past is used for present and public projects.[35] His reasons for saying this are twofold: first because they are ethically unqualified (for the earlier brief discussion of the narrative function of ethical choice, see pp. 40–41); and second, their collective efforts to see history as a scientific pursuit of 'the truth' means avoiding the ' . . . temptations of literary writing, the excesses of philosophy of history, and the seductiveness of ideology . . . '. For these reasons White suggests professional historians will become increasingly irrelevant not just to how the content of the past is organised but also to how it is expressed in the public realm.[36] This view is, of course, at variance with that of most professionals in the world of galleries, archives, museums and heritage who want even more input from professional historians.[37]

However, the 'temptation of literary writing' I just mentioned continues to do its tunnelling work because narrative crosses time, place and all academic disciplines. It is readily seen in the huge variety of public histories, even those that *appear* not to 'tell a story' (like collections of relics in glass-topped display cabinets).[38] In all this the key issue remains the epistemological assumption that proper, that is, **objective** or scientific history will shine through in proper modes of expression, and if it does not then it is because the expression is a tainted medium. And in the case of experiential history it is tainted by virtue of its popularity and 'good fun' element.[39]

Of course, the only connection most people have with the past is through media such as TV, radio, publicly narrated history such as museums, heritage sites and, as we shall see in the next section, other modes of spectacle and pageant such as role play and first-person interpretation. Following the example of Raphael Samuel, Ludmilla Jordanova claims museums and heritage sites illustrate the complexities of public history but they also raise the question of what epistemological purpose museums, heritage sites and collections of relics and memorials serve.[40] Here again the issues of narration come to the forefront as we endeavour to define the chronotopic signature of any individual museum. That some museums are experiential and others are not tells us a great deal about the epistemological awareness and beliefs of their 'managers'!

Normally a great deal of public history investment is required to create and cement national narratives in the shapes of 'national galleries', folk museums and memorials to major events. They are sites deliberately associated with a variety of senses such as nationhood and also, as appropriate, mourning. Most are emplotted as romance or tragedy. As Jordanova surmises, these modalities represent genres of history defined in terms of *topoi* or motifs (nostalgia, 'seize the day', 'nationhood', 'co-operation', 'class', 'race' or 'gender' consciousness). Matters like the connection between truth and reference rarely arise in these narratives although memorials to politically divisive events can, like the proposal for an Enola Gay exhibit in Washington in the mid-1990s memorialising the atom bombs dropped on Japan in 1945, generate extensive debate. However, the variety of ways in which public history narratives are constituted means that the historian who elects to work in those environments has to constantly face the larger question of the relationship between reference, truth, narrative making, revisionism and socially useful myths.

▸ **Performance: Re-enactment, 'first-person' history, games**

There is growing interest in what Peter Burke has called the 'performative turn' in historical studies – history theorised as drama, ritual, festival, theatre, pageant and even architecture.[41] While most historians probably still think of this in terms of Hayden White's notion of historians emplotting the past as some kind of drama, the notion of history as theatre or symbolic action is most obvious in historical re-enactment; historical role-playing is popular in schools. But there is also history gaming and 'first person historical interpretation' – as in folk museums and what I will call 'histouric' sites. Examples of the latter include the Black Country Living Museum in the West Midlands in Britain, Colonial Williamsburg in the United States, the Anne Frank House in Amsterdam, the Ulster-American Folk Park near Omagh, Northern Ireland, or any historically preserved buildings virtually anywhere.

All this raises important questions about how history is shaped through the range of narrative choices (the aesthetic, emplotment, **ethical**, voice, timing and other choices) by the historian (as well as the stately home administrator, the curator and the museologist) and for what purposes. Moreover, as with other forms of publicly consumed and participatory history, what do such 'historical experiences' do with and to concepts such as 'reality', 'truth' and 'objectivity'? Indeed, are these concepts of any relevance given that many aspects of performance history invite the contribution of those who would otherwise be simply spectators?

As noted in the previous section, the ultimate in historical experience is affective in the shape of talking to someone from the past – even though we 'know' they are retired teachers or students in their vacation and that they are all working from a character script. The **fact**ual learning experience is largely irrelevant. 'Talking to the first person interpreter' about whether there will be a revolt in the American colonies or what it was like to work in an early-nineteenth-century iron foundry in the Black Country in England is less about 'finding out the factual truth' and more about having fun. History thus becomes play and often literally 're-creation'.

The awareness among historians of the epistemological consequences of first-person interpretation is now well established with a growing number of analyses of its practice and the impact it is having on a nation's (and a class, race or gender's) historical consciousness.[42] In one sense this is not surprising given the influence of the British historical thinker R.G. Collingwood – though he was writing some 60 years ago.[43] Placing the historian squarely at the centre of the historical process asks how and from who do people derive the meaning of their lives? His answer for the historian is to understand the intentions of people in the past by endeavouring to 're-think' their thoughts. As noted, this is now almost a staple activity in history classrooms, and role-playing as an empathic act is its favoured form.[44]

Of course there are at least two dangers with such re-enactment (empathy). Collingwood's historical approach imposes a philosophy of history that perhaps focuses too much on the actions of agents (agency). This, as we saw in the last chapter when I discussed **intentionality**, action and agency, is fraught with problems. Specifically, Collingwood's historical procedure emphasises what are 'common sense' (i.e., under-theorised) notions of human nature. Indeed there is no questioning of the assumption of such a thing as 'human nature'. But the second danger might be more important. What Collingwood called the 'plain method' of history was to look to thoughts in the context of dominant ideas and events. This meant if we know the facts the historian should be able to work out their meaning via a kind of 'history of thought' mechanism. In other words, facts have their rationale fixed in them. So, while first-person interpretation is undoubtedly a way to rethink the expression of history, it remains freighted with the epistemological assumption that while it is not proper history it still conforms to the epistemological model for 'discovering' historical knowledge. It brings once again to the fore the issue of 'telling' and 'showing'.[45]

▶ Digitised representations

In 2004 the journal *Rethinking History* hosted a forum entitled 'History and the Web'. In introducing it, the editor, David Harlan, argued that Roy Rosenzweig's 2001 suggestion that the web might '... reshape the ways we research, teach and write history' could happen, but that it had not yet.[46] While we have an almost unlimited library of data, both primary and secondary, literally at our fingertips, it has not yet changed how we 'research, teach and write history'.[47] From developments so far it seems it will not. Commentators like David J. Staley are sure, however, that digitising history should generate new thinking as well as practice by replacing the conventional notion of linear prose storytelling with the mental equivalent of scientific collection and discovery, cutting all the verbiage down to the minimum. Here history would turn into the reporting of data, which will increasingly be visual, re-enactments, atlases, and so on.[48]

However, the 'digitisation turn' continues to grow in historical practice. The allure of making history aural, written, visual and apparently 'interactive' is perhaps too strong in our Westernised culture, hooked on technology and sensory gratification. As to whether it directly influences historical thinking, it is only likely if, as David Harlan suggests, it fosters a new historical sensibility but one, I would add, that must fundamentally confront the epistemological equation of reference, explanation, meaning which is then summarised and delivered in a narrative.

The epistemological issue apart, however, the novelty of digitised representations of the past is that history is no longer shaped in the form of an analogue.[49] What seems to be new is the way in which the consumer (reader, viewer) can break down the order in which the narrative and the events described therein can be consumed. It is true that the emergence of the 'graphical user interface' whereby the user can move objects on the screen is an important element. Indeed, it is a commonplace belief that the nature of the expression of digitised representations allows the reader to dispense with the author's preferred textual structure assuming they have one, and derive a meaning from it different to the one of either the real or the implied author.

Yet the underlying logic of digitisation remains firmly that of the constructed narrative – even though it may be 'virtual'. The simple rule seems to be that you get the narrative the originator of the virtual digital history wants if the choice available on the screen interface (choices of icons, buttons, etc.) is directed towards a specific end. Often users will not realise that they are being 'narratively managed'. This is no different to a print text. The print author 'directs' the reader down a particular narrative path using the range of narrative choices with which we are now familiar – emplotment, argument, ideology, focalisation, order, timing, agency choices and so on. The Burkean performative and Landsberg's prosthetic are elements that work just as powerfully as in the 'old print based history'.[50]

Nevertheless, the problems of epistemology will not go away. When the 'hypertext' is claimed to be radically different in epistemological terms, it is because it makes more complex the issue of **intertextuality**. Normally intertextuality has no meaning in history – it is not a term historians use. We prefer instead the notion of contextuality. This refers to both the historiography and the placing of events in the context of other events. Historiography is that to which reference can be made for the confirmation or the rebuttal of an argument. The context of the event is 'the historical background'. But, as I have suggested, in a hypertextual historical representation, the problem of extracting 'the meaning' is actually no more complex than it is with printed text because of the ease with which the text consumer can jump about, dip into, skim, use the index and so on. The form of hypertextual expression only appears to provide the ultimate in the self-construction of historical meaning. Thus, regardless of whether we read printed or hypertexts, we are always thrown into a world of intertextual as well as intratextual relations (not forgetting context). Historical meaning is something we extract not from one single text (*intra*textually) but from both the text and the other texts to which it refers and with which it communicates (*inter*textually).

The 'hype' normally associated with 'hypertextual' history should not, therefore, be swallowed wholesale.[51] Hypertext history does have certain formal advantages. It provides huge amounts of material from which teachers can select for classroom purposes. Presentation can have sound, video clips, a glossy presentation and so on. However, all this does not allow the student to control his or her own 'learning experience' as is often claimed. This is not necessarily a bad thing if we believe that maintaining a narrative thread is useful, and lesser abled students need careful coaching. Indeed, most digital histories merely translate mimetic materials like journal articles and books to the new medium – simply becoming more accessible and providing deeper 'archival troughs'. The advent of e-books is pedagogically useful as well as being student friendly in terms of advanced search facilities. But the practical result is that hypertext historical thinking is probably less innovative in format than either a film or in many museums. This is because of the continued iron grip of epistemology. It is certainly too strong a claim to say that the new media requires the re-invention of the discipline. Indeed, digitised representation gives the lie to the notion that all new modes of expression must automatically disrupt our epistemological expectations.

▶ Conclusion

What I have explored so far is the logic of history as an authored narrative representation defined in terms of its content/story, narrating/narration and mode of expression. I have argued that the content/story of history cannot be exclusively limited to reference to 'what happened'. This is because the listener, reader or viewer expects **followability** in the story, which is provided by a series of epistemologically driven and connected narrative functions that knit the sequence(s) together. This provides it/them with both explanation and meaning – as we shall see in the next two chapters. Hence, the truth (as the result of explanation and meaning) that we seek in any narrative arises through the coherence of the story that the historian has imposed on those sequences of content selected for their story world. Epistemological historians (a.k.a. empirical-analytical) expect, of course, that there is always truth to be 'found' because it is assumed *the* story must be back there and it is discoverable and verifiable according to the evidenced sequence of events and actions. And even when data is slim, following sound epistemological thinking and practice, the constructionist feminist, for example, will invoke theory to make up the empirical slack.

I have suggested that because the relationship between content/story, narrating/narration and mode of expression is ultimately the result of an epistemological decision on the part of the historian, explanation and meaning, rather than simply following on from reference, derives, therefore, from the narrative drive towards coherence. This is, of course, the product of the figurative, emplotment, ethical and ideological choices and narrational decisions made by the historian. Moreover, the mode of expression selected by the historian is constituted by another set of narrative choices, which both reflect and at the same time modify content/story and narrational decisions. At its most basic the logic of history lies in the historian making content/story, narrational and expression decisions through the continuous loop of reciprocity and aesthetic over-determination between the past and the mode of expression selected for the history.[52] The choice made between alternative and perhaps competing modes of expression is a fundamental decision made by all historians. Because, seemingly, the textual choice is made for most historians it only serves to hide what is still a choice that has crucial epistemological consequences. That epistemological, cultural and especially professional forces push historians towards this decision in no way diminishes the significance of that choice – or the fact that it is a choice.

It is now time to turn to the implications and practicalities of this history narrative model. This involves re-addressing several 'fundamental beliefs'. These include the distinction between historical reality, reference and representation, the nature of the relationship between narrative, explanation, meaning and the utility of **experimental history**. And finally we need to examine the consequences of the narrative logic of history in the matter of objectivity, truth and relativism. These issues will be examined in the next three chapters.

5 The Past, the Facts and History

As Frank R. Ankersmit noted over 20 years ago, **epistemological** approaches to **history** have always been concerned with the criteria historians deploy for **truth**, the accuracy of historical descriptions, **explanation** and **meaning**.[1] Narrativist approaches to history, however, focus on the linguistic instruments deployed by historians in understanding and interpreting **the-past-*as*-history**. Epistemology is concerned with the **correspondence** between historical statements and their **referents**. Narrativist history is concerned with history as a **story–discourse** connecting activity. But this does not mean that epistemological history is 'realist' and narrativist history is non-realist or idealist – or fiction. For narrativist approaches to history are, as I will explore in this chapter, concerned with the relationship between **reality**, reference and **representation**.

Briefly, I will examine how this rethinking of the logic of history affects seven key historical concepts:

1 reality
2 reference/**facts**
3 representation
4 explanation
5 meaning
6 **objectivity**
7 truth

In this chapter I will examine the first three concepts. These are normally cast in terms of a *commitment* to the knowable historical reality of the past, the *belief* that the past must be empirically available in the form of reference and, the *practice* of representation in the historical text.

▶ Historical reality

The *commitment* to 'reality' might appear to be unproblematic in history. It seems reasonable to assume the past was once real and as such should be amenable to 'being known' through its **empirical** verification. This means its epistemological connection to history ought to be trouble-free. According to conventional thinking, the only genuine problem can be a lack of evidence, which may make 'knowing exactly what happened' just a bit difficult at times. But even then by the comparison and verification of the evidence that is available, and with the use of **inference** and clever theorising, historians can get pretty close to the story of what happened especially if the evidence is well attested and is never (or hardly ever) in dispute.

But we are all very well aware that capturing the past as it was is not exactly that straightforward. This is exemplified in Sue Morgan's *The Feminist History Reader* (2006), in which over two dozen feminist historians collectively demonstrate that historical categories do not necessarily have to be part of the past to be part of history. As Morgan says, 'The recovery of women as subjects of, and agents in, the making of history, and the simultaneous decentring of the male subject has prompted widespread re-examinations of the most fundamental of historical presumptions, not least through vastly democratising the vision of who and what constitutes historical discourse.'[2] As feminist history demonstrates, the reality of the past is only the starting point for the creation of a culturally significant history.

So, how do historians cope with the now unreality of the reality of the past (it was once real but is not anymore)? Ricoeur expends much effort in defending the survival of the past in what he calls 'the trace'. This is composed of data, which are re-worked by the historian through a sense of duty to the past. His argument is at its least convincing when he says that though 'constructing the past' the historian's intention is to 'reconstruct it'. He seems to acknowledge the epistemological inadequacy of this argument when he says history and fiction are 'interweaved', with history making use of fiction and fiction history to figure time via a variety of **narrative** functions like **emplotment**, **voice**, implied reader.[3]

Understood in terms of the-past-*as*-history, 'the trace' has to be turned into a narrative discourse to be 'knowable'. This is why virtually every philosopher of history, apart from Ricoeur, at some point is concerned about it. Realist philosophers of history have followed in the footsteps of early-twentieth-century logical positivists like Bertrand Russell and the early Ludwig Wittgenstein, who limited their idea of truth to that which can be validated by empirical research into the trace. These, like Gardiner, McCullagh, Bunzl, Searle, Zagorin, Carr, Dray, Norman, Zammito and so on maintain there is an epistemological continuity between the real past and the present history of it.[4] This means historians can pretty much tell it like it was – they can get the story straight. Of course even the most realist of philosophers know that it can only be done in and through language. As G.W.F. Hegel famously noted, history records what actually happened (*res gestae* or the content) *and* it is always a representation as a narrative or verbal account (*historia rerum gestarum* or its form). So the notion of history as reference and representation is hardly new.[5]

But what is still often forgotten is that Hegel pointed out that the past and its historical representation are produced synchronously. The congruence of historical reality – things that actually happened – and their narrative clearly complicates the status of both. However, the realist position maintains that the world exists separately of our representations of it. It is, of course, hard to disagree with this. By way of illustration, I feel pretty confident (like you?) that the present is real and so, in all likelihood, was the past. But I am far from secure in believing that past reality can be regarded as ultimately knowable for what it really or even most likely means.

Reconstructionist historians, as realists, assume historical knowledge is largely independent of how they narrate and write. Indeed, they argue, it is dangerous to maintain the past cannot be **reconstructed** pretty much as it actually was, even though it is in the form of a narrative. While few reconstructionists would say the past was as history says it is, the category error with which we are familiar is ignored. Hence for reconstructionists and even the most sophisticated **constructionists** (because ultimately they also endorse some version of correspondence theory), the reality of the past does not change as we represent it. But this is not and never has been the case. As we shall see when I discuss the nature of representation, there is confusion between the concept of description and representation that derives from the false assumption that history is about description, **empiricism** and analysis, but is not about representation. The claim is then made that historians, who question whether what we say or write can correspond with past reality as it actually was, are anti-realists. In fact we are all anti-representationalists.

The realist philosopher John Searle recognises this situation when, he says, there is nothing epistemic about reality.[6] Although Searle does not go on to pursue this point, historians should not equate a belief in reality with the correspondence theory of knowledge. **Realism**, in other words, is not a theory of truth (see pp. 116–121). Indeed, to assume that knowing what happened defines truth is simply wrong. Reality is about our **ontological** existence – our 'being' (past and present) but is not about epistemology – our knowledge. Historians, like most people, get confused because they tend not to see beyond the situation where correspondence theory (working backwards, as historians tend to do) *implies* a belief in realism. But it is perfectly possible to endorse a belief in reality (as I do) and yet also have grave doubts about correspondence theory as a way of accessing the truth. As the leading philosopher of truth Donald Davidson has argued, being labelled as a realist or anti-realist is pointless. This is because he sees no difference between a correspondence view of truth, and the idea that what we say/write 'represents'.[7]

In other words, realism does not entail correspondence with 'truth' because truth is not the name of a relationship of correspondence between language statements and reality. That the notion of the 'true representation' of past reality is a contradiction is suggested by the fact that there are a large number of modes or systems of representation and expression for the 'same' reality. This is why we have different **modes of expression**. This is not to say reality changes with its form of expression. But its nature, such as we can 'know it', does.

The major contemporary critics of the concept of reality entailed as correspondence are the pragmatic philosopher Richard Rorty and Frank Ankersmit. Like all anti-representationalists Rorty denies that reality causes language to work as it does. In terms specifically of history, Frank Ankersmit argues there are two compulsions – reality *and* language.[8] This position, I think, means we can argue in favour of what we might call the process of **narrative supervenience**. In broad terms the philosophical concept of 'supervenience' refers to the **order**ing of a 'dependency relationship' between properties in the world. To be precise, a group of properties is supervenient on another set when a change in the first set creates change in the second, but not vice versa.

Historians, though not used to this nomenclature, actually use the concept of supervenience all the time especially when they imagine, for example, that complex social, economic and cultural structures (classes, races, nations, levels of technology, etc.) are supervenient over (the lives of) individual human beings/**agents**. Historians do, of course, regularly deploy organising concepts in their **story space** like class and race (and more detailed constructions like subalternism). Given this, we should be able to understand how history – as a narrative making activity – supervenes (imposes on) the past.

But what about 'the real'? The concept of realism is as much an artistic endeavour, as it is anything else. Modes of expression such as writing, film or the visual can and no doubt will continue to emphasise 'truth' and 'be authentic'. Film can be 'realist' in just the same way as written history claims to be. But, like history, this is because film relies on complicated compositional rules to which the consumer is habituated and which makes their contrived nature invisible. Thus, because both written and filmic history narratives rely on devices like linear plots, closure, omniscient narrators (who deliberately ignore their act of narration) and so on, realism is only ever understood as reflecting the world, and is never grasped as a discursive creation. In order to unmask realism, its narrative rules have to be confronted.

Consequently, narrative supervenience, as a way of explaining the relationship between the reality of the past world and the history we devise to represent it, is as cognitive as any statement of **justified belief** or analytical conclusion. As the Philosopher Louis Mink famously observed over 30 years ago, historians would be ill-advised to relegate narrative to the level of 'a merely literary grace' for, as he said, the narrative is ' . . . a primary cognitive instrument'.[9] Taken together, each function within what is now well-known to us as the triad of **content/story**, narrating/narration (such as epistemological choice, emplotment, ethical choice, factualism, authorship, **focalisation** and time order) and **mode of expression** enables the historian to map and explain in an intelligible way the connections between actions and events.[10] At this point a few historians will no doubt say 'yes, but what about the facts?' Surely the only proper link between the reality of the past and history is inference from the **sources** (factualism). I shall examine that now.

▶ Reference/facts

The *belief* in reference is a narrative function that we first came across in Chapter 2. It should be very clear by now that 'reference' is not just literally a referring to the past. It is also the belief that we can accurately represent an object or event that was once located in space and time. In other words, empiricism cannot work its way around the situation that past reality can only be accessed as a language. This is the problem with facts. Facts carry the connotation that they exist 'outside of narrative'. Phenomenologically this is not the case. In narrativist thinking, facts are events under a description (representations of reality). As the poststructuralist feminist historian Joan Scott famously said, experience is always contested and contingent. So, even such seemingly neutral concepts like reference and experience are themselves 'produced' as concepts. Reference, after all, *refers* to some 'thing'. It is not that 'thing'. Equally, though perhaps less obviously, 'experience' can only be understood as we process it conceptually.

First, facts are similarly constituted entities. They are 'hand built' from the raw data. And second, because of this, facts have no voice of their own. Data can refer to 'what happened' but that is all it does. This is obviously important if you want to know 'what happened'. But it has little utility in any other way. No matter how detailed and precise is the data, or that it took 5 years of working in an archive to 'discover', such material has no utility until it is encoded and given meaning (a signification) in an explanatory narrative. This confronts us with the fact that '*the past*' does not exist except in the form of 'the-past-*as*-history': this is why there are, in other words, only histories.[11]

What is more, the existence of different histories has much to do, as Claire Norton has pointed out, with the protocols of academic history writing and reception.[12] Using examples of sources that have been variously construed as both history and fictive stories, Norton raises again the question of what White calls 'the fictions of factual representation' in history.[13] However, asking how historians can verify the accuracy of the correspondence between reality and perception is only half the issue. The other half is how audiences construct and recognise 'historical reality'. Norton offers, following Rorty and others, '. . . a pragmatist theory of justification' based, as she claims, on actual practice.[14]

In essence Norton argues it is less strict reference and analysis and rather more the beliefs of communities of competent historians that creates the relationship between past, the facts and history (deploying the apparatuses of footnotes, acknowledgements, the voice of the well-known historian, etc.). Her analysis leads to the conclusion that until we also acknowledge the problematic nature of the relationship between historical reality and reference the situation whereby reference and realism are not at all the same thing will remain obscure to us. Now, while recognition of this should lead us away from confusing past reality *with* reference and reference *with* knowable reality, it leads us on to a particularly significant feature of reference.

This is that reference is normally defined and used by historians in such a way as to suggest that both the narrator and the story/discourse is entirely reliable in an empirical and, *therefore*, a truth-acquiring sense. The very concept of reference, in effect, constitutes the reality–representational connection or correspondence. Thus a historian may offer several evidentially attested statements of justified belief but this act *in itself* does not *necessarily* carry within it 'the conclusion that...'? Certainly 'the weight of evidence' can suggest a proposal for a likely and plausible meaning but the act of reference *itself* only ever establishes a relation between a 'referring expression' and the referent it purports to represent. This is where narrative becomes central to history thinking and practice.

The explanatory and interpretative history narrative – though factually heavily laden – is still more than the sum of its referential parts. Thus, for constructionist historians it has independence in terms of the concepts that always accompany factual statements. Statements that are offered 'in evidence' are always used by constructionists, in support of some theory or another as the American historian Lee Benson famously acknowledged in the Preface to his distinguished early social scientific history *The Concept of Jacksonian Democracy: New York as a Test Case*.[15] Although his book examines the impact of egalitarian ideas on New York politics between 1816 and 1844, he conceived it to be an essay on the clarification of historical concepts. Specifically, he said he was attempting to resolve two questions, namely what empirical data could be 'logically' designated by the concept 'Jacksonian Democracy', and does the concept help historians to understand the course of American history after 1815?

Benson concluded his book with a chapter entitled 'Jacksonian Democracy – Concept or Fiction'.[16] Explicitly rejecting the concept (the fiction?) of Jacksonian Democracy he replaced it with 'a more adequate and realistic concept'.[17] His more realistic conceptualisation was to disassociate the democratic tendency of the period from the party of Jackson by looking at the role of individuals (as he said 'who caused' the egalitarian revolution rather than 'what were the causes'). This is not to doubt that Benson did not exhaustively sift evidence and modify his theory in the process. But at some point he had to fish or cut bait and he fished with the theory of historical **agency**. Eventually Benson reached the point when he thought 'the evidence' matched 'the theory' and *vice versa*. But most importantly – as the category distinction between the past and history amply demonstrates – Benson's narrative about Jacksonian Democracy still differed *in kind* from his factual statements even when they are considered as empirical propositions about the *likely* nature of past reality.

Recognising that historians invariably deploy narrativism, Frank Ankersmit uses the word to refer to the analysis of the historical text as a whole and, in the process, endorses the judgements of Hayden White and Louis Mink that there is always a cognitive gap between 'what happened' and the 'historical text'.[18] That this is the case has little impact on those (few) empiricists who insist that such an argument must entail historians ignoring evidence, or retaining a theory despite the evidence, or must end up failing to recognise the difference between useful and less useful data. The other implication is that epistemic **sceptics** in particular deny the rationality of analysis.[19] The reconstructionist historian and archivist David Henige says we historians cannot

> ... evade our responsibilities to test evidence ... before we draw conclusions. Nor does it [epistemological scepticism] warrant putting ourselves constantly at the centre of our enterprise, forcing critics to sight in on an ever-moving target. Least of all does it allow us to pontificate on the fragility of knowledge in order to excuse indolence in addressing loose ends, elusive sources, or irksome discrepancies.[20]

Implicitly rejecting the position of archivists like Bernadine Dodge, Henige implies that what he calls 'postmodern' historians are feckless and afraid of hard work in the archive. But in saying this he is not really answering the key question raised by most philosophers of history today: how does the relationship between reference and narrative work?

Philosophers of history as diverse as Ankersmit, White and Mink agree that historians are in error if they believe history is 'concealed' in the facts and that telling a history is a matter of digging out and making explicit what is already there. It follows that, like works of art, historical story spaces can only be compared with each other, and not some original reality. This is most obvious in autobiographies and biographies when the **author-historian** imposes a construction on the data of their own or others' lives. It becomes even more obvious when, like Lee Benson, historians crank up (or down) from agents and historical characters to entities like classes and nations.

To understand the nature of reference, therefore, we have to take what seems to be the counter-intuitive step of detaching it from the concept of 'knowable reality'. Reference suggests an existential correspondence to past reality. But yet it is a linguistic sign. It follows, therefore, that a concept like 'The American Civil War' is not a vast chunk of historical reference that was 'discovered' by historians – which it forever corresponds to and which shaped US history between 1861 and 1865. Most historians will acknowledge that it is an interpretative tool of cognition and as such its meaning and our understanding of it change as it is revised or, to be more accurate, re-visioned over time. Indeed, the data from that period of the American past has had different meanings for historians at different times and in different places. As William Pencak argues, the triumph of the term 'Civil War' 'as the dominant signifier of the events of 1861–1865' was a complex and slow *historical* process.[21]

Northerners at first talked of 'rebellion' or 'the War for the Union'. Southerners talked of 'The War for Southern Independence'. Then during the late nineteenth century 'the War Between the States' emerged (and which is still the preferred term among many Southerners). From the 1920s the term 'Civil War' became the most popular description. The Civil War is thus a sign intended to grant equality between the combatants and to signify contemporary unity. The term is only understandable when it is **historicised**. It is then understood perhaps as less a description of events than an interpretation of them. The interpretation that *uses* the term is deployed, arguably, as an effort to debunk the Southern mythmaking process of contented slaves, states rights and the peaceful re-unification of the federal state.

In effect the American Civil War as a description of events did not take place – what did was a victory for Southern racism? As Pencak concludes, the Civil War did not take place and the South won it. We should always remember that there is never any determinate meaning in the past. Over time the meaning of reality, what is *now* 'reference' and what is likely to become conceptualisation and then representation are increasingly difficult to distinguish. To deploy another paradox, words do not always mean what they say. Just what do the terms 'the Alamo', the 'sands of Iwo Jima', the 'American Revolution' or the 'War on Terror' really *mean*? We can never know.

This much we learn from the 'postmodern' approach to the referent, which emphasises the structuralist insights of Ferdinand de Saussure. In the early years of the last century Saussure pointed to the lack of a 'natural correspondence' between the world or content (in history terms *res gestae*) and word or form (*historia rerum gestarum*). More recently Elizabeth Deeds Ermarth has noted how language operates differentially.[22] Like Saussure, words for Ermarth are only 'signs' defined by their difference from other words in a sentence. These signs have three elements. First, they are composed of the signifier (the word) and the signified (the concept the word represents). Second, the signifier is the linguistic sign and the signified is the concept represented by the sign. And the third is, of course, the referent to which the sign and the signifier connect and which – in structural terms – is the least important element. This structuralist view of language notes only the structure of the connections between signifiers that are culturally generated (see the definition above of the American Civil War). Although we use words as though they are referential, such usage is based on conventional social meanings and/or values.

Saussure's primary insistence on *langue* means rejecting the historical or diachronic dimension of language in favour of the structural, or 'synchronic' as he calls it.

Saussure's ideas concerning the relationship between words and their constructed meaning result first in the belief that language works according to its own rules and is unrelated to the 'real world': past or present. And second, words do not automatically or naturally correspond to the their referents. The relationship is therefore arbitrary, being fixed by social convention (or, in the case of the American Civil War, the arguments of people, politicians, journalists and historians over generations). The poststructuralist movement of the last 30 years or so has further emphasised the problematical, aporetic connections between reality, reference and representation by emphasising the nature of texts (sources and history books) as being replete with gaps, silences and hesitation over of meaning(s) and signification. None of this implies a denial that certain events occurred or that we cannot refer to them. That, as I hope is clear by now, is not the issue.

You will recall that in the Introduction to this book I noted briefly what the French cultural theorist Roland Barthes called the 'referential illusion' by which we ascribe to one category (history) features that are only attributable to another (the past). You will remember Barthes' point that historians tend to combine that which is signified (the representation) with its referent thus constituting an arbitrary signifier–referent association. Barthes insisted that in 'objective history' the 'real' is never more than a hazy signified. Hence we have history defined as a textual 'realistic effect' whereby reference only attains meaning when it becomes representation. I called this a 'category mistake' because the category of reference does not belong to the same category of that of a connected prose narrative.

It is worth considering further at this point Barthes' concept of the 'reality effect' because of its centrality to understanding the disputed status of history as a referential undertaking.[23] He argued that that which historians take for the real past in their writings can, as it is a narrative, only be a reality-effect (in the narrative) generated by their belief in the correspondence theory of knowledge and truth. The logic of his argument was that history has no privileged access to reality through reference because its overall constitution makes it no different – *in the process of that constitution* – from fiction. The turning of the past object into a historical subject of study is an inevitable deformation of that object despite its direct reference to events and existents in the past. It is the deliberate omission of the narration function in history that creates this effect. As I tried to demonstrate in Chapter 3, the narrating function is one of the central pillars of history creation. As Barthes claims,

> On the level of discourse, objectivity – or the deficiency of signs of the utterer – thus appears as a particular form of imaginary projection, the product of what might be called the referential illusion, since in this case the historian is claiming to allow the referent to speak all on its own.[24]

The epistemological status of history *as a **discourse*** is thus exposed and deflated; the empirical can now be prioritised above other narrative functions *only* by virtue of its self-proclaimed claim to truthfulness. Barthes is arguing that this is an epistemological ruse by which the referent is placed beyond the artifice of the narrative elements of content/story, narrating/narration and mode of expression. The past, in effect, has no continuing identity except *as* history. In other words, the past only 'exists' when it is narrated (and read, viewed, performed and/or witnessed).

In rejecting this Barthesian argument, empiricists insist that the essence of **referentiality** has less to do with language than a detailed empirical knowledge. Put simply, we can know history is truthful because (a) reference is not an illusion just because it is a representation and (b) people in the past were pretty much like us. So, if we can figure out what people are thinking and doing today then we can do the same for people in the past. This is based on the principle that human beings act intentionally to achieve objectives. Thus the realist philosopher of history Frederick Olafson argues that the essence of history is the translation into narrative of the real action in the past.[25]

For Olafson, history is nothing more than the narrative reconstruction of the chain of past human actions in a cause and effect relationship. More recently Mark Bevir has supported this position arguing that the historian can have objective knowledge of the past by reconstructing individual human volition (in the history narrative).[26] This rational action theory (even if weak – as in Bevir) accepts not only that people act purposefully but that their actions can be mirrored in the structure of the narrative (as in Ricoeur's rationale for emplotment). The implication is that *the* story (of **intentionality** and action) generates events and these can be revealed in the history.

Certainly reconstructionist historians view the past as working according to the logic of action and agency. For them explanation is built quite simply on the direct reference to the agent's motivations and intentions that produced outcomes (events). This is the mechanism that provides *the* story of the action. Consequently the narrative provided by the historian can mimic the action-story of past events through reference.[27] Hence we have the central principle of **reconstructionist history**: 'to know *the* action (truth) is to understand *the* story (its meaning)'. Unfortunately this fails to address the central issue of history: representation.

▶ Representation

In the nineteenth century the question and *practice* of the representation of 'the real' emerged as an issue with both 'the novel' and 'the history'. It is not a coincidence that they became the two dominant modes in Western bourgeois culture for connecting reality and reference. The novel developed as a realist mode of expression from Balzac, Flaubert, Eliot and Stendhal through to the realist novel and naturalism (with its scientificist pretensions), and in history via the efforts of Enlightenment-inspired Gibbon (history as example) and Ranke (history as demonstration). Eventually, in the twentieth century, a plethora of 'varieties of history' developed. Both 'the history' and 'the novel', as modes of expression, were developed through the conviction that they could comprehend and represent 'the real' by examining the social relations of agents and the structures that shaped their lives in time and space.[28]

Both 'the history' and 'the novel' attempted to describe and explain the turning points and climacterics of human existence in terms of economics, society, politics, culture and technology. As it worked out, whichever was 'most realistic' in their apprehension of 'reality' could then lay down the ground rules for that knowledge. Although the novel has been described in terms of a 'classic realist' text, actually it was history that embodied that description. **Mimésis** became history's key characteristic while the voice of the author (the poet's voice) diminished in audibility. However, like the realist novel, history fed on the false impression that it gave that the documentary references or trace(s) (the direct quotation in particular) were somehow the essence of realism.

What was neglected was how the trace 'stood for' the past. But this did not last very long into the twentieth century with the rise of situated history – social history from below – and the attack on the bourgeois concept of agency because of the experiences of capitalist industrialisation. As the aims of history changed so did the understanding of reference. Moreover, despite the artifice of the silent narrator it became clear very quickly that the historian was actually the omniscient voice. Only the profound prejudice that flew in the face of the constructed nature of the history text could maintain the fiction of its pure referentialism.

Perhaps the major twentieth-century development concerning the nature of representation was the realisation that the analogue effect of the text was crucial to the constitution of its meaning. In terms of a history text the reader may be convinced by reference to that which happened, and consequently they may 'believe' they have read 'the truth'. Nevertheless, history is also all about persuasion (poetic effect). Thus, as Ricoeur suggests (following Aristotle), a 'compelling impossibility' is often preferable to that which, though possible, is unpersuasive.[29] Thus, the convincing metaphor (the literally impossible) is preferable to the simple factual statement that *in itself* carries no meaning. It seems increasingly plausible to more and more historians that the truth (strictly the truth-effect) of any history is the product of its textual construction and reception of the content, as much as reference itself.

The narrativist theory of history thus acknowledges reality, reference and representation as working reciprocally. It also accepts that our **reader-response** to the text will, among other considerations of an **intertextual** nature, be to the content/story such as emplotment (tragedy, romance, comedy or whatever combination) that the author-historian has deployed. As Ricoeur insists, the fear, happiness, loathing or indifference readers experience is inscribed *in* the events *by* the composition as it moves *through* the sieve of the representation.[30] Of course reader-reception theory as espoused by Barthes suggests that the 'literary competence' of the reader, as well as the nature of intertextuality, also directly creates meaning. This is exemplified in the distinction between the first-year undergraduate's 'historical competence' compared to that of the PhD candidate. The meanings they get from the same history text will always be different.

Now it is these sorts of considerations which prompted the historian Hans Ulrich Gumbrecht to suggest that to 'to think seriously' about our historical knowledge we should keep an open mind about the relationship between reality, reference and representation.[31] This is what Hayden White prefers to think of as issues of 'presentation'.[32] Gumbrecht suggests what we imagine to be past reality may turn out to be only an intertextual cultural or social construction that has been incarnated as historiography. As we shall see, this raises a number of questions about explanation, meaning, objectivity, **subjectivity** and **relativism**. As I noted in Chapter 2, the concept of historical representation can best be approached through Ankersmit's concept of 'narrative substances' and the notion of story space. By acknowledging these, our attention is shifted from the absolute primacy of research and referentiality to their role *within* the narrative construction of the whole text.[33] It is here that issues relating to the modes of expression also become significant and the matter of 'realist representation' emerges.

Of course for many contemporary thinkers, representation is the crucial element in knowledge creation because reality is something we cannot 'know'. As Jean Baudrillard has argued – perhaps too radically for most historians – reality is an invention of modern Western reason ' . . . unknown to other cultures'.[34] His reasoning is that once we reflect upon the idea that even if objects exist outside of us ' . . . we can know absolutely nothing of their objective reality' for ' . . . things are given to us only through our representation'.[35] He maintains that arguing about the objectivity of external things is, therefore, a hollow exercise. In this sense history becomes 'pointless'. He calls this activity – so basic to what historians do – a 'definitive illusion'.[36] He concludes that whilst human consciousness claims the privilege of being the mirror of reality this is an impossible situation because a mirror is part of the object it reflects. And this is the trap from which history cannot escape.

However, if Baudrillard remains unpalatable (though increasingly not for all historians) the logic of narrative supervenience prompts us to have sympathy for Ankersmit's notion of narrative substance and its connection to reference.[37] Uncontroversially Ankersmit argues that the historical text is composed of many statements of justified belief that offer an accurate description of events and happenings in the past. These evidential traces are derived from the sources and, when processed and arranged appropriately by the historian, constitute the 'facts' of the past.

But, as Ankersmit goes on to point out, while single statements of justified belief can be verified the history itself cannot be because it has the epistemic status of an interpretative narrative – not a singular statement. Histories are not just collections of statements (descriptions of events), plus analysis (inference as to what those descriptions of events might mean). History is a highly complex representational structure of narrative functions of which empiricism and inference are but two technical elements. Hence, as Ankersmit argues, the historical narrative can never provide a site for the 'testing' of truth and objectivity in conventional empirical and analytical senses. A history, as a complete text, cannot be reduced to the level of an analysis that can only work with statements. To repeat, history is not a statement, but an **aesthetic**, figural representation.

So narrative interpretations fulfil the function of organising knowledge, which means as narrative substances they can never be true or false according to referential criteria alone. Hence 'historians' debates' over the meaning of Athenian democracy, or 'the causes of the English Civil War' are not over the actuality of the past but about narrative interpretations of the past. What this means is that statements of justified belief can maintain their 'truth-acquiring' status in respect of their correspondence to each other, but that quality does not translate to the overall epistemological nature of the narrative. The narrative remains a (category of) representation and aesthetics and the facts remain (a category of) data and their reference.

Thus, to give an example, I pluck at random from my bookshelves, *A People's History of the United States* and *A History of Australia*.[38] Both of these titles constitute a story space and any number of individual narrative substances that result from the narrative function decisions made by their authors. Indeed, the fact that there are so many different histories of the United States and Australia (and any other historical topic you can think of) is because there never was such a 'thing' as a people's history of the United States until the historian created it. The same applies to a history of Australia. Or, for that matter *The Mind of the South*, *Working Class Americanism* or *An Economic History of the USSR*.

One is thus tempted to say that any symmetry between the reference (to reality) and its representation in a narrative history is purely accidental. Hence, 'a people's history of the United States' never existed 'back there' to be detected and rescued. As Ankersmit reminds us, narrative substances are representational proposals about the past. If this seems like bad news, it should not be. We are not abandoning the faithfulness of reference to past actuality. That remains. Historians like everyone else want to know what happened. There is no room for the denial of the reality of the past nor our referential-based beliefs. But what I am saying is that acknowledging the problems concerning the relationship between reality, reference and representation actually makes us *better* historians. It also frees us (or it should) from the tyranny of those people (not just historians) who would take chunks of 'reality', designate them as 'facts', then claim they automatically connect and then can only 'mean one thing'. Only by grasping the nature of representation can we achieve some understanding of the connections we make between reality, reference and representation. This also has the added benefit of making historians epistemologically sceptical – as well as being sceptical empiricists.[39]

That history is *about* the past is a convenient way to recall all of these arguments. In history, if we seek 'genuine truth' or 'the real meaning' we will remain disappointed. An important consequence of this is that we cannot actually learn 'from the past. We can certainly learn different things from 'history', but not the reality of the past'. Understanding this reduces the confusion that results from insisting there is a determinant relationship between reality, reference and representation. In other words, as epistemological sceptics we must continue to rethink the 'reference → explanation → meaning → narrative' formula.

▶ Conclusion

In this chapter, I have suggested that recovering the past is complex because 'the real' has to be converted into a narrative that by its nature cannot correspond directly to 'what happened'. But this does not produce a conflict between the referential function of the content/story and the processes of narrating/narration. I have argued that past reality, reference and representation must be viewed as a coherent whole. In so doing I suggested, noting the contributions particularly of Barthes and Ankersmit, that the two compulsions of reality *and* language must be viewed together as producing a 'historical reality' rather than 'the reality of the past'.

I claimed that historians do not work with given historical objects like 'the American Civil War' about which they then try to offer an accurate representation. I suggested, rather, that 'historical reality' is the reality effect of the history narrative. In other words, 'past reality' and 'historical reality' are different. In none of this have I suggested that tried and tested historical skills are inappropriate. Indeed, referentiality demands that those skills remain intact. However, my conclusion is that there can be no 'realistic representation' that can be generated by reference alone.

So, how can historians explain the meaning of the past under these circumstances? I turn to this in the next chapter.

6 Understanding [in] History

We have now begun to confront the primacy of that form of **explanation** that connects **reference** (evidence) with **meaning** and explanation exclusively through the process of **inference**. In this chapter, I will describe how the conventional definitions of historical understanding in terms of the two key concepts of explanation and meaning need to be re-thought.[1] As we shall see, one of the most significant results of the **narrative turn** has been the emergence of a new approach to **the-past-*as*-history** derived from the emerging and growing compulsion to undertake **experimental history**.

▶ Explanation

Pared down to its essentials, 'historical explanation' means disclosing why certain historical events occurred (and, by implication, not others), understood as a succession of statements of **justified belief** that are causally connected and which together will provide the explanation that best fits the evidence.[2] This procedure of 'best fit' provides the 'argument behind the explanation' starting with the historian scouring the **sources** 'looking for' potential explanations of change over time.

This 'best fit' process of 'historical analysis' inclines to be one of two kinds. First, the process may be quasi-scientific in nature, tending to impose law-like regularities on past events. This is the preferred orientation (though not exclusively) of **constructionist** historians. **Reconstructionist** historians reject this 'scientific' or 'structural' approach in favour of 'human **agency**', maintaining that the way to explain past events is to explore the human reasoning and **intentionality** of action behind them whilst acknowledging there may be larger social, economic and political structures within which agency operates.

It is here that we see that the concept of *the* given **story** of the past, as opposed to the **fictively** derived **emplotment** of 'historical **reality**', has little relevance to **history**. For most of those historians who believe the **narrative** carries *the* explanation (usually understood to start and end with an **objective** account of the **facts**) derived by non-narrative means, the **ontology** of the text is irrelevant to knowledge creation and is only pertinent when *the* explanation needs to be delivered. This process is reinforced for those historians who endorse 'scientific historical explanations' by the thinking of Karl Popper and Carl Hempel with their beliefs that explanation implies a law-like mode of explanation.[3] This 'science-like' mode of explanation is cause and effect in nature, being specifically hypothetico (propositional)-deductive (inferential). It is realist, referential and verifiable. It is built on the **correspondence theory** of knowledge. This form of historical thinking is usually formulated via the notion of the covering law. This is a generalised explanation for events that presupposes a universal law of human behaviour (as evidenced by observation).

An example of this would be Joel Perlmann's book *Ethnic Differences*, which is a detailed assessment of 12,000 members of four ethnic groups in Providence, Rhode Island, the intention being to explain the (covering law) relationships between ethnicity, education, and economic and social advance during the period 1880–1935.[4] Perlmann uses a wide range of **empirical** data drawn from school records, census data, tax books, occupational data and city directories plus a research design that deployed the statistical analysis of multiple regression. For example, school variables were regressed on parent occupation, property values, family size and ethnicity. His conclusion is that historians cannot readily generalise in a covering law fashion. In fact Perlmann thinks that to explain ethnic differences found in American social history it is better to explore individual ethnic experiences '... with a comparative perspective and an eye on theory...'.[5] So, even the most sophisticated statistical analysis cannot produce 'scientific history' even if the desire was there.

Even the most sophisticated constructionist forms of interpretation and explanation tend to be viewed by reconstructionists as crude inventions. Reconstructionist targets have included the Marxist school of history (that seeks class as the explanatory variable in change over time) and the *Annales* school of history that has argued for a scientific approach to the study of the past since the 1920s. Another is the hard-core social science and economic history that spawned a variety of forms starting with the New Social History of the 1960s and cliometrics (statistical histories). Yet another is the latest wave of **poststructuralist**-inspired feminist history. Despite reconstructionist opposition, the last 30 years has seen the emergence of a new and richly complex set of histories indebted to social science disciplines especially sociology and anthropology.[6]

The most recent development in this debate is the rise of the '**new empiricism**' or 'practice theory'. According to Gabrielle Spiegel this is a historical practice that acknowledges the impact of the linguistic turn but which 'seeks to move beyond its initial formulation' to 'focus on questions of how society undergoes constant transformations in both its material and conceptual realms'.[7] Whether new empiricism or practice theory they have tried (largely unsuccessfully) to return to 'the real' while acknowledging the role of language in history writing. Arguably the new empiricism is neither fish nor fowl and like all such efforts will presumably fail to square the circle of **epistemological** and narrativist theories of history.[8]

How can historians explain anything convincingly given all of these problems? Well, most historians, even though they are fairly well assured that history can never be a 'true interpretation' of the past, continue to plough their empirical-analytical furrow. This is because they believe that only through that method can they inch closer to the true nature of the past. They believe in the progress of history as a discipline because of their faith in the four basic principles of classic realist historical explanation:

1 Empiricism can justifiably constitute history as an epistemology.
2 The evidence will allow the fair-minded historian to discover *the* story within (hence the process ends up as being objective).
3 The judicious use of inference, social theory and concept can provide for historical explanation.
4 The composition of the history narrative is a function of the first three beliefs.

However, if we assume history is a **historicist**, authored, literary representation then historical explanation (and meaning, objectivity and **truth** as we shall see) can only be constituted through the narrative functions that I have outlined. As I have suggested, viewing history as a **content/story**, narrating/narration activity places empiricism and analysis within the much bigger framework of the narrativist philosophy of history.

The founding principles of the narrative logic of history should by now be starting to very clearly emerge. Briefly, we can summarise them as six principles:

1 History is an unavoidably historicist undertaking.
2 The historical narrative is an interpretative act that supervenes the empirical and inferential through the principle of inclusion.
3 The act of narrative making in history shares the same characteristics as any other realist narrative mode of literature.
4 History narratives impose a meaningful structure of explanation on the past.
5 The history narrative tells a story by 'showing *a*' rather than 'demonstrating *the*' correspondence to the past.
6 Historical narratives are built out of statements that describe the past which, through their precise configuration, define the narrative explanation.[9]

Confusingly the first principle – historicism – has acquired several different meanings over time. But its definition here emphasises the presentist manner in which reality, **referentiality** and representation are fictively 'made' to connect by the historian (in a text, a graphic novel, a museum exhibit or whatever other **mode of expression**). To view history as a historicist exercise is to recognise its uncertain epistemological status. It is because of its historicist nature that we have debates over 'what is history?' and why history after 'the modernist event' (events that apparently defy adequate description and explanation) has been an issue that shows no sign of disappearing from the agenda.[10]

As the philosopher of history William Dray said half a century or more ago, the key to historical explanation is telling *a* story (not necessarily *the* story) explaining how some thing could have happened rather than why it did.[11] He thus compared the concepts of 'how-possibly' and 'why-necessarily'. The former is the logic of narrative, the latter the logic of covering law positivism. For example, when explaining the economic impact of the development of the railroads in nineteenth-century America (an old favourite of hard-core social science/cliometric conceptually constructionist 'why necessarily' historians) the story is *in effect* told in terms of 'how-possibly' connections. Of course, there is never going to be a resolution to the conflict between 'how-possibly' and 'why-necessarily' modes of historical explanation. Indeed, a **'new empiricist'** would probably say they could be compromised or different circumstances that dictate one or the other should be employed. But if we assume we cannot clone past action as textual history, then narrative explanations of 'why-possibly' do tend to make more practical sense.

Today, historical explanation is essentially a debate about narrativism understood, I think, in terms of content/story, narrating/narration and mode of expression. But this does not mean narrativism should be viewed as some sort of alternative to 'proper' empirical-analytical history. Only if historians believe they can escape 'back to the past' would they seriously doubt that they write explanatory narratives in the here and now and that they involve epistemological choice, **emplotment**, figuration, argument, ethical decisions, and so on. Because the vast data set that is 'the past' cannot be rendered in all its richness, it has to be selectively raided and presented, and the only mechanism for that is narrative. Only once we acknowledge this can we gain a better insight into the complexity of historical explanation and meaning – to which I now turn.

▶ Meaning

Historians normally start with the evidence of past actions and events which are usually (though not invariably) incarnated as texts. Thus an article in *The Times* in late January 1924 reporting the death of Lenin might be used as evidence of the attitude of the British press to Lenin's demise. This relic of the past could be deployed (depending on the epistemological orientation of the individual historian) to reconstruct or construct the historical object in which they are interested (the death of Lenin as received by the British press).[12] This would be done to reconstruct (or construct), as Mark Bevir says, '. . . ideas or meanings from the past'.[13] But, as Bevir rightly notes, historians tend to have incompatible views about what constitutes a historical meaning. One historian might, for example, dismiss another's object of study as unimportant so that the history that results is meaningless. So, what (according to Bevir and others) is the generally accepted nature of historical meaning?

At the risk of oversimplification, it is widely acknowledged that deriving the meaning of an act or event ultimately depends on discovering the intentionality (of who is) behind the action. In an exchange between Mark Bevir and Frank Ankersmit in 2000 it became clear that Ankersmit had doubts about Bevir's assumption – held by most practitioner historians – that meaning *is* knowable intention. In other words, Ankersmit doubted historians are in possession of *the* meaning of the past when they know *the* intentions of agents in the past. He questioned the definition of meaning as knowable intentionality as based on the common-sense belief that knowing the intentions of people in the past is no more difficult than knowing the intentions of people in our present everyday life. For Ankersmit it is always going to be an open question as to whether intentions are 'discoverable' and even then capable of becoming 'objectified' in a text. As well as Ankersmit more recently, linguistic, narrative and ethical turners are also indebted (among others) to Hans-Georg Gadamer who maintained language could not be 'used' as a form of instrumentality like a tool, but rather language directs or even controls us. Indeed in the 1930s, the literary theorist I.A. Richards argued words have no meanings that can be said to belong to them.[14] Because words possess no intrinsic meaning it is always up to the **reader** to create specific definitions.[15]

The implication of this long-standing debate is that the agent-author (and also the **author-historian**) is no longer the centre or origin of meaning (knowable intentionality). To grasp the range of meanings available in texts we must understand their relationships to other texts or, more accurately, the discursive formation in which they (all) exist. The authority of the author is lost (their **voice** is drowned out) in the larger **discourse** in which their intentions are understood (misunderstood?) by the historian as/and reader. So, is there any 'realist determination' of meaning in history, especially given the free-play of the signifier–signified relationship, the referential illusion and reader-reception theory?[16]

You will recall from Chapter 2 White and Ricoeur's argument that metaphor is fundamental to interpretation and meaning creation. I suggested there that the role of metaphor in language was to provide the site where the world met the word (where reality meets meaning). Consequently, we always see **the-past-'as'-history**. I argued that history is a linguistic substitute 'standing-in' for the past. This suggests the 'literal meaning' of the past is hardly a straightforward concept in interpreta-tional and meaning-generating terms. Indeed, the notion of 'literal meaning' has no place in history thinking and practice. So, while we tend to assume that the historical text is an example of literal meaning because it is (apparently) made up of facts (statements of justified belief), philosophers of both 'continental' and Anglo-American 'analytical' kinds have been long concerned with the complexity of the connection between language and reality. The philosophy of language has long been the battleground for what 'meaning means'.[17]

It can be argued that words generate meaning in two ways. First, in terms of what they directly signify. The meaning of 'Henry VIII' in a sentence in a history of the Tudor dynasty is fairly clear. 'Henry VIII' was a particular person who did certain things. But words do not just refer to objects in the real world. They also create meaning through their relationship to other words in a sentence. So a word can be a reference – what it stands for like 'Henry VIII' stands for a person. But for a more complete picture of meaning creation we need both reference (by a word to an object) and we need to 'make sense' out of the reference. An important part of this is that the meaning of the historian's statements are always offered with the aim of encouraging a particular belief in the reader's mind. Here again we have the perennial conflict between author intention/reader reception, implied author/implied reader.

Now, a brief acquaintance with the speech act theories of the mid-twentieth-century English philosopher J.L. Austin makes it clear that doing things with words is much more complicated than we might think pointing to what he regards as the *performative* nature of language.[18] Thus, when we say something, and this includes historians (such as I am doing at this precise moment), we *perform* speech acts that work at different levels. The single sentence Austin called the *locutionary act*. But in producing such a sentence we are not, as I just noted, simply making a statement of fact. For example, a historian may say, 'The wartime situation of African–Americans contradicted the ideals of equality and justice for which Americans were fighting' thereby referring to that group of people in the American Revolution (1776–1783). This is not simply a factual statement of justified belief but is (as I read it) also a warning to the reader that the ideals of the American Revolution were being subverted just as they were being established?[19]

This additional level Austin called the *illocutionary act*, and history, of course, works on both the locutionary and the illocutionary levels. Hence there is no defin-itive single and exhaustive meaning even when making what appear to be factual statements. But it does not end with the illocutionary act. The sentence I just quoted also possesses a third *perlocutionary* **order** or level, which is the consequence of the warning implicit in the illocutionary act. This is another level of meaning that might, for example, persuade the reader to behave/believe differently. Increas-ingly historians are becoming aware of the misleading simplicity of much history, writing not least because of the empiricist investment in simplistic polarities such as 'true or false', 'fact or value', 'meaning or no meaning'.

For, as I hope I have made clear, there is still an immense professional invest-ment in empirical or sense-data knowledge (reference) among historians. But this investment ignores the fact that every statement concerning the given nature of past reality is *always* located within a much broader historical narrative **story space** constructed from content/story, narrating /narration and mode of expression. So, to know 'the meaning of what happened' can only be pursued in ways that are strictly controlled by a process of knowing that is a complex mix of the past, the personal, the cultural and the linguistic. Hence the beliefs held by historians are never simply warranted by reference.

Despite many historians still finding this notion hard to take, the philosopher Immanuel Kant (1724–1804) famously argued that perceptions without concepts do not constitute knowledge. Consequently, the primacy of 'empirically derived meaning' lives on only because we still fail to see how our ontology affects our understanding of meaning creation. So, beyond Austin and his speech act analysis, what can we say about the nature of the relationship between language (history) and experience (the past) in terms of meaning creation? Well, we can accept, for example, the observation of Richard Rorty that reality and language are inescapably coupled, but not in a correspondence, a cloning or a **representationalist** way. This is because of the functioning of the story space, the non-existence of the *tertium quid* and the role of 'as' in the-past-*as*-history.

To complicate matters further there are also the well-known problems associ-ated with **hermeneutics** to consider. The first problem is concerned with what are the 'rules' for understanding what the author 'really means'. The second and directly related issue concerns how we interpret the rules and how we apply them. Clearly, applying a rule changes what we wish to know. Martin Heide-gger, though not the first to note the problem, describes it as the understanding of (past) existence being dependent on understanding the effects *of* the world of existence. Unlike science – which assumes we can effectively step *outside* the 'hermeneutic circle' to locate the foundation of meaning via 'hypothesis testing' – history is always trapped.[20] The reason is the historicist one that historians cannot step outside history (the act of interpretation). Thus, one historian's interpreta-tion of class (or 'the war on terror') is another historian's denial of it. Histor-ical understanding only exists *in* history. From this we can thus legitimately infer that history is neither scientific nor objective. It also means that histor-ical interpretations proceed from other interpretations. In other words, explan-ation and meaning starts with the process of explanation and meaning. H-G Gadamer reinforces this idea when he claims that truth emerges from the traditions (histories) through which 'things' like the past are understood (hence the-past-*as*-history).

However, this does not convince realists like C. Behan McCullagh, who has long provided the clearest exposition of the conventional understanding of 'historical meaning'.[21] McCullagh argues that if we can justify our historical descriptions we can know the most likely meaning of the past. McCullagh, sustained by his belief in knowable intentionality and action theory, argues the meaning of a past text can usually be grasped and represented accurately if we look for its 'conventional meaning' as derived through a knowledge of its context.[22]

Prior to disposing with them, McCullagh notes seven possible problems that epistemological **sceptics** offer to rebut his realist analysis of meaning.

1   Languages are not uniform so there is no 'conventional' reading of any text.
2   Contextuality gives way before **intertextuality**.
3   Texts may be seen as products of discourses (the 'real' is not the measure for accuracy, etc., but other texts; consequently, the intentionality of the author cannot be known).
4   Only the reader can create the meaning of a text (hence there cannot be a conventional meaning).
5   All summaries of texts must be **subjective**.
6   Textual readings can be biased.
7   The meaning of text is to be judged by its coherence not its credibility.

McCullagh answers each of these criticisms by upping the dosage of empiricism and increasing the voltage of inference. In effect, he pursues a thoroughgoing hermeneutic agenda and methodology. He does this as follows:

1   The first criticism is answered by historians' extensive knowledge of the relevant language as used by the relevant group in the past.
2   The second answer is to contextualise through comparison with other texts by deploying more evidence (more texts).
3   The third is to question the notion of the displaced author and that it is feasible to know the author's intentions again through context and comparison and by 'finding the best explanation of all the relevant evidence'.
4   McCullagh argues there can be 'objective meanings' in texts and they can be discovered through his responses to the first three criticisms.
5   The fifth criticism can be rejected if the historian provides 'general summaries of texts' which are ' . . . both accurate and comprehensive'.
6   The sixth criticism can be resolved by ensuring inferences are justified and the practice of other historians to point out biased inference (personal, cultural, class, race, gender, or whatever) when it appears.
7   The seventh criticism is answered by turning to the evidence and the processes of contextualisation, verification and comparison.[23]

So, based upon the premise of

1   the honest historian
2   as large a range of evidence as possible
3   contextualisation
4   comparison
5   sound summaries
6   verification
7   the circling shoals of other historians.

the explanation of actions and events in the past can be undertaken satisfactorily in terms of locating their most likely meaning.

McCullagh's analysis, though clearly sophisticated, reveals the limits of any positivist orientation. This is not just because he deploys a 'when did you stop beating your wife' approach (when did you stop contextualising, verifying, evidencing . . .), but because it pays insufficient attention to the logic of content/story, narrating/narration and mode of expression considerations. In other words, there is no sense in McCullagh's analysis that a historian can still believe in justifying historical descriptions while also accepting that it is only one element in a process of historical knowledge creation.

Like Ricoeur before him, Frank R. Ankersmit in his book *Sublime Historical Experience* (2005) questions McCullagh-type hermeneutic approaches to meaning. He starts with the argument (rehearsed by a number of other thinkers not least and perhaps most famously H-G. Gadamer) that historians (like everyone else) start with language and move to experience – the reverse of McCullagh's position. In Gadamerian mood (experience is understood in language) Ankersmit argues that we understand the meaning of the past only in as much as it has 'obligingly taken on a linguistic appearance' and what is outside this 'house of language' of necessity ' . . . exceeds our comprehension'.[24] Ankersmit thus forces us to consider the argument that cause and effect do not connect reference and meaning. The concept of the 'sign', so beloved of structuralists, reminds us that the signifier may 'stand for' both what is represented by the sign *and* its meaning.

Thus the notion of intertextuality (competing with contexuality) holds that the (linguistic) meaning of history texts and relics is always intertextual because their meanings mutually and reciprocally determine (over-determine) each other. Thus, the meaning of one historian's interpretation of 'the origins of the Cold War' is not only dependent on her/his representation (interpretation) but also on other representations of the 'the origins of the Cold War'. One of the most interesting and challenging aspects of history is its comparative (intertextual) nature. As Ankersmit argues, when we want to know what 'historical meaning' is we always have to start with 'representation' and the reader's experience of the text.[25]

We should not infer from this that we cannot have generally satisfactory under-standings of events, texts or actions. We can readily make do with 'probable authorial meaning' as Terry Eagleton describes it.[26] But to accept this is not to swallow the much more doubtful hermeneutic notion that trails it, which is that the meaning of history exists *entirely* outside its powers of narrative representation. Unless we are wary we can easily fall into the trap of believing that facts have a built-in 'historical meaning'. Following the argument of Hayden White, I suggest they can only attain such a meaningful status when fitted into *a* story.[27] Or, to put the same argument slightly differently, bearing in mind the metonymic nature of historical thinking and practice, establishing the meaning of the past is never simply dependent upon a naïve notion of correspondence.

Does this automatically mean being a realist is a pointless waste of time, as Baudrillard maintains? Well, no. Being 'realist' usually works to our advantage so long as we do not extend it beyond what it can usefully do. For the **deconstructionist** historian this means a belief in **realism** does not entail confid-ence in knowable meaning through correspondence theory. Equally, it does not mean epistemological doubts require one to be an anti-realist. An anti-realist refuses to accept there is a mind/language-independent reality. The deconstruc-tionist historian is not anti-realist but, as we shall see in the next section, an anti-representationalist, and it is this that permits her or him to explore the past in new and experimental ways. In other words deconstructionists believe past reality cannot be (a) explained *exhaustively* in empirical terms and its meaning thereby discovered because (b) our only access to it is a complex and ultimately a failing form of representation. Rather than foreclosing on history, this opens up all kinds of exciting and challenging possibilities for engaging with the past.

► Experimental History

Part of the twentieth-century critique of realism, especially in literature, is that it deceives by masking its status as art. It does this, as we have seen, through the category error of suggesting it is a facsimile of *the* story. However, once we acknowledge that there is no given meaning defined as *the* knowable real story in the past we can, if we wish, develop new ways for acquiring *a* meaning for the-past-*as*-history. But this is fraught with problems. As the literary theorist Wolfgang Iser maintained, there are always 'indeterminacies' that in every narrative (real, fictive or fictional) are represented by gaps that directly affect both the processes of explanation and meaning creation.[28] Not everything in a history can be explained. It is normal that such gaps must be left to the reader to 'fill in' as part of the meaning creation process (you will again recall Barthes and reception theory, the readerly text, the implied author, the implied reader). All histories are, by definition, unfinished and crude even though the reconstructionist and (only to a slightly lesser extent) the constructionist are both driven by the desire for closure (through an empirically driven certitude that is meant to short-circuit any reciprocity between the text and its reader).

The nature of the-past-*as*-history ought to make historians more amenable to open-ended history: that the past is ultimately lacking in meaning – or, to be more precise, 'knowable' meaning. Closure is, after all, only the yield of the history narrative (regardless of whether it is expressed as the historical text, graphic novel, experiential museum or whatever), and so what we are confronted with is that 'historical explanation and meaning' is a property of the history text. Of course the past remains the empirical material with (upon) which the historian works (even in experimental history there is normally reference to a once real past). But the upshot is that as there is no direct correspondence between the past and history. There is no 'natural' epistemic continuity between them despite bulky reference and even direct quotation from sources.

This *is* the understanding of Hayden White, Frank Ankersmit, Arthur Danto and Louis Mink unlike that of David Carr and Paul Ricoeur – who argue for a continuity or extension between the past and history. Carr says he is not claiming ' . . . that second order narratives (like history) . . . simply mirror . . . the first order narratives that constitute their subject matter'[29], but he disagrees that the narrative form is what is produced in literary genres in order to be imposed on non-narrative reality.[30] The Carr and Ricoeur position is the safety net for all new empiricists/ practice theorists.

Eventually the historian has to choose between accepting that our explanation of the meaning of past reality results from the functioning of narrative (including the element of reference), or it does not. Perhaps the only way to make a choice is to think of a narrative as a cultural and linguistic activity that transforms one state of affairs into another. In the case of history this is the transformation from a subject *of* existence (in)to an object *for* representation. This is the narrative turn that takes us from the empirical knowledge of the real past to the ontology of the historical text and its narrative functions. The narrative turn is not, of course, a dangerous descent *into* discourse that deforms the reality of the past. Such a conception both oversimplifies and misconstrues the process of representation.[31] As should be clear by now, realising that history is a mode of representation draws our attention to the underlying epistemological assumptions that shape our knowledge and understanding of both the past and the limitations of history. It is commonly asserted that 'knowledge is power'. This is only a partial truth. It might be more accurate to say that understanding how knowledge is created is power.

Using the term 'historiographic metafiction', Linda Hutcheon argues that we get multi-levelled, pluralistic histories rather than *the* history – a history that is self-consciously fictive rather than unknowingly so.[32] This situation is most obvious in experimental history, where the narrativisation of past events is not buried and the past no longer appears to speak for itself. Experimental history requires that the reader participate in fashioning meaning by engaging with the creative authorial process. Indeed, in this sense all history is experimental. This is because history is always constructed as narratives made up of emplotments from sequences of events with preferred beginnings, middles and ends.

Take a question such as 'how representative and legitimate a spokesman for American values and interests was Woodrow Wilson during the Great War?' The data alone cannot answer this question because it requires the emphases and narrative making decisions of the historian. This is probably why there is a different answer from every historian. In this example it depends upon how much significance a historian places on Wilson's religious commitment or, say, his beliefs in American exceptionalism – a concept which itself can be emplotted in different ways.[33] So, there are no answers in the past only probabilities or, more usually, possibilities. This is why an increasing number of historians are exploring the ways in which they can connect content and form. And once a historian does that, then *experimentation* emerges.

To start with, experimentalism welcomes plausibility in its narratives over more narrow empirical justification. Thus, one of the most disputed kinds of history available today is that of 'creative non-fiction'. This is writing that may be factually accurate and, therefore, not strictly fiction, but is overtly written for **aesthetic** as well as explanatory reasons (and even for 'pleasure'). Most often critical non-fiction history is manifest in modes of expression that are non-textual, like film and TV, but cartoons, postage stamps and pop-up books are relevant here too. Perhaps the most infamous recent book-length textual example is *Dutch: A Memoir of Ronald Reagan* by Edmund Morris, which was populated with fictional characters within what was otherwise a conventional biography. Many historians and readers were self-righteously upset by this act of epistemological betrayal, as the author did not tell the readers what he was doing.[34] In other words, he 'pretended' to be writing a strictly **mimetic** history, ignoring his own **diegetic** voice.

Most historians tend to recognise the work of writers and filmmakers like Alice Walker, Tom Wolfe, Studs Terkel, Joan Didion, Thomas Keneally, Alexander Kluge or Milcho Manchevski as unhistorical. This is because reference to the past is unattributed, or not offered according to conventional referencing criteria or, if it is, it tends to be fictionalised. Or they may well mix the diegetic and the mimetic. But what all these writers and filmmakers have done is seek meanings not *solely* defined by the referential. This is an argument offered regularly by Frank R. Ankersmit and Robert A. Rosenstone, who complain that most historians still subscribe to a classic realist conception of the writing of history intending their accounts to be copies (mimes) of what actually happened in the past.[35] Once that idea is dismissed, historians are free to invest in a vast range of possibilities. If we genuinely wish to engage with the concept of 'what the past means' we have to take on board the central importance of the ontology (the being, nature and functioning) of narrative (and how it changes in its mode of expression at the behest of the author).

Robert A. Rosenstone, arguably the leading advocate and exponent of experimental history, summarises all this when he says

> Experiments in writing history? An oxymoron surely? No writers have clung more firmly (desperately, even) to traditional forms than those academic historians whose professed aim is to accurately reconstruct the past. While the discipline has in the past century undergone an enormous expansion in methodologies of research . . . opening up fields and topics little dreamed of by earlier generations . . . the means of presenting the findings of historical research has altered little. The monographs and synthetic works that historians produce continue, for the most part, to tell the past as stories narrated in the third person, linear stories with a clear sense of cause and effect, and a beginning, a middle and an end.[36]

Most historians would still not accept what Rosenstone is saying for reasons familiar to us from the discussion of modes of expression. Rosenstone points out that twentieth-century challenges to realistic representation (impressionism, cubism, constructivism, expressionism, surrealism, abstraction, the New Wave, **postmodernism** . . .) have generated new ways of seeing, telling and creating meaning. Historians, arguably, cannot be isolated from these developments. What Rosenstone is saying is that an understanding of 'writing history' has opened up an intellectual space for innovative history thinking and practice.

Thus, he noted in 2004 that for ' . . . the past three decades, the possibility of innovative historical writing, the notion of playing with new forms of narrative, has floated around the edge of the profession'.[37] But he had to acknowledge that ' . . . little innovative historical writing has appeared in print'.[38] The major outlets for experimental narrative have been in other modes of expression. Indeed, other modes of expression have often been claimed to be the cutting edge of experiment – graphic, digital, film and TV. But, as we know, more often than not such modes remain epistemologically unchallenging. Of course, for many (most?) historians epistemological challenge is not what they signed up for. As a result experimental history cannot yet be accommodated, much less the effort made à la new empiricism to sanitise and domesticate it. And, of course, sanitisation and domestication are essential precursors to 'measurement for research funding purposes'.

So, why experiment with history?

Experimental history is about different ways of seeing and telling. It is often happily opaque rather than miserably clear. It is not always referential but is poetic. It is rarely an exercise in theory, but it is never under-theorised. It can illustrate paradoxes such as 'subjective realism', which is no more of a paradox than 'empirical reality' (except that does not acknowledge itself as such). Perhaps the key facet of experimental history is that the experimentalist narrator intervenes for overt purposes. Indeed, in practice, experimentalism often emerges from the disharmony between the narrative voice of the author-historian and the way in which the text is **focalised** as, for example, with Rosenstone's intervention with the lives and voices of his characters in *Mirror in the Shrine*. But, in the end, no listing of the attributes of experimentalism will exhaust what it is. Indeed, different historians at different times (in their careers) will experiment for many different reasons – and they may/will return to empiricism and analysis (for what are usually secular epistemological reasons and purposes). There are as many different intentions behind experimenting as there are kinds of experiment.

Some experiments will engage with different modes of expression like experimental film, the graphic novel, dramas or pantomime. Written texts may employ different typefaces, or stream of consciousness textual effects, or produce literary pastiche, montage and even sur-narrative. Indeed, reading fiction such as Salman Rushdie's *Midnight's Children* (a novel that re-arranges beginnings middles and ends) or Martin Amis's *Times Arrow* can tell us more about the nature of history than reading hundreds of full metal jacket empirical texts. As might be expected, self-reflexivity has a strong appeal for experimentalists. As Greg Dening suggests, history can be seen as the rejection of reification in order to make the past live by its (unavoidable) transformation into words, paint and dance (to 'trans' 'form' but also to transgress forms).[39] History is, in this sense, the transfiguration of the past. Or, as Hayden White described it in the late 1990s, a 'figural realism' – a series of studies in the **'mimésis** effect'.[40]

While analogies are not necessarily helpful I am tempted by the impressionist movement that began in mid- to late-nineteenth-century France when the likes of Cézanne, Bazille, Cassatt, Degas, Monet, Manet, Pissarro, Renoir, and so on were hostages to innovation and who confronted institutionalised aesthetic orthodoxies. The parallel with history experimentalists appeals to me. But are experimentalists really that innovative? After all, as an advocate of experimentalism I am not suggesting deposing all extant conceptions of history. Is experimental history, then, just an extension of the possibilities that already exist in the empirical-analytical orthodoxy? Equally, is experimentalism an inevitable development given our postmodern cultural and epistemologically sceptical condition? Indeed, is experimental history not a rupture but a confirmation of our own place in time? Or is it an underground terrorist movement intent on blowing up the railway lines of empiricism? All this suggests, I suppose, that there are as many narratives about experimental history as there are narrators.

But the impressionist analogy niggles. It is still unsatisfactory. We can see this when we consider experimental history in terms of the nature of its experiments.[41] Plainly, while the authorial function cannot be excised from experimental history any more than it can be from traditional approaches, different voices can be employed. The autobiography of Henry Adams is an early if rather constrained example of experimentalism written as it is by its subject in the third person.[42] The convention of hidden and omniscient narration can be explored by self-consciously using it. Self-conscious playing (ludic history) with the **timing** of the text to defamiliarise the reception of the past is always permissible and is to be encouraged. There can be acrostic history, cryptic history and anagram history. Thus a crossword, properly constructed, can be a mode of historical understanding.

Chopping up the linear narrative is increasingly common, its origin is in modernism's self-consciousness – as with Walter Benjamin's *Arcades Project* written between the end of the 1920s and unfinished in 1940. Using the arcades of Paris as an analogy, in the main section of 36 elements with titles like 'Mirrors', 'Flâneur' and 'Fashion', Benjamin tried to resolve the problems he saw with his Marxist philosophy of history and its organisation of the past. He believed, for example, that the process of montage would serve his aim of explaining the movement and purpose of historical time.[43]

The numbers of examples of experimental history has grown substantially in the past decade with the publication of texts like Hans Ulrich Gumbrecht's *In 1926: Living at the Edge of Time*. Ignoring the conventional 'beginning, middle and end' formula, Gumbrecht pieced together 51 entries or fragments of reference to the past and, avoiding totalisation, offered a picture of 1 year – 1926. Gumbrecht's objective was to confront the verities of correspondence and linearity saying the reader should not ' . . . start from the beginning' as there was no beginning. As he said the point of the exercise was to make ' . . . at least some readers forget, during the reading process, that they are *not* living in 1926'.[44] And, most pertinently, he asked what could we do without knowledge ' . . . about the past once we have given up the hope of "learning from history" '? In abandoning the classic realist narrative with its omniscient and silent author, linear cause-and-effect modes of explanation and meaning, we are suddenly open to any form of imagining and representing history – even synchronically as in his book. There is no coherent 'picture' of the past anymore – not even an 'impression'. This lack of sequentiality in deranging our sense of agency and action (cause and effect) demonstrates we are, perhaps, moving towards a postist kind of history.

Synthia Sydnor's article 'A History of Synchronised Swimming' published in the *Journal of Sport History* over 10 years ago, and creating quite a stir at the time, is an arresting history experiment that utilises Benjaminian thinking and which is a self-conscious experiment in making a history narrative.[45] Sydnor offers a heavily referenced and epistemologically realist 'modern text' with, as she says, 'post-modern concerns' that are semiotic specifically that in, as she says, ' . . . through, and out of language we create, discover, invent and signify our world'.[46] Deploying a pastiche narrative form, Sydnor defamiliarises the conformation of history thus promoting greater freedom than is conventionally allowed for the reader to construct their own 'history' of, in this case, synchronised swimming.

Robert Rosenstone's *Mirror in the Shrine* is a recounting of cultural contact that is a commentary upon the smoothing out function of conventional history.[47] Sven Lindqvist's *A History of Bombing* also confronts the smooth narrative making of history, defining his experiment as a book that is a labyrinth with 22 entrances and no exit, where readers choose their own pathway through the text.[48] Meaning is entirely – or so it seems – in the mind of the reader. As far as I am concerned, there is an implied author in this experiment and (according to my reading) it is the West's holocaustal and genocidal character. But it does not have to be.

What experimental history does through its fresh emphasis upon the nature of representation and expression is not just force the issue of explanation and meaning but also challenge empirical-analytical concepts of objectivity and truth. In this sense experimental history is primarily political. Indeed, we have reached a point where we might wish to do away with the term 'experimental history' and adopt a term like 'expressionist history'. Such a change in terminology would not only acknowledge the connections between content/story, narrating/narration and mode of expression but it would turn our attention from 'representation' towards 'knowledge through expression'. I suggested when I discussed different modes of expression in Chapter 4 that they do not necessarily reflect a radical epistemological choice. But *new* modes of expression can result from epistemological choices, and allow us to pursue them.

Expressionist historians could thus, perhaps, render 'the truth' of the past as a presentation of expressive possibilities that acknowledge the horizon of expectations of the consumer of the history.[49] Presumably for the reconstructionist whose horizons of expectation are empirical-analytical, expressionist history makes no sense, and similarly for the constructionist. For the deconstructionist the history experiment's expressive deployment of its narrative functions is as much the centre of attention as its ostensive engagement with the past. So, experimental history is not really in the business (necessarily) of giving a new impression of the past. While experimental history makes no sense to conventional reconstructionist and constructionist thinking, it does in deconstructive terms if only because it draws our attention to 'sublime historical experience' that Ankersmit notes, or what I would call the 'malleability of expression'.[50]

▶ Conclusion

Today histories that deliberately explore their own literary constructedness with their intentionally authored and voiced character are more common. Consequently, there is no longer a single, utterly convincing answer to the question: What is History Today? Thus, for some historians it is not an absolute requirement that prospecting in the sources and deploying new methods, theories and conceptualisations is the only and professionally authorised route to engaging with the-past-*as*-history. Historical explanation and meaning can also be achieved through the recognition of history's artifice, located in its timing and ordering, the re-situation of its **referentiality**, the ontology of its textuality, and its political purposes and expressions. The great and giddying fear among the rump of the empirically absolutist consequent upon such an answer is that the history that results deviates from their accepted notions of explanation and meaning (producing the history equivalent in art of Fauvism [the wild beasts)]?).[51]

But the question has now been posed. Henceforth, can history still only be 'judged' according to the classic realist empirical-analytical calculus? The charge is often levelled that experimental history, in particular, obscures explanation and meaning and is, consequently, at best a conceited and at worst a pointless activity. Experimentalists/expressionists would respond that the greater hazard and most dangerous recklessness are the *belief* in constancy of explanation and that *the* meaning that supposedly flow from it. Experimental/expressionist history acknowledges the discordant in our own lives, its ironies, and most of all the inadequacies of realist representation. But, perhaps most disconcerting for conventionalists is the undermining of the notion of certainty in our understanding of the past. Nevertheless, explanation and meaning is now challenged in textual history as it is in other modes of expression and, clearly, they cannot all be judged according to the same set of arbitrary empirical and analytical rules. But if our epistemological scepticism has confronted explanation and meaning, then what happens to truth and objectivity?[52] I turn to this in Chapter 7.

7 The Oar in Water

Since Plato the notion of 'the oar in water' – the way the oar seems to bend/break in water – has reminded us that, when considering issues of **objectivity**, **truth** and **relativism**, the circumstances of seeing affect our perception. This suggests rethinking the connections between **explanation** and **meaning** in **history**. The realist will say that an object will not necessarily be perceived identically at all times, but this does not affect the **reality** of its true nature. So, while the past must be cast in a 'historical' **narrative** that does not alter the shape of the past. The anti-**representationalist** response is that if the object can *only* be understood in a medium that refracts its reality (the past can only ever be represented through narratives about it – see the **hermeneutic** circle) then knowledge is always relative – in the case of history to the process of narrative making.

With the nineteenth century, however, came the 'age of positivism' (the victory of science in terms of objective and method) which broadened the gap between literature and history even though in both the greatest 'author-ity' remained the writer and their style.[1] But so powerful was the cultural force of science and scientific explanation even in literature that by the end of the nineteenth century, literature itself had succumbed to the power of the real through the literary movements of '**realism**' and '**naturalism**'. In effect, the banality of (primarily middle-class) reality and existence edged out what, since Aristotle, had been assumed to be the 'revelatory nature' of literature.

But historians generally were not interested in revelatory universal truths and insights into human existence (notable exceptions were Marx, Spengler, Toynbee, etc.). The vast majority of historians were interested in the limited knowledge of 'what happened' through **empiricism**, specifically **fact**ualism. Eventually, empiricism was joined to social theory, which then crushed all before it. Indeed, even the notion of authorship was quietly disposed of. Authorship was taken to mean **subjectivity** rather than objectivity, and relativism rather than truth. Dreaming about the possibilities in the past was not something historians did anymore.[2]

In the first 60 years of the twentieth century, history was worked through a variety of empirical and analytical grinding machines. These included economic and social history, the *Annales* School, Marxist constructionism (in almost all its forms), cliometrics and cultural history, and empiricism coupled to analysis reached its peak in the first phase of women's history. Literature and history were now totally separate disciplines with, it was claimed, distinctive **epistemologies**. However, through the early 1950s Paul Ricoeur offered an important brief analysis of history, truth, objectivity, relativism and subjectivity in which he questioned this notion though he eventually fell back on the side of the empiricist angels.[3] But it was the intellectual revolution of the 1970s and especially the publication of Hayden White's *Metahistory* that produced the breakthrough (or disaster depending on your point of view) that ushered in the **narrative turn** in historical studies. In effect, what White was proposing was a narrative *re*turn. Employing the work of literary scholars like Kenneth Burke and Northrop Frye on archetypal **emplotments** and Stephen Pepper on root metaphors (**tropes**), White demonstrated how major nineteenth-century historians produced history (creating **story spaces**) in the same way as literary scholars.

Up to the present day this thesis has generated a continuous and often rancorous debate about what historians do and think. The claim that history was a literary form occurred against the background of a variety of European philosophical developments such as structuralism, **poststructuralism**, new historicism, **deconstruction**, **postmodernism** and a variety of 'turns' like the linguistic, narrative, **aesthetic**, **ethical**, and most recently the compensatory efforts of the **new empiricist** re-turn. With issues like explanation, meaning, objectivity and truth in the melting pot the stakes are still high.

During this period most historians clung to the philosopher David Carr's judgement (as shared with Paul Ricoeur) that the historical narrative must retain *the* structure of the events described. This is the fundamental basis of the belief that the historical narrative can be objective and truthful. In other words, the history narrative aims to be – ultimately – symmetrical with past reality. White's judgement was that historians should no longer (naively) believe that statements about the past '**correspond**' to a pre-existing body of 'raw facts'. He argued that what constitutes the facts themselves is the problem which, in his view, could only be resolved by the act of figuration/aesthetic choice. Moreover, because the gap between the past and the history is unbridgeable via *the* **story**, if we want to retain a notion of truth, we need to seek out its mechanism in our narrative making. But this produces a new definition of 'objectivity' and '**historical truth**'. This is why White became, and remains, such a controversial historian. It is also why he is probably the most famous historian-philosopher of his generation.

White's argument suggested a lack of neutrality that deconstructionist history openly acknowledged, believing empiricists had not demonstrated objectivity and truth in their accounts despite the testable statement of justified belief. Concomitant with this has been the general failure to understand the nature of content/story, narration/narrating and **modes of expression**. Conventional history thinking generally had rejected the significance of the relationship in history between form and content by concentrating on empiricism and **inference**.

In effect, however, what the Whitean revolution has produced is a **new history** in which increasing numbers of historians produce experimental history in new modes of expression. So what happens to the primal claim that history must be objective? Let us see.

▶ Objectivity

As we know, **reconstructionists** and **constructionists** seek to be objective in their knowledge acquisition through the mechanism of explanation that best fits the available evidence. The response of the narrativist is to say that is fine as far as it goes, but the definitions of objectivity (and truth) implied by this mechanism do not sit well in an interpretative (hermeneutic) discipline that is about far more than just getting the facts straight. And, moreover, to our cost we forget the nature of history as a conduit between the self as a subject and the past as an object.

But what do most historians mean when they talk about 'objectivity'. Basically, objectivity has been understood in four related ways. First, it is acknowledged to be a state of mind of the honest, fair-minded and judicious historian who is steeped in and led by the **sources**. The second understanding concerns methodology and **representation**. The honest and judicious historian deploys a method and a form of representation in which '(objectively derived) discoveries' (in the archive) are described fairly (as history). And, third, as C. Behan McCullagh puts it echoing the still widely accepted view of E.H. Carr, we have objective knowledge when we know what a text means. From this historians can legitimately claim that their professionalism and procedures for understanding the evidence and thereby objectively delivering 'truthful interpretations' of past texts control the boundaries of 'proper history'.

Objectivity is also generally thought of as being the opposite of bias. There is a sort of inverse ratio between them. It is usually claimed that if we can minimise bias we maximise objectivity. The fallacy in this is the unjustified belief that a given body of data will contain its own 'given story' from which any deviation constitutes a bias. Discover the story, and the history will be objective. This is akin to a self-fulfilling prophecy. Apart from exaggerating the likelihood of 'knowing the story', the concept of bias/objectivity (as polar opposites) demands that we raise ourselves from any normal state of **ontological** commitment. So we are required to step outside our beliefs, ideologies, arguments, **emplotments**, theories and authorial decisions.

To do this we must never take any evidence at face value.[4] Historians are also aware that when they enter the archive they carry political baggage with them. But, as they go through the methodological procedures of comparison and verification they are self-conscious about being the honest historian who only ever strives (but in all modesty rarely achieves) explanations to best fit. If pressed every historian will tell you their own 'archive story', which ranges from the exhilaration of Deborah A.

Symonds when trapped in the Scottish Record Office to Durba Ghosh's account of her feelings of exclusion and alienation as an 'Indian' woman in colonial archives.[5]

It is no doubt right to be aware of the problems historians have with their experience of the archive, as well as recognising their efforts to be fair, even-handed and painstaking in establishing accurate **reference**. But, of course, being self-conscious and following 'objective procedures' cannot resolve Ankersmit's point about the epistemological distinction between a **justified belief** and a created history narrative. The 'objective procedures argument' assumes, in effect, that nothing of significance happens between 'knowing the data' and 'creating the history', maintaining that if the evidence is adequate one explanation will be superior to any other and, by definition, it is likely to be the one objectively derived (and true) narrative.[6] But, taking the opposite tack, as the feminist historian Joan Scott has long argued, the absolute appeal to reference is never enough. Indeed it is misleading given that it does not break the epistemological stranglehold of which objectivity and truth are central planks. For Scott, to better understand the nature of the (gendered) past it needs to be 'read', as it can only be read, within the textual substance we call history with all the authorial assumptions and narratives choices that go into making it.

Despite the respect for objectively derived data, the history of history in the West amply demonstrates that gender and cultural bias has existed in male, white, metropolitan, bourgeois history from the seventeenth through to most of the twentieth century. Historians created the history of those aspects of the past in which they were/are personally interested (and often which their publishers have suggested they write about). Unfortunate though it might be, the desire to see historians counter personal and cultural biases is a counsel of perfection. Though bias is deplorable when it leads to the omission or 'invention' of data, the ontological commitments of an individual or a culture make dispositions and proclivities inevitable to some degree. In reply to this latter argument the empirical-analytical trump card is the historian's commitment to rationality. But, desirable though rationality is, this is a red herring because it is rational thinking that has produced the doubts many historians hold about the exclusivity of empirical-analytical history. To acknowledge and work within the human condition is not to be irrational or endorse irrationality.

What I am saying, I suppose, is that 'bias' (positioning) exists from the outset in the initial epistemological choices of historians. While epistemological **sceptics** will never be certain about the status of knowledge, non-epistemological sceptics will be sure that objectivity is within their grasp if not always absolutely achievable. The epistemologist who believes in objectivity will – by definition – have an ontological commitment to justification. The epistemological historian of nineteenth-century British foreign policy who wants to discover the most appropriate explanation for the collapse of the Ottoman Empire will presumably, at some point, examine the evidence of Disraeli's contempt for Slav nationalism. She or he may then feel justified that they have inched 'forward' in an objective way towards an objective conclusion. This is a belief that can only be justified by the outcomes: a circular argument indeed.

Paul Ricoeur has summarised some of our understandings of objectivity when he argued that we expect 'a certain objectivity which is proper to it' in and through the methods of history.[7] His argument not only stressed the objectivity of method but also acknowledged 'the role of the historian's subjectivity . . .' in the 'elaboration of history'.[8] The terms of the historian's subjectivity, as Ricoeur acknowledges, encompass many choices. These include data, the appropriate theory (including the preferred theory or sense of causality), the imposition of the historian's imagination on the past and, of course, the distance between the historical agent as 'the other' and the historian. But Ricoeur hoped that recognising all this would generate a 'good' subjectivity whereby the 'historian's craft educates his subjectivity'.[9] Ricoeur concludes, importantly, by also noting the subjectivity inherent in the reception of the history by the reader who ultimately provides the historical meaning.

The deconstructionist historian holds that historians always live in a state of **subjective** or relativist knowledge, because, as Ricoeur argues, that is just how we exist. The past cannot be 'known' except through an immensely complex variety of different story space and narrative making strategies of which reference is only one. The others include those with which we are now very familiar: methods but also arguments, emplotments, aesthetic choices, ethical beliefs, the **order**ing of the **timing** of the narrative, **voice** and **focalisation**, and the constraints of different modes of emplotment. In addition to the **fictive** structuring process there are also personal orientations related to gender, class, race, nation, culture, the desire for research funding, promotion, publication, peer respect and so on. No doubt getting the facts straight is crucial, but this has to be viewed within a much bigger framework, not least that the past has to be (re-)created as an 'object' of the historian's mind. The reading of the textual relics of the past means constituting them as an object of study by the historian, and this is unavoidably a subjective activity. This only becomes a radical claim if it is assumed that there can be an objective reading derived by other means.[10]

So, if we dismiss objectivity from our vocabulary, what are we left with? Well, I have constantly stressed that it does not mean historians are no longer concerned with the evidence of past events or have automatically lost all sense of right and wrong. Events can be described accurately as having happened and, by that measure, not every interpretation is as good as any other. But the crucial point is that because the historian takes past reality and explains its meaning in a way that makes us experience it, it can only be undertaken through the creation of a particular story space. Subjectivity can be defined, therefore, in terms of the process of narrative making that allows us experience the past. Every literary act is subjective because it is authored.

It is the function of the reader to determine for herself or himself why some views of the past are plausible, satisfactory or convincing and others are not. All historians and consumers experience the past differently and this forces us to represent it differently. If we simply try to describe the past (as objectivity demands) we do not get very far (this happened, then that . . .). Description allows us to refer and predict (the subject and predicate of statements of justified belief). But we do not only do that in history. What we actually do is represent or, as I prefer, express the past. You will recall the basic argument here, which is that the historical narrative does not distinguish between subject and predicate – represented and its representation are not the same as subject and predicate.

So, to cope with history as a narrative we have to rethink the *primacy* of the empirical-analytical notion of objectivity. In a universe where historians have to construct the question to which the answer is the text before us, we have to acknowledge how we (as historians) have expectations about both the forms of explanation and the meaning derived therefrom. But, if we accept that our defin-itions of explanation, meaning and objectivity may never be agreed upon, what happens to the concept of truth? Certainly for the reconstructionist and probably also for most constructionists, if we dismiss objectivity in hermeneutics (the science of interpretation) then surely we are destroying the firewall that protects history from lies and a variety of viruses such as poststructuralism, relativism, postmodern theory and empirical denial? Without objectivity don't we lose all grip on truth?

▶ Truth

The subjective nature of history (as an authored narrative making activity that attempts to reconstitute, reconcile and explain past reality) means re-orientating our thinking from epistemological to ontological terms.[11] In the understanding of truth this means rejecting the belief that there is an epistemological hierarchy between a subject and an object and replacing that notion with a sense of conti-guity. In other words, the historian as a subject and **the-past-*as*-history** as an object need to be viewed hermeneutically – as sharing the same ontological space. Hence, as Jacques Derrida so famously pointed out, there is no directly accessible authority beyond the text.[12] Because the historian quotes the references this does not place her or him 'outside' or 'above' history. This is because she or he is an active parti-cipant in its creation. What this means is that we cannot generalise from 'the fact' to 'the history' in terms of 'truth'. This is because of the metonymic nature of language and the reader's inevitable (to some degree) re-writing of all texts. Hence, the way truth is regarded by empiricists (as the **correspondence** of experience to its description) has to be modified. Instead of regarding attested evidence *as* akin to truth, it is merely evidence *for* the possibility of truth.

But first, just how does the empirical-analytical historian define truth? You will recall that the assumption is that communicating *the* truth in history is essentially *re*-telling *its* story. The history must be pretty close to the truth *of* the past because it is honestly undertaken 'best fit' history. So, re-telling *the* story starts with the laudable desire to be truthful. Here again partiality on the part of the historian must be avoided – hence the need for objectivity of approach. Clearly, however, this definition does not exhaust the nature of '**historical truth**'. Nevertheless, as the foremost 'philosopher of truth' in history, C. Behan McCullagh defines objectivity as knowledge of what a 'text' means defined in terms of the justified statement of historical belief.[13] Upon this basis we can reasonably assume that historical descriptions are probably true. In addition, McCullagh defends the belief in representationalism – that reality (reference) can be represented accurately in language. This argument forms the basis of the four major theories of 'historical truth' that historians are free to deploy.

The first theory of truth is the one with which we are most familiar: correspondence. These days even the most unreconstructed reconstructionist accepts that correspondence in a facsimile or full-blooded **mimetic** sense is unlikely. They accept that a complete linguistic picture of past reality is impossible. But ultimately correspondence results from the bedrock belief that the real world exists beyond our selves *and* how we describe it. So, the reasonable option must be to accept that we can provide explanations and meanings that are fairly and objectively derived and which reasonably fit the data. This is all well and good but plainly correspondence starts to fail beyond the factual level. In other words, if correspondence fails at the level of the narrative substance then a different kind of truth is created in the narrative. This is no longer a correspondence form of truth.

The second version of truth is correlation and it is the one favoured by most historians. This is actually a moderated correspondence theory. Still believing that sentences will ultimately connect with past reality, the assumption now is that our perceptions are caused by reality. In other words what we reasonably believe about the past does not have to correspond precisely with reality but is generally caused by it. We know this to be the case as our perceptions actually make sense because they co-relate to and with each other. By cross-checking our sources (through comparison and contextualisation) we can determine how reasonable are our beliefs. Thus the mindset of the historian is to believe that the evidence 'strongly supports' their descriptions. So when the historian John Burnett claims that in the late 1870s in England and Wales beer consumption rose to 40.5 gallons a head, this is 'suggested' by the evidence.[14]

The third form of truth is coherence as found in constructivism/constructionist history. This further loosens from the grip of correspondence and also correlation but is still firmly realist in orientation. Because the past(-thing-in-itself) is not knowable (as Baudrillard argues) correspondence (even if it worked) cannot be known (to work), and even correlation will not do more than imply the likelihood of a meaningful connection between the past and its description, so there is a need for a more flexible theory of truth. This tips the balance towards those historians who wish to inject a sense of the constructed nature of history into their understanding of the past. The philosopher-historians Michael Oakeshott and Leon Goldstein both argued (following the logic of the hermeneutic circle) that knowledge cannot be separated from the knower and their experience of life. The result is a situation in which, notwithstanding correspondence and correlation, the historian literally makes history and the most they can hope for is to do it plausibly, rationally and coherently and with appropriate deference to the empirical.[15] Essentially coherence/constructivism holds that the evidence can only clue us to likely hypotheses as to the nature of the past but neither the evidence nor the hypothesis can be identified (in either a correspondence or a correlation sense) with the past itself. So the best historians can do is to construct (place a construction on) the past.

In many respects the constructivism/constructionist search for truth is the most convincing account available for most historians.[16] Certainly of the three forms or theories of truth I have described the narrativist theory of history (which I am explaining in this book) is a literary elaboration of the constructivist position. But it is one that, by acknowledging the authorial and narrative function activities of the historian, doubts the constructionist belief that theories can prise open the truth of the past. In other words, history constructs *a* truth; it does not re-tell it.

The fourth kind of truth and perhaps the most unsatisfactory is the consensus theory. Surely, you may think that correspondence–correlation–coherence is a potent truth-acquiring brew – good enough to see off all epistemological sceptics – so why do we need another? Essentially, the consensus theory of truth holds that if historians as a group of honest, fair-minded, reasonable, objectivity and truth-seeking individuals agree on something then it must be a virtual guarantee that it is right. But while this may work at the level of confirming a justified belief (that the Battle of Crecy was fought on August 13, 1346), it patently does not apply at the level of interpretation. An interpretation might be that Edward III of England won the Battle of Crécy because of the power of the English Longbows sending thousands of arrows a minute with each hit equivalent to a shot from a powerful handgun. It may not be universally agreed. But if it were so agreed then the consensus theory of truth would be operating at its most forceful.

Of course it is all much less clear-cut than this four-truth model suggests. This is because the question remains: if truth in history does not take the form of correspondence, correlation or coherence then its truth must result as much from the metonymic organisation of the history narrative as it does from anything else.

In effect we have a deflated variety of truth in which meaning is prior to truth. For the sake of brevity we can call this narrative truth. As Michael Lemon argues, history is always an account.[17] He says 'by true' we do not mean all the facts in the history are true (which we will ask at some point of course) but that the account as a whole is 'true'; that it does not omit things which are clearly relevant or includes things which are not. So, all the facts in a history can be accurate and carefully chosen for their relevance and significance, but the account itself need not end up being 'true'. It seems that, because history is a form of realist literature, its truth claims need to be judged by criteria beyond the four versions we have just noted. So what is the best way of approaching the nature of truth in history?

As will be clear by now, we need to begin by acknowledging the functioning of narrative. What we should call 'narrative truth' or 'historical truth' (always placed in inverted commas) does not reject empirical-analytical methods for finding out what happened and offering explanations that best fit the evidence. But, unlike the restricted empirical-analytical notion of truth so elegantly described by Richard Rorty as the 'mirror of nature', increasing numbers of historians are shifting towards a concept of 'historical truth' derived from an understanding of **narrative constructivism**.[18]

Jerome Bruner has argued we all make the world (past and present) through our capacity to create narratives.[19] We are also aware, from our reading of Gadamer, White, Ricoeur and Ankersmit, that the aesthetic is where we must look for truth in its broadest meaning beyond 'this happened, then that, because . . . '. This suggests that 'historical truth' is a form of truth in which empirically attested statements do not exist independently but that their meaning derives from their functioning *within* the narrative.

Therefore, attested data – empirical factualism – does not in and of itself constitute truth in history. Truth in history is much more complex because it is that yield of its authorial functions (of which reference is only one). Hence it is that truth in history is part ideological, part emplotment, part aesthetic choice, partly a function of authorial voice and focalisation, in part the result of the timing of the text, **intentionality** (of both the agent and the **author-historian**) and so forth. Put at its simplest truth in history is a function of content/story, narrating and narration and **mode of expression** as the author-historian poses questions, creates expectations and offers conclusions.

The fear that accompanies this definition of 'historical truth' is that it will become a function of 'good stories' that in themselves have little to do with what actually happened. That this fear is unwarranted is because the narrative logic of history retains reference within the content/story function maintaining all its compulsions and authority at the level of statements of justified belief. Having said that, the mode of expression selected by the historian will dramatically confront textualised empirical-analytical assumptions about truth. But, as the pro-film history theorist Robert Rosenstone has argued, when dramatic history films like Edward Zwick's *Glory* (1989) create a history, they still communicate important and valuable information about the past and how we deal with it.[20]

Nevertheless, the fear that constantly lurks in the minds of empiricists concerns the existence of competing narratives that refuse to accept the authority of the data with its one given story. This apparently terrifying situation is actually very common, as one would expect in a constructed narrative. For example, the narrative in Genesis is irreconcilable with that of evolutionism or, even more confusingly given that the dispute is rarely over statements of justified belief, the narrative of economistic Marxism is incompatible with that of post-Marxism. This incompatibility will never be resolved for the simple reason that the different narratives are generated, in this example, by competing sets of historicist epistemological assumptions.[21]

It can be argued that knowing how 'historical truth' works requires understanding and accepting history as a **performative** act. In Seymour Chatman's analysis 'the story' (what he calls the *fabula*, a term he borrows from Russian formalists) is where the truth of the history (as opposed to the truth of single statement of justified belief) emerges.[22] The content/story contains the references to the events in the past but that is no more important than, for example, the emplotment. Indeed, for Hayden White, viewed as verbal artifacts, histories and novels are indistinguishable. So, it follows that, for 'historical truth' defined as 'knowing what happened and what it most likely means', results from the operation of all the elements within the content/story (which includes reference).[23]

Of course in practice the operation of the other two elements in the triad, namely narration/narrating and mode of expression, complicate all this. Dependent upon the historian's epistemological choices, the 'truth' of the history *may* be retained as it shifts through a variety of modes of expression (ballet, formal history text, film, painting, comic, website, and first-person museum interpretation) because the story remains coherent and essentially the same one. Events and actions remain what they were/are even if they are words, gestures or images. But there is always a degree of deformation and transformation as the content/story is imaginatively translated into different modes of expression if only because each mode has its own particular physical demands.

Because, as we know, textual and filmic history both possess analepsis or 'flashback' and prolepsis or 'flash forward', their cognitive truth-effects will be different. The justifiably famous textual history of African-Americans by John Hope Franklin *From Slavery to Freedom* (first published in 1947) cannot be rendered in film and possess the same kind of 'truthfulness'. This is not because of the 'failings' of film but the nature of Franklin's history cast in a different mode of expression and produced for that expression. The fact that many 'history stories' are transposed between modes of expression is, perhaps, the best reason for arguing that 'the history narrative' is a structure that is not reliant on any particular one. And, most importantly, it is important to remember that, as I have already suggested, the textual is not and never should be privileged *relative* to other forms. It seems appropriate, therefore, to conclude this chapter with a brief comment on the issue of relativism.

▶ Relativism

I hope it is clear now that the historical narrative encompasses much more than the single statement of justified belief. 'Historical truth', on the other hand, as I have argued, refers to truth experienced and engineered by the narrative and story space logic of history with all its content/story, narrational authorial intrusion and modes of expression demands. Consequently, the idea that truth in narrative is only a kind of rhetorical persuasion through the cunning use of metaphors should be dismissed for the misunderstanding it is.[24] It is worth noting that relativism is not the same as subjectivism. By relativism is meant the belief that what is true (or desirable for that matter) depends on external circumstances. This does not entail subjectivism, which follows from the principle that truth or un-truth do not depend on the actual state of reality – hence 'historical truth' is a function of 'history'.

Another misunderstanding is that relativism is an obstacle to discovering the 'true origins' of, say, baseball, or 'the causes' of the American Civil War. Rather, I would define it as the acknowledgement of there being many points of view, cultural locations, authorial creativities, 'historical truths' and the arbitrary nature of signs and significations. I have no problem with 'situated knowledge' in the arts and humanities, or with that relativism which makes absent the concept of certainty. Nevertheless the notion of relativism as being integral to the historical enterprise – because of the latter's narrative construction – is still widely feared as interrupting the current of meaning between *the* past and *its* history.

But such angst flows only from a failure to understand history as an authorial act that makes the connection between subject and object. The 'relativist model of history' is the one that the experimentalist will certainly feel most at home with, but all historians should be able to cope with it as well. History viewed as a historicist and relativist undertaking is a liberated intellectual activity because it is no longer exclusively tied to notions of positivist/scientific reliability. The pragmatist philosopher Hilary Putnam argues that as fact dissolves into values, relativism in history opens up more possibilities than it closes down.[25] Henceforth we can explore history as politics, as parable, as experiment, as allegory and above all, acknowledge it as the constructed story it is.

Indeed, can it be anything else if we accept that the historian is at once a creator and creation of an ideology, culture, gender or whatever? Ontologically we exist relative to place, time, concepts, circumstances, personal ambition, race, language and so on. Our knowledge of the past is situated relative not only to the data or its construction as a narrative, but also to its intertextuality and to the discursive formation(s) in which we exist. Historians, by and large, are not metaphysical relativists who believe there is no independent reality back there outside our minds. However, epistemological sceptics are relativists who accept that knowledge of the past is constrained by forces they cannot control but which they can recognise. Such historians take issue with crude empirical notions of objectivity and truth and are willing to engage with history as a socially useful meaning-creating activity. It is not a matter of 'what the past tells us', but what we think it is 'good to believe' as we create history.[26]

In acknowledging the inherent relativism of history thinking and practice – from epistemological choice to the timing of the text through to the selection of mode of expression – epistemological scepticism permits the examination of subjectivity and the identity of the author-historian while still telling us what happened. The empirical specificity of history can still be there to be explored in the 'conventional ways', but – and this is the crucial point – it does not have to be, to still 'qualify' as history. In rethinking the conventional definition of history to acknowledge its triadic structure of content/story, narration/narrating and mode of expression, the historian has a new freedom in creating knowledge and understanding.

▶ **Conclusion**

The issues of objectivity, truth and relativism remain central to historical analysis. But, if we assume history is a narrative representation created by an author-historian about the past, we need to understand how she or he creates the-past-as-history despite the empirical-analytical insistence that historians are ciphers and the past is somehow using their minds as conduits. I have noted how this epistemological position produces the peculiar notion that history can be (must be) an objective discipline that deals only in truth or falsity. To adhere to the 'auteur theory of history' is supposed to promote subjectivity, deny objectivity, is an admission of relativism and is a perverse rejection of *the* accepted standards of historical method.[27] *Happily this is not the case.* No longer is reference more important than, say, emplotment or argument. Indeed, without applying the concept of 'the author' to the process of creating history all we would be left with is a crude and stultifying epistemological conception of where history comes from and, worse, where it is going.

Conclusion

In this examination of the state of historical knowledge, I have argued that our understanding of the structure of the work of **history** demands the recognition of the nature and cognitive significance of its **content/story**, narrating/narration and **mode of expression**. I have explored this in terms of the **epistemological choice** of the historian, specifically their attitude to the **narrative turn**. Deploying the familiar **reconstructionist, constructionist** and **deconstructionist** epistemological choices or genres open to historians, I noted how the conventional equation for reconstructionists and constructionists relies on the determining authority of **empirical reference** (evidence or **sources**) which leads to **explanation** and then **meaning**. This process claims to be undertaken with analytical **objectivity** aimed at producing the **truth** of the past. The results of this conventional thinking are then reported in the form of a **narrative** cast as '*the* story of . . . '. Although a few historians today will argue they are perfectly well aware that they cannot locate the story, the plan remains to find it. As Ricoeur pointed out, beneath every history construction there is a reconstructionist aim.

My position has been that of the deconstructionist who argues that this conventional empirical-analytical epistemological approach fails to take adequate account of the narrative logic of history. This, in turn, raises issues concerning **reality**, **reference**, explanation, meaning objectivity and truth. In the analysis of the narrative logic of history offered in this book, I have tried to account for the mix of Genette's three elements of story, narrating and narrative by translating it into a structure that reflects the epistemologically challenged thinking and practice of historians. It is central to Genette's analysis of narrative that the process of narrating is, in effect, the **author's** production of ' . . . narrative action and, by extension, the whole of the real or fictional situation in which that action takes place'.[1] This, the **story space** created by the historian out of the action of the historical agent, is, plainly, not a replication of the past. It is the past narratively turned into history: **the-past-*as*-history**.

Following the work of Genette, and other leading narrative and history thinkers like Ricoeur, Chatman, White, Mink and Ankersmit, I suggested understanding narrative opens up the relationship between the real, reference and **representation**. Using the three-tier model of *mimésis* of Ricoeur, I argued that history is always subject to a **mimetic loop** through which the past is turned into history. In arguing for this logic I suggested that the arc that takes historians from the archive to meaning is fraught with the kinds of issues and difficulties that are ignored in the histories of reconstructionists and constructionists. While there is no doubt deconstructionist historians accept and deploy reference and **inference**, they address a wide variety of other **narrative choices** that are made by the historian.

I have suggested that rather than examine narrative as a cognitive instrument, all reconstructionists and too many constructionists still tend to argue that deconstructionists do not give enough credit to them for their levels of sophistication, self-consciousness and narrative awareness.[2] In response to that, and the claim that narrativists abandon the truth-claims of history, I argued that the deconstructionist recognition of the **fictive** and **aesthetic** nature of the historical narrative is a corrective only to the absolutism of the statement of **justified belief**.

For reconstructionists and constructionists, history (history defined as the form of the past) is inferior to the past (content). This exemplifies the fallacy that, for all its **referentiality**, the historical narrative is not a linguistic copy of the past. As **semiotic** and symbolic representations, histories cannot, by definition, be 'discovered' or be 'truthful' in any sense that does not acknowledge their fictively constructed nature. Though they possess referential, sentence-length descriptions (statements of '**fact**'), histories are premeditated **discourse**s and literary constructions all the way through. Hence, the 'reality of the past' can only be engaged via the aesthetic turn. Even reconstructionists must make narratives. Even for them history is an experience and activity produced by the **ontological** contiguity between **author-historian** and the past. In other words, historians are an unavoidable part of the history they produce.

In most circumstances (apart from when the demands of **experimentalism** dictate otherwise) it continues to be important that factual statements can be demonstrated to be empirically true/false. Although there is a potent **ethical turn** to be found in all histories, there is also a cultural imperative that we get the facts straight and do not deny the well-attested evidence. Deconstructionist historians do not downplay the functioning or the difficulty of research. Nor do they deny that there are many sophisticated historians who recognise the problems of the silent archive, or that there is no useful role for high-powered theorising. But, fundamentally, history is historiography and **historicist**. In other words, the **correspondence** situation, while generally desirable, is irrelevant to the **diegetic** *process* of writing history.

The issue, therefore, is not one of the facts (or lack of them), or potential dishonesty on the part of the historian, but of how we use what we have according to the conventions and rules of engagement of a particular historical practice. So, there may well continue to be a cultural need to believe in 'truthful history' rather than what I have called 'historical truth'. But if truth is conceived only in empirical-analytical terms we will continue to misunderstand how the **narrative constructivism** of history works and how it provides for our historical cognition. Because the historian cannot deliver the reality of the past through statements of justified belief alone, it is imperative that we understand the nature of **narrative supervenience**.

It is no surprise, then, that the central issue in historical thinking and practice today is the question of **representation** and the **performative** nature of history rather than questions of positivism and covering laws. Historians are now aware as never before of the aesthetic as well as the classic realist dimensions to history. As has been famously observed, probing the limits of representation is now the key to understanding the nature of history. This has been heightened by the **postmodern** and specifically the **poststructuralist** avowal of the crisis in representation along with the 'death of the author', the failings of the signifier–signified relation, and the problematic connection between **form and content**. But to this list must be added **reader-response theory**, **relativism**, the role of **trope/figuration**, **intertextuality**, the consequences of the **linguistic turn**, and the emergence of epistemological **scepticism**. Indeed, the overall effect has been to reject crude **mimetic** historical thinking in favour of a **new history** that acknowledges its fictive nature and the absence of the *tertium quid*. This is despite the rearguard action of the **new empiricism**. The benefit has been to place the relationship between the sources, reference and representation on a new footing. This is the enduring legacy of many history theorists, most notably Paul Ricoeur, Jacques Derrida, Roland Barthes, Hayden White, Louis Mink, Arthur Danto, Robert Rosenstone, Keith Jenkins and Frank Ankersmit.

Each in their different way has argued that historical representations only become plausible as they are narrated. Creating followability in a story is the central processing aspect of historical cognition. To argue there is cohesion in *a* history is not, of course, the same as saying that as we recognise it we are grasping *the* cohesion of the past. All that history can do – as with all narratives – is represent or impose an **order** through interpretation. I pointed out that this is different to description (what happened or 'factualism'), which has no investment in followability and understanding, explanation, meaning or truth. How we conceptualise past reality as a representation is the most significant element in determining what we will 'find' on the level of the represented. This is the consequence of the revolution wrought by the metahistorical approach to history.

Following the logic of Genette, I suggested a story is constructed out of past events and existents (the content). I described this as the content/story dimension of history. I noted that the historian functioned as an author who narrates the past by making a number of decisions concerning a range of narrative functions, the specificity of which arise from their initial epistemological choice. These include decisions about aesthetic/figurative, **emplotment**, mode of argument/explanation, ethic/political/ideological strategies of explanation and appropriate referential and causation judgements. Next, historians make authorial decisions about the process of their narrating and narration. These decisions centre on **voice**, **focalisation**, **tense/timing** (order, **duration** and **frequency**), **intentionality** (text, action, **agency**, characterisation). Finally, the author-historian has to determine the nature of the mode of expression to work with and in. The primary modes I noted were written texts, film and photography, television and radio, graphic novels, comics, history magazines, public histories including museums, heritage sites and memorials, various forms of **performance** and digitised representations.

Content/story, I maintained, was a category derived from Hayden White's model of historical writing and the representation of the past. However, rather than only stressing figuration, argument, ideology and emplotment as White did, I argued that it was necessary to include epistemological choices, story followability and reference. Content/story is thereby defined as the locus for the organisation of any set of events and the decisions and actions of historical agents by the historian founded on the principle of a followable story *about* such past events. This notion was outlined by William Gallie, although for him knowledge of events would generate *the* story. Defining *the* story as the discovery of the most likely meaning of the past (which is also a workable empirical-analytical definition of truth) prompted Hayden White and Louis Mink to argue in a fashion similar to Gallie. Of course they suggested there was nothing in the past to constitute anything other than *a* story. But all were agreed that the content of the past could only be grasped when storied. Hence we arrive at the implication that the conventional notion of reference → explanation → meaning → narrative is, in effect, challenged. The narrative functions within the category of content/story that I briefly described included the initial epistemological choice of the historian, aesthetic or figurative decisions, emplotment choices, argument ethical decisions and empirical **referentiality**.

Given that the determining feature of history is its logic as a narrative cognitive instrument, I argued that the function of 'telling' demands an understanding of how the author-historian narrates. I suggested that the historical narrative is experienced (**subjectively**) by the consumer (implied reader) and, arguably, this generates a meaning that is ambiguous, not always being the same as that intended by the author (implied author) or, for that matter, the past. The delivery (the narration) of the text by the author I characterised as the creative force behind the explanation, meaning and truthfulness of the-past-*as*-history narrative. Inevitably this re-situates the role of referentiality. I noted this had a twofold consequence.

First, it becomes necessary to reconsider the idea that it is 'the past' that invariably and ultimately produces history and, second, I suggested we need to note that history is a fictive construction. I noted two consequences of this. First, the historian is not a conduit for the past. And second, we should not be comparing 'history non-fiction' with 'literary fiction'. I have argued that there are two types of narrative – the 'non-history narrative' and the 'history narrative'. But, as I have tried to demonstrate, the authorial functions for both are identical. If, therefore, we wish to argue that 'history' is a different kind of narrative than 'fiction' just because its content once really existed, then we will have to demonstrate that the authorial functions for each are fundamentally different. But, regardless of whether it is a historian or a non-historian writing, the fundamental mechanics and rules of authoring a narrative do not change.

Further, I argued that the fundamental operating procedure in 'doing history' was not one of strict determination but reciprocity or over-determination. In other words, history's commitment to **referentiality** and truth are not primal, but equally they are not impaired or impugned by its status as a narrative. The implication for history and historians is that the 'what' of the story is located in the events and existents of the past, but the historian-author generates meaning as she or he narrates the-past-*as*-history. But I also noted that because the process of telling is never simply limited to the textual, there are many different forms or modes of expression available to the historian. Further, I suggested that although what happens to history in terms of its explanatory value is less determined by its mode of expression than the initial epistemological decision, different modes of expression would over-determine and re-orientate the content/story, narrating/narrative relationship.

In consequence, the belief that history and fiction are polarised is false. It is false because it is the result of an irrelevant comparison. I said this is irrelevant because it follows from the failure to acknowledge how the historian has to create a history story space (the universe created by the historian about the past). Moreover, it is the nature of narrative to encompass all forms such as history (and non-history whatever form that takes – magic **realism**, autobiographical fiction, graphic novels, ballet, diaries, etc.). The whole point of narrative is that it substitutes itself for the real and its memory. As Ricoeur suggests, not only can memory not retain that which is to be remembered 'pure' but the act of retaining a memory means transforming (literally trans-form) that which is remembered into a narrative (form) which will make the memory 'memorable'. Through the process of content/story creation and the functions of narration the past is trans-formed into a form – a mode of expression – that becomes the physical and intellectual incarnation of the-past-*as*-history.

The model of historical thinking and practice offered in this book is based, then, on the notion that history cannot connect knowing what happened with what it means without understanding the nature of representation and the constitution of the historian's story space. We have seen that this entails an acquaintance with the mechanisms whereby writing and telling include the established practices of empirical investigation and analysis. Without question, the reality of the past is a fundamental constraint on the nature of the history. But, invoking the work on the nature of narrative primarily of Gérard Genette and Seymour Chatman I have argued that all historians will gain in their understanding of the connections between 'what is told' and 'how it is told'.

I suggested that Genette's analysis of non-realist literature was significant for the logic of history thinking and practice. I explained how for Genette the order of precedence in fiction is story then narrating but – in a way that is significant for the logic of narrative historical explanation – how content and story, narrating and narrative are simultaneous activities. As a fundamental and highly practical insight into historical thinking and practice, this argument reveals how the narrative does not follow on from the discovery of the story. In other words, it is impossible to have a history narrative in isolation from a story and its narrating. As a result of this logic, I argued that history could only start with the decisions of the author whose job is to connect content/story with *and through* the processes of narrating and narrative.

While I argued that ultimately the process and nature of this transformation is determined by the epistemological choices of the historian, I also suggested the mode of expression in itself would not necessarily alter that initial choice. Hence it is quite wrong to imagine that the chosen expression will automatically 'change' the nature of the history (after the 'expressive turn' as it were). The mode of expression reflects the epistemological choice (for or against) of the historian. Thus digital history will be reconstructionist in form and content if it is created by a reconstructionist. Of course, all media of expression are flexible and open to a huge variety of forms and contents hence my argument that the mode of expression and what was done with it *may* feed back upon the other key narrative elements. It is always possible that, as with Robert A. Rosenstone, working within a particular mode of expression (in his case, film) will directly influence the historian's awareness of the epistemological potentialities and possibilities within the discipline. Indeed, this is clearly the case with Rosenstone, whose study of film made him rethink the nature of history which then fed back into how he saw history on film, and film on history.

The consequence of all this, in terms of the twin functioning of reference and representation, is that they over-determine each other. I argued that the nature of that over-determination derives from the principle that the representation (history) has the same ontological status as that which is being represented (the reality of the past as reference). In other words, following Gadamer, I suggested that the aesthetics of any history is the product of the contiguity of author-historian and the past; hence the-past-*as*-history. As we know, it can be legitimately argued that a detailed knowledge of the past is of no value whatsoever. If the first philosophy is ethics, then empirical knowledge cannot generate it. At best it can illustrate it and then usually in a highly selective manner. If, however, we want a discipline that can guide us (though not help in predicting the future) then we need to endorse a history that welcomes experimentalism, the first principle of which is that the historian, the history narrative and the past are ontologically and self-consciously connected.

For me, the future of history involves rethinking the ontological connections between the past and the understanding of it through a reconsideration of objectivity, truth and relativism. Conceived in terms of the logic of narrative, history's objective and truth-seeking character demands an acknowledgement of the immanent relativism in our engagement with the past. As we have seen, the truth of the past can only emerge through its representation and is not produced exclusively through reference and inference in any correspondence type of way. In producing history we can still be faithful to the established rules of source analysis, method and appropriate theorising. However, I have argued that it is only due to a history viewed in all its rich variety of content/story, narration and expression and by acknowledging our epistemological choices that we can we derive a meaning for the past that is socially useful.

There seems little doubt that in Western societies history is highly regarded. But the paradox, still hardly acknowledged, is that we cannot move outside its story space to gain entry to the past in order to fulfil our many expectations. Understanding the 'real' nature of the past is always going to fail because history cannot escape its own act of creation. While it can refer to past 'reality', that reference is tied to the experience of its own narrative construction. So, while the past can be approached and, arguably, become a subject of study, it can never be known except through the narratives we create about it. This leads to the conclusion that it is the limits of our narrative making that constitute the ultimate confines of our understanding of the past.

Glossary

▶ **Aesthetics/aesthetic turn**

The understanding and examination of the space between the **representation** and what is represented. See also the **narrative turn**.

▶ **Agency (structure)**

Often polarised as two distinctive approaches to historical **explanation**, historians can elect to favour one over the other: agency *or* structure. Equally they can attempt to understand the past as the interaction of agency *and* structure. Structures can be political, social, economic, ideological or whatever the historian wants them to be.

▶ **Author-historian**

The individual whose function it is to generate **narratives** within which **reference**, **explanation** and **meaning** are created. The author-historian creates a **story space** as the location of their **content/story**, narration and **mode of expression** choices.

▶ **Characterisation**

The historian characterises **stories**, events and historical agents (often through the **emplotment** of action) for purposes of **explanation** and **meaning** creation. Characterisation is a major **fictive** undertaking. See also **voice**.

▶ **Constructionist history**

One of the three primary genres of **history** (cf. **reconstructionist** and **deconstructionist history**). Constructionist historians cover a vast range of interests and methodologies. However, they all tend to propose relationships between events in the past, which will then be validated through empirical research. For constructionists, history results from the conceptual interface constituted between **empiricism** and **explanation**.

► Content/story

One of the three elemental features of **history** (see also **mode of expression**). Content/story is the content of the past explained as a **story**. It is impossible to conceive of a history where content and story are separated out.

► Correspondence theory

This is a theory of **truth** that equates empirical knowledge (see **reference, reality**) with **meaning**, assuming the adequacy of the representational medium (usually natural language). See **representation/representational**. The debate over correspondence theory centres on whether the one-time existence of a past reality does or does not validate the notion that the truth of past events can be found in the agreement between the word and the world. The majority of historians accept correspondence theory to some extent. See **reconstructionist, constructionist** and **deconstructionist history**. The latter group dissent from this belief.

► Deconstructionist history

A genre of **history** defined by the adoption of several **postmodern** assumptions about the study of the past. By definition, this means questioning a number of key modernist beliefs which underlie **reconstructionist** and **constructionist** approaches to the past. See **correspondence theory, content/story, fictive, experimental history, narrative supervenience, form and content, story space, relativism** and *tertium quid*.

► Diegesis/diegetic

This refers to the telling aspect of **history** specifically (a) to the **story** in history. There are two levels in every hi-story (as in all literature) the intra-diegetic (in the story) and extra-diegetic (above the story). Another use of the term (b) is to designate the mode of narration or **discourse**. Diegesis is usually compared with **mimesis**. Whether it is acknowledged or not, all historians work within this written **representational narrative** structure.

▶ Discourse

A discourse is broadly defined as a language terrain (written, spoken, filmic or whatever) that is concerned with how a **story** is told (see **aesthetics/aesthetic turn, author-historian, diegesis/diegetic, focalisation, story space, tense/timing** and **voice**). Discourses encompass a vast range of concerns and come in many kinds – **history**, gardening, cookery, aerodynamics, **epistemology** and, of course, linguistics (the analysis of discourse as a language system). A key figure for historians in understanding discourse is the theorist Michel Foucault who suggested a discourse is a mechanism for establishing and organising power. Thus a **reconstructionist history** discourse will prohibit certain historical activities that will be insisted on by **deconstructionist history** practitioners. The concept of discourse is useful if only because it reminds historians that their product (as a kind of history discourse) – how they tell **the-past-*as*-history** – is a creation for disciplinary purposes. See **experimental history** as a dissenting mode of historical discourse.

▶ Duration

Historians have to make decisions about the speed at which they will narrate their **history**. Duration is the 'real time' elapsed in the **content/story** (of the past) and the amount of discourse time (space and time allocated to it) in the history. The duration choice historians make regulates the speed of the **narrative** in relation to the events told. This is a significant feature of the narrative construction of all histories.

▶ Empiricism

The acquisition of knowledge by means of sensory input, which is then turned out as statements of **justified belief** based on **inference**. See **sources, explanation, meaning** and **truth**.

▶ Emplotment

This is the **author-historian**'s mode of organising the evidence of the past to explain it as an archetypal **story** type (tragic, romantic, farce, epic). See **agency, aesthetic turn, empiricism, explanation, form and content, linguistic turn, narrative supervenience, narrative turn** and **representation**.

► Epistemology/epistemological/epistemological choice

Epistemology addresses the foundations, theory and nature of knowledge and its acquisition. There is no single epistemological mode for **history** and historians although each historian after they have made their epistemological choice is likely to insist theirs is the most appropriate one. See **reconstructionist, constructionist,** and **deconstructionist history**. While most historians are wary about insisting on certainty in interpreting the **sources**, they are less deferential or modest about their epistemological choice.

► Ethical turn

This is the recognition that all histories are extended ethical statements. The reverse argument begins with the **epistemological choice** that opts for the empirical-analytical model with its self-proclaimed demand for **objectivity** over **relativism**. This requires the rejection of the notion of **history** being an overtly ethical activity. From this position, history is defined as a search for the **truth** rather than a moral intervention. The ethical turn, however, accepts history as a more complex activity of authorial intervention which demands strategies for **explanation** that include the ideological, political and moral. See **narrative choices**.

► Experimental history

This is any form of **history** that expressly confronts the nature of the connection (as a **representation**) between **reality** of the past and its **correspondence** in the text (or in any other **mode of expression**). By definition, experimental historians make **epistemological choices** that challenge those of **reconstructionist, constructionist** (and maybe also) **deconstructionist** historians. Like the art movements of impressionism, naturalism, surrealism and cubism, experimental history is not necessarily anti-realist but it is anti-representational.

► Explanation

This is the process whereby historians tell us what, how and why things in the past happened. There is no single avenue to historical explanation given the availability of the variety of **epistemological choices** open to the historian, although **reconstructionist** and **constructionist** historians would tend to say there is no legitimate choice. **Deconstructionists** would be equally insistent there is. The modes of explanation thus differ markedly. The primary forms are scientific (see, for example, **facts, empiricism**) and non-scientific (see, for example, **aesthetic turn**, content/story, **emplotment, followability, narrative** and **trope**).

▶ Facts

Facts are assumed to be true statements about the **reality/realism** of the past. In effect they are the products of statements of **justified belief**. Facts do not, therefore, pre-exist in the **sources** or evidence. Facts are constituted but are understood by most historians (see **reconstructionist** and **constructionist history**) to be essentially reflective of *the* state of how things *were*. For the **deconstructionist**, facts are defined somewhat differently as events/happenings under a description. This is not just nit-picking. Facts – as statements of **justified belief** – have to be described and presented in a **narrative** to have any meaning.

▶ Fictive

The fictive is often defined in terms of what it is not – it is not factual. But this is a definition of fiction, which is what **history** is not. Fiction is intentionally not true (see **truth**; '**historical truth**') whereas history is meant to be true. Hence, while works of fiction can have true statements (of **justified belief**) in them, histories cannot have fictional statements that are unconnected to evidenced past **reality**. In these senses, history and fiction are not comparable. By fictive is meant a discourse that is imaginatively created (as opposed to being an empirical reconstruction). Perhaps the whole point of acknowledging history as resulting from the triadic structure of **content/story**, narration/**narrative** and **mode of expression** is to recognise that it is imaginatively – fictively – constructed.

▶ Focalisation

Associated with the concept of **voice**, focalisation is a primary function of the **author-historian**. It is the telling of past activities of agents and events, thereby producing **meaning** by regulating the flow of appropriate information usually in terms of 'seeing' from the point of view of the subject of focalisation or the focaliser. There are three types of focalisation – internal, external and zero.

► Followability

This term refers to the quality of a (hi-)story as a 'directed' series of successive actions and events that draws the **history** reader/viewer/listener to the **explanation**. Followability is a central feature of the content/story.

► Form and content

This term defines the relationship between the form/design of the **history** text and the content of the real world events, agents and existents represented in it. How an individual makes that connection is the result of their **epistemological choice**. Hence, **reconstructionist** historians see content determining form (**reality** produces empirical-analytical history). The **constructionist** is not quite so empirically determining allowing for the interventionist role of concept and theory. The **deconstructionist** would ask whether the two concepts do, in fact, constitute a duality much less that form is the function of content.

► Frequency

A further significant feature of the temporal organisation of the **timing** and **duration** is frequency. This is concerned with the 'repetition' of events for explanatory purposes. There are four modes of telling: the singulative, repetitive, iterative and the irregular.

► Hermeneutics

This is a process that can be defined as either a methodology for interpreting the **meaning** of texts or, more broadly, as the philosophy of interpretation. See also **relativism** and **mimetic loop**.

► 'Historical truth'

The subject of a variety of definitions, it can be defined in empirical-analytical terms or as that which results from **narrative constructivism**. It may best be thought of more broadly as the intention of the historian to be honest and say honest things about **the-past-*as*-history**.

► Historicism/historicist

For the majority of historians, historicism is the understanding of historical periods in their own terms. What for **reconstructionist** and (for many though not all) **constructionist** historians is a major problem is judging the past not in its own terms but by our own presentist – historicist – terms. **Deconstructionists** are not particularly worried about this, believing it is to be in some degree unavoidable.

► History

That **narrative representation** intended to provide a coherent and **order**ed body of **explanation**s and **meaning**s about the past produced by the historian.

► Inference

The activity of arriving at a conclusion (the inference) from a set of premises/ assumptions. Most historians have premises/assumptions which they 'test' in the **empirical** data. A collection of inferences can add up to an argument. The inference acquires legitimacy once it achieves the status of **justified belief**.

► Intentionality

The connection between (a) a human state of mind (see **agency**), (b) its **representation** (see **mode of expression**) and (c) its referent (see **reference/ referentiality**). Knowing the nature of intentionality is a central aspect of histor- ical **explanation**. The **inference** and interpretation of intention from evidenced human action is a notoriously difficult activity.

► Intertexuality

This is the notion that **meaning** derives not simply from a single text in isolation, but from the situation of the text among others – literally as a text-inter-text. Intertextually, therefore, texts have no completely independent meaning.

► Justified belief

A belief justified according to a range of acceptable criteria such as **empirical reference**, adequate **inference**, **truth** conditions, ethics and so on. Justified belief needs to be distinguished from truth.

► Linguistic turn

This is the move in historical **explanation** to an emphasis on the functioning of language (see **poststructuralism**, **deconstructionist history**, **meaning** and **trope**). The shift has substantial implications for concepts such as **objectivity**, **truth**, **relativism**, **meaning**, **justified belief** and, ultimately, the definition of **history**.

► Meaning

The notion of meaning starts with the way words (in language) hook onto both **reality** and to other words. Thus, the meaning of a word such as 'revolution' cannot only refer to 'the real' but also to other words with which it also connects to create meaning (understanding). Thus to know 'what happened' – **empirically** or as **justified belief** – can at best only provide partial meaning. Indeed, it is always also possible to construct different meanings for the language–word connection (see **intentionality**, **semiotic/semiotics**).

► *Mimésis*/mimetic/mimetic loop

This is the activity of imitation. In **history** mimésis is usually defined as the textual imitation of past human action. From a **deconstructionist** perspective (as opposed to a **reconstructionist** or **constructionist** one) history is not mimetic because mimésis assumes the one-time presence of the past can be imitated in that completely different form called history. The problem with *mimésis* (showing) is that a **narrative** is unable to imitate the past because texts are linguistic in their form, and language can only duplicate itself. Historians cannot escape the mimetic loop as described by Paul Ricoeur which is the over-determining process inherent in his model of mimesis$_1$, mimesis$_2$ and mimesis$_3$. See **form and content**; **hermeneutics**.

▶ Mode of expression

This is the medium or form in which the **author-historian** depicts their **history**. There is a clear reciprocity between the **form** chosen for the **representation** and what is being represented (see **form and content** and content/story). Modes of expression vary – film, ballet, sculpture, literary texts, photographs, digital representations and so on.

▶ Narrative/narration

Not limited to any discipline, narrative (a.k.a narration) is the communication (telling, recounting) of a sequence of happenings or events by establishing a **meaning**ful connection between them. The connection between author and consumer via the structure of the narrative (see content/story and **mode of expression**) is central to the process of narrative making and understanding. See **fictive, focalisation, history, intertextuality, explanation, narrative choices, narrative constructivism, narrative supervenience, narrative turn, representation/representational, story, story space, tense/timing** and **voice**.

▶ Narrative choices

The recounting of a series of past events with the intention of understanding and explaining their **meaning** results from the **author-historian**'s individual powers of **fictive narrative** construction. In effect this means the **history** narrative is the product of a substantial-range complex and (in varying degrees) (un)self-conscious choices made by the historian as they construct their narrative about the past. The historian 'makes sense' of the past through those narrative-making decisions and turns (see **linguistic turn, narrative turn** and **ethical turn**). That history's logic is that of making narratives – so all histories work within a common (and formal) functional narrative structure – explains why their meanings are invariably different.

▶ Narrative constructivism

This is the product of a radical constructivist approach to writing **history** which assumes that historical knowledge is a mediation of the historian's experience of engaging with the past, as opposed to the epistemological notion of the past itself producing its own history. See **objectivity, relativism** and **subjective/subjectivity**.

▶ Narrative supervenience

Supervenience (referring to the **order**ing relationship between properties in the world) explains how historians elect to argue that certain forces in the past supervened over (or determined) others. The logic also applies to the construction of **history**. Historians use the concept of supervenience all the time when they prioritise certain narrational organising concepts and especially when **deconstructionists** claim that history (as a **narrative**) supervenes the past.

▶ Narrative turn

One of the many turns in **history** (see **linguistic turn**, **ethical turn** and **aesthetic turn**), the narrative turn challenges the priority of **reference**, **explanation** and **empirical** and analytically derived **meaning** over **narrative** construction. After the narrative turn, for **deconstructionists** in particular, questions of **representation** become central to historical understanding.

▶ New empiricism/ist

A recent move to rehabilitate **empiricism** and analysis (see **inference**) under the presumed anti-realist onslaught of the versions of historical explanation that have been influenced by continental philosophy and **poststructuralism**. See **deconstructionist history**. The main aim of new empiricism is to domesticate and then, perhaps, commit to obscurity all metanarrative understandings of **the-past-*as*-history**.

▶ New history

It seems that every generation of historians produces a new history. These are usually reactions to conventional beliefs and practices. Thus at the start of the twentieth century in the United States a new history emerged that was self-conscious and supposedly **relativist**. The Annales School was self-proclaimed to be a new history in the 1920s and 1930s; similar is the cliometric and social science (statistical/measurement/social theory orientated) **history** of the 1960s. The 1990s and 2000s produced yet another new history (see **narrative turn**). Deconstructionist historians would claim their new history is the most substantive to date because it confronts basic **epistemological** assumptions.

▶ Objectivity

Possessed of a confusing number of differing **meaning**s, objectivity is commonly assumed to mean knowledge of the past thing-in-itself for what it is without any embellishment or the intrusion of a false consciousness, bias, ideology or other deviations from honest **representation**. While there are formal methods for the (hoped for and intended) objective acquisition of **justified belief**, this does not automatically mean **history** is an objective mode of inquiry. The reasons are legion, not least because history is selective of its data, **fictive** in its creation, is a **narrative construction**, is not mind-independent, is culturally **relativist**, is authored and so on.

▶ Ontology/ontological

This refers to the branch of metaphysics that deals with the state and nature of being (of people, places, contexts, **narratives**, the past) and existence. It also explores how the human mind constructs structures and categories for organising **reality**. All humans have ontological choices. Thus knowledge of the ontology of the narrative is of particular interest to **deconstructionist** historians and has little appeal (or value) to **reconstructionists**.

▶ Order

This has two meanings. It can refer to the order in which the historian undertakes the tasks of content/story, narrating and narration. As Genette suggests the **narrative** (narrating) act initiates *both* the **story** and its narrative, which then become indistinguishable. The second meaning refers to the distortion between the order in which events in the past occurred and the order imposed upon them for explanatory purposes. Thematic and problem-orientated histories are obvious examples in which anachronisms such as analepsis and prolepsis are deployed.

▶ Performance/performative

Because **history** is a mode of realist **narrative**, its effects in terms of **explanation**, interpretation, understanding, and **meaning** creation can only be judged through its performative effects upon the narratee. Such effects are inevitably broad and will encompass the expectations of the consumer in terms of the genre of history. Performance can also refer to physical actions as in first-person narration.

▶ Postmodernism

Postmodernism describes the present condition of knowledge acquisition. Suffused by its anti-Enlightenment epistemological scepticism, postmodern **history** works playfully to expose the presumptive and yet utterly contingent nature of the primacy of **empiricism** and analysis that is essential to the intellectual terror machine of modernism. As you may judge from this definition, postmodernism is also inflected with irony and hyperbole as mechanisms of defamiliarisation. See **experimental history, deconstructionist history, author-historian** and **relativism**.

▶ Poststructuralism

This is an epistemically sceptical, late-twentieth-century intellectual and philosophical movement that is a central pivot of postmodern analysis (see **deconstructionist history, epistemology/epistemological/epistemological choice** and **postmodernism**). Because poststructuralism confronts the full range of modernist and Enlightenment **history** thinking as encapsulated in the empirical-analytical epistemological model, the vast majority of historians have little time for it or its practitioners (see **reconstructionist** and **constructionist history**).

▶ Reader-response

This refers to a variety of wide-ranging theories of reading **meaning** into and from texts. See **discourse, intertextuality, hermeneutics** and **intentionality**.

▶ Reality/realism

Reality is assumed to be 'how things *are*'. There are two corollaries. The first is that how things *appear* does not constitute reality or realism (the real can be different to what it seems). Second, how things appear is irrelevant to the nature of how things are. Reality is mind and language independent. This produces a dual concept much favoured by **reconstructionist** historians, that (a) there is **objective** reality (back there) *and* (b) such an objective reality can be adequately represented (in the here and now). At this point, what **deconstructionist** historians like to point out is that (b) does not automatically follow from (a). If deconstructionists are correct, this raises all kinds of problems about what is **truth** in **history**. See **linguistic turn**, all the glossary entries relating to **narrative**, and also **reference/referentiality**, **relativism**, **representation/representational**, **story**, **story space**, **subjective/subjectivity** and *tertium quid*.

▶ Reconstructionist history

An **epistemological** approach or genre, which views **history** in **realist**, **referential**, **empirical**, **truth** conditional, **objective**, **correspondence** (transparency of **narrative**) and non-theory, terms.

▶ Reference/referentiality

The reference a historian makes in an expression stands for the subject/object to which it refers. Or, to put it in **semiotic** terms, a referent is the subject/object designated in language by a signifier (a sound/**mode of expression**/ concept) and which together constitute a sign (which is to all intents and purposes a **meaning**). When placed in a sentence with a predicate, the reference can possess a **truth**-value. However, **deconstructionist** historians are fond of pointing out that the referent and, by implication, reference/referentiality are cultural and ideological constructions. Hence there is no 'natural' connection or **correspondence** between reference/**reality** and meaning.

▶ Relativism

Often confused with bias, relativism acknowledges the 'situatedness' of knowledge. This ranges from the rejection of the notion of the **representation**al **correspondence** between the world and the word, through situational ethics, to the linguistic and **narrative** creation of historical constructions such as gender, race, class and nation, as well as the constructions historians place on the **sources**. See also **objectivity** and **reference/referentiality**, **representation/representational** and *tertium quid*. **Deconstructionist** historians would argue that relativism is in some degree unavoidable and, rather than explaining how it can be 'overcome', understand and work with it, using it to advantage in engaging more fruitfully with the past. **Reconstructionists** and many **constructionists** would regard this as dangerous nonsense.

▶ Representation/representational

The central issue in historical understanding today, representation forces historians to address how the past is turned into **history**. Because history is a **narrative** written about the past it is necessary to understand its cognitive functioning as a form of representation. Essentially, a representation is not 'the thing in itself' but a 'stand-in' for it. This suggests we cannot know the **meaning** of an object except through its representation. In this sense a historical narrative is a highly complex and radically constructivist representation of the past. Hence historians cannot 'tell the **truth**' in strict **correspondence** terms about the past because of the **narrative turn**. See **deconstructionist history**, **linguistic turn**, **mimesis** and all entries relating to **narrative**.

▶ Sceptical/scepticism

Essentially scepticism can be defined in terms of lacking and acquiring knowledge (see **epistemology**). **History** is an activity founded on scepticism in that **reconstructionist** and **constructionist** historians tend to work on the principle that they believe they can gain knowledge only through what is evidenced to them and then explored via a variety of 'assumptions' and/or concepts. Such knowledge is then 'tested' in its detailed verification and comparison (see **empiricism**, **sources**). Knowledge not so provided is **unjustified belief** and, therefore, epistemologically unsupportable. Epistemological scepticism (generally favoured by **postmodern** and/or **deconstructionist** historians) is the position that there are narrow and strict limits to the empirical-analytical mechanism for gaining knowledge such that its outcomes like **truth** and **meaning** are never vouchsafe. The limits to knowledge arise not merely from the contingency, situatedness and the relations of power implicated in its acquisition but also in its transmission as a representation, especially as a **narrative**. See **hermeneutics**, **historicism/historicist**, **reality/realism**, **relativism**, **representation/representationalism**, **objectivity**, **poststructuralism** and **subjective/subjectivity**.

▶ Semiotic/semiotics

This refers to the study of signs, how they are created and the nature of (the resulting) signification (**meaning** can be defined as the inter-relationship of signs). Thus, all languages and **discourse**s such as **history** are symbolic **representation**s of **reality** and constitute our 'meaningful' access to it ('the past' in the case of 'history') by creating expressions as descriptions, ideas and so on. A basic grasp of semiotics reveals there are no given meanings.

▶ Sources

Those referred to as 'primary sources' are evidential relics or any vestigial remains left from the past. Secondary sources constitute historiography. Sources are not *the* origin of historical **meaning**. Though clearly highly important and necessary given the realist literature of **history** they remain only an element within the overall **narrative**-making process. They are not of themselves sufficient for history.

▶ Story/stories

Conventionally distinguished from **discourse**, story refers to what is told – the narrated events, existents and so on (discourse refers to how it is told). Story is directly implicated with discourse in terms of style, **mode of expression** and content/story.

▶ Story space

The story space is the **author-historian**'s **fictively** constructed **narrative** model of when, why, how, what and to whom things happened in the past. Story spaces, whether ostensibly realist or overtly fictional, operate according to the precise rules of narrative making and are shaped by the author-historian's experience of the past and how they imagine it to have been. The **history** story space, though **referential**, is contrived according to the **narrative choices** the historian makes.

▶ Subjective/subjectivity

A term that refers to the character of the concepts, mechanisms or methods for acquiring knowledge being dependent upon the manner in which they are applied (usually determined by the person applying them: see **objectivity**). Regarded as something to be avoided by most historians, **deconstructionists** would, however, say it cannot be avoided, but should be explored and, finally, incorporated into 'doing **history**'. See **experimental history**.

▶ Tense/time/timing

A key **author-historian** function, tense/time refers to the turning of the real time of the past into the **story** time of the **history**. It is one of many strategies of **explanation** deployed by the historian. According to Seymour Chatman this temporal turn saturates every aspect of writing.

▶ *Tertium quid*

An undefined 'thing' that is related in some indefinite way to two other defined and definite things but distinct from them. The *tertium quid* in **reconstructionist history** is the 'empirical **correspondence**' presumed to exist between language (the 'word') and **reality** (the 'world'). For constructionists it would (more complexly) be the 'empirical-analytical correspondence'. **Deconstructionists** doubt the existence of the *tertium quid* and are happy to live with the consequences. See '**historical truth**'; **truth**.

▶ the-past-*as*-history

This is a neologism that describes the **deconstructionist** sense of the relationship between the past and **history**. Specifically it describes how, given that the past and history are different **ontological** categories, the former, which is now beyond our contact, can only be grasped through the latter, which is our construction. Hence it is that our knowledge about the time before now is only possible through the-past-*as*-history.

▶ Trope/figuration

Figures of speech that work by deploying words in such a way they create and change **meaning**. **Deconstructionists** regard troping as an important cognitive device in turning the past into **history**. The notion of trope/figuration does not, of course, create the past but it does have a role in shaping how we understand it.

▶ Truth

Although an immensely complex concept, generally truth is taken to be the match between a proposition and the **reality** to which it refers (see **referentiality**; **justified belief**). However, because **history** is a mode of **narrative**

representation it has no absolutist **epistemological meaning**. See **correspondence** the-past-*as*-history *tertium quid*, 'historical truth', **facts** and **meaning**.

▶ Voice

A key concept defined as 'who tells the **story**?' and, importantly, which also encompasses the 'speech acts' of the narrator, thus influencing every aspect of the creation of the **history** understood as a **narrative**. This includes the creation of the triad of **content/story**, narration and **mode of expression**.

Notes

► **Introduction**

1 Prose refers to 'ordinary' or 'everyday' 'non-verse' language. It is usually written. Prose, unlike verse, has no formal metrical arrangements. There are a great many 'historical explanation' texts available. Useful as a starter is Paul Veyne, *Writing History, Essays on Epistemology*, trans. Mina Moore-Rinvolucri (Middletown: Wesleyan University Press, 1984 [1971]); R.F. Atkinson, *Knowledge and Explanation in History* (London: Macmillan, 1978); Arthur Danto, *Analytical Philosophy of Knowledge* (Cambridge: Cambridge University Press, 1968); and two books by W.H. Walsh, *An Introduction to Philosophy of History* (Westport, CT: Greenwood Press, 1984 [1967]) and *Substance and Form in History* (Edinburgh: Edinburgh University Press, 1981). See also William Dray, *Laws and Explanation in History* (Oxford: Oxford University Press, 1957) and 'Philosophy and Historiography', in *Companion to Historiography*, ed. Michael Bentley (London: Routledge, 1997), 763–782. A comprehensive introduction to history as a discipline and practice is Michael Stanford's *A Companion to the Study of History* (Oxford: Basil Blackwell, 1994), and up-to-date and collected from the pages of the journal *History and Theory* is *History and Theory: Contemporary Readings*, ed. Brian Fay, Philip Pomper and Richard T. Vann (Malden and Oxford: Blackwell, 1998).
2 One of the best examples of how this works is in Dennis Dworkin's excellent analysis of the historiography of class in *Class* (Harlow: Pearson, 2007).
3 E.H. Carr, *What is History?* (London: Penguin, 1987 [1961]); Geoffrey Elton, *Return to Essentials: Some Reflections on the Present State of Historical Study* (Cambridge: Cambridge University Press, 1991) and *The Practice of History* (London: Methuen, 1967). This debate and the future direction in which history was moving (and has moved) was described in great detail by Keith Jenkins in his *On 'What is History?': From Carr and Elton to Rorty and White* (London and New York: Routledge, 1995). All students of history are strongly advised to seek out this text for what is probably still the very best introduction to the fundamental developments in historical thinking.
4 William Gallie, *Philosophy and the Historical Understanding* (London: Chatto & Windus, 1964), 105.

5 For an excellent short introduction to many of the issues concerning narrative and history that have exercised the minds of historians in the past 20 years, see Hans Kellner, 'Narrativity in History: Post-structuralism and Since', *History and Theory* 26 (1987): 1–9.

6 See Martin Kreiswirth, 'Narrative Turn in the Humanities', in *Routledge Encyclopedia of Narrative Theory*, ed. David Herman, Manfred Jahn and Marie-Laure Ryan (Abingdon and New York: Routledge, 2005), 377–382 and Martin Kreisworth and Thomas Carmichael, eds, *Constructive Criticism: The Human Sciences in the Age of Theory* (Toronto: University of Toronto Press, 1995). The interest in narrative grows apace. See Jürgen Straub, ed., *Narration, Identity and Historical Consciousness* (New York: Berghahn Books, 2005).

7 George B. Tindall, *America: A Narrative History* (New York, London: W.W. Norton, 1988).

8 Paul S. Boyer *et al.*, *The Enduring Vision: A History of the American People* (Boston and New York: Houghton Mifflin Company, 2005), 1.

9 Ibid.

10 Perhaps the best introduction to issues of representation in what is for many an age of scepticism about our ability to 'know' in the arts and humanities, and especially in history is Linda Hutcheon's *The Politics of Postmodernism* (Abingdon, New York: Routledge, 2005 [1989]). Though not as useful, see also Alun Munslow, *The New History* (Harlow: Pearson, 2003); Alun Munslow, *Deconstructing History*, 2nd ed. (London and New York: Routledge, 2006 [1997]); Alun Munslow, *Routledge Companion to Historical Studies*, 2nd ed. (London and New York: Routledge, 2006 [2000]).

11 Hutcheon, *The Politics of Postmodernism*, 59.

12 Elizabeth Deeds Ermarth, *Sequel to History* (Princeton, NJ: Princeton University Press, 1992) and 'Beyond the Subject: Individuality in the Discursive Condition', *New Literary History* 31, no. 3 (2000): 405–419.

13 Paul Ricoeur, 'Narrative Time', in *On Narrative*, ed. W.J.T. Mitchell (Chicago: University of Chicago Press, 1981), 168–186; Paul Ricoeur, *Time and Narrative*, trans. Kathleen McLaughlin and David Pellauer, vol. 1 (Chicago: University of Chicago Press, 1984), 3–51.

14 Gérard Genette, *Figures* (Paris: Seuil, 1966), 258.

15 Hayden White's key text is his *Metahistory: The Historical Imagination in Nineteenth Century Europe* (Baltimore: Johns Hopkins University Press, 1973); Ricoeur, *Time and Narrative*, 3–51.

16 Kalle Pihlainen, 'The Confines of the Form: Historical Writing and the Desire That It Be What It Is Not', in *Tropes for the Past: Hayden White and the History/Literature Debate*, ed. Kuisma Korhonen (Amsterdam and New York: Rodopi, 2006), 55–67.

17 Among the leading analysts of history as a conceptual literary undertaking is Reinhart Koselleck, *Futures Past: On the Semantics of Historical Time*, trans. and with an Introduction by Keith Tribe (New York: Columbia University Press, 2004); see also Dorrit Cohn, *The Distinction of Fiction* (Baltimore and London: Johns Hopkins University Press, 1999); Linda Hutcheon, *A Poetics of Postmodernism* (New York and London: Routledge, 1988) and *The Politics of Postmodernism*. A recent examination of the relationship between history and fiction is offered by Ann Curthoys and John Docker, *Is History Fiction?* (Sydney: University of New South Wales Press, 2006).

18 Cohn, *The Distinction of Fiction*, 15.

19 Ibid., 156.

20 Sande Cohen, *History Out of Joint: Essays on the Use and Abuse of History* (Baltimore and London: Johns Hopkins University Press, 2005).

21 Michel de Certeau, *The Writing of History*, trans. Tom Conley (New York: Columbia University Press, 1988 [1972]), 6.

22 Callum G. Brown, *Postmodernism for Historians* (Harlow: Pearson Education, 2005).

23 Martin McQuillan, ed., *The Narrative Reader* (London and New York: Routledge, 2000), 18–21.

24 Colin Davis, *After Poststructuralism: Reading, Stories and Theory* (London and New York: Routledge, 2004); Mark Currie, *Postmodern Narrative Theory* (Houndmills: Macmillan Press, 1998).

25 As an introduction to the matter of epistemology I recommend all historians read at least one of the following: Jonathan Dancy, *An Introduction to Contemporary Epistemology* (Oxford: Blackwell, 1985); Linda Alcoff, *Epistemology: The Big Questions* (Oxford: Basil Blackwell, 1998); Robert Audi, *Epistemology: A Contemporary Introduction to the Theory of Knowledge* (New York: Routledge, 1998), and David Cooper, *Epistemology: The Classic Readings* (Oxford: Basil Blackwell, 1999).

26 J. Appleby, L. Hunt and M. Jacob, *Telling the Truth About History* (New York and London: W.W. Norton & Co., 1994), 1.

27 David D. Roberts, *Nothing But History: Reconstruction and Extremity after Metaphysics* (Berkeley: University of California Press, 1995).

28 Roland Barthes, 'Le Discours de l'histoire', *Information sur les Sciences Sociales* (1981 [1967]), 6: 65–75, *Comparative Criticism – A Yearbook*, trans. with an introduction by Stephen Bann (1981); Stephen Bann, 'Analysing the discourse of history', *Renaissance and Modern Studies* (1983), 27: 61–84.

29 See Murray Phillips, 'An Athletic Clio: Sport History and Television History', *Rethinking History: The Journal of Theory and Practice* (forthcoming, 2008); also Munslow, *Deconstructing History*.

30 David Cannadine, ed., *What is History Now?* (Houndmills: Palgrave Macmillan, 2002); see also Michael Kammen, ed., *The Past Before Us: Contemporary Historical Writing in the United States* (Cornell: Cornell University Press, 1980); Juliet Gardiner, ed., *What is History Today?* (Houndmills: Macmillan, 1988); Peter Burke, ed., *New Perspectives on Historical Writing* (Cambridge: Polity Press, 1991); Peter Lambert and Phillipp Schofield, eds, *Making History: An Introduction to the History and Practices of a Discipline* (London and New York: Routledge, 2004); Bentley, ed., *Companion to Historiography*.

31 Having said that, every history student is probably well aware of the 'learning outcomes' they are expected to demonstrate in their history assessments, which seems to suggest there is only one officially approved way – one genre to employ – in thinking about and doing history. This is certainly the situation in the United Kingdom, where it has become official government policy to make them and their teachers aware of the preferred 'skills and qualities of mind' they must demonstrate. These are based upon a nationally imposed History Benchmarking Statement (there are such statements in all disciplines). Student historians are expected to understand basic research techniques, the nature of 'historical inquiry' including the detailed knowledge of a specialist topic, demonstrate an understanding of the ambiguity and limits of historical knowledge, deploy established techniques of historical research and analysis, be aware of current debates on interpretations, and be able to critically evaluate arguments, assumptions, concepts and data in order to make reasoned judgements. But there is little in all of this about understanding the epistemological connections between reference, explanation, meaning and narrative. I suppose that is why historians like me write books like this. That you, as a history student (or even an academic historian), has been recommended this book to read suggests lines of communication are opening up and we are moving towards a more secular understanding of the nature of history.

32 See Douglas Booth, *The Field: Truth and Fiction in Sport History* (London and New York: Routledge, 2005), for an excellent examination of the three epistemological orientations.

33 As we shall see, the factual statement is not the unproblematic connection to the past reality it is usually supposed to be. The reason is that such statements only derive their meaning in a larger narrative understood as a representation of the past. This does not necessarily deny the utility of factual statements or cast doubt on the requirement to be empirically accurate. Without entering into a debate about what philosophers call 'truth-conditional semantics' it is worth noting that not all sentences are either true or false, as with statements about morality, taste or probability. See Max Kölbel, *Truth Without Objectivity* (London and New York: Routledge, 2002). Also see Chapters 6, 7 and 8 passim.

34 C. Behan McCullagh, *The Logic of History: Putting Postmodernism in Perspective* (London and New York: Routledge, 2004); C. Behan McCullagh, 'Bias in Historical Description, Interpretation, and Explanation', *History and Theory* 39, no. 1 (2000): 39–66.

35 John Searle, *The Construction of Social Reality* (London: Allan Lane, 1995), xiii.

36 Geoffrey Roberts, 'Postmodernism Versus the Standpoint of Action', *History and Theory* 36, 2 (1997): 249–260.

37 Arthur Marwick, *The New Nature of History: Knowledge, Evidence, Language* (Houndmills: Palgrave, 2001), 29.

38 Jerzy Topolski, 'The Role of Logic and Aesthetics in Constructing Narrative Wholes in Historiography', *History and Theory* 38, no. 2 (1999): 198–210.

39 D. MacRaild and A. Taylor, *Social Theory and Social History* (Houndmills: Palgrave, 2004), 3.

40 Ibid.

41 Aviezer Tucker, *Our Knowledge of the Past: A Philosophy of Historiography* (New York: Cambridge University Press, 2004).

42 John Belchem and Neville Kirk, eds, *Languages of Labour* (Aldershot: Ashgate Publishing, 1997), 3.

43 Ibid.

44 Bryan D. Palmer, *Descent into Discourse: The Reification of Language and the Writing of Social History* (Philadelphia: Temple University Press, 1990).

45 Ibid.

46 Ibid.

47 Barbara Bush, *Imperialism and Postcolonialism* (Harlow: Pearson Education, 2007).

48 Hans-Georg Gadamer, *Truth and Method* (New York: Seabury Press, 1975).

▶ 1 Narrating the Past

1 Frank R. Ankersmit, *Sublime Historical Experience* (Stanford, CA: Stanford University Press, 2005), 245.

2 Jerome Bruner, *Actual Minds, Possible Worlds* (Cambridge, MA: Harvard University Press, 1986).

3 Richard Rorty, *Truth and Progress: Philosophical Papers*, vol. 3 (Cambridge: Cambridge University Press, 1998); Richard Rorty, ed., *The Linguistic Turn: Recent Essays in Philosophical Method* (Chicago: University of Chicago Press, 1992 [1967]); Richard Rorty, *Objectivity, Relativism and Truth: Philosophical Papers*, vol. 1 (Cambridge: Cambridge University Press, 1991); Richard Rorty, *Philosophy and the Mirror of Nature* (Princeton: Princeton University Press, 1979); Donald Davidson, *Inquiries into Truth and Interpretation* (Oxford: Oxford

University Press, 1984); Donald Davidson, *Essays on Actions and Events* (Oxford: Oxford University Press, 1980). As a pragmatist, Davidson does not deny knowledge given the generally accepted and universal nature of language – even though it is the mechanism through which we engage with the real – arguing all language relations are based on an 'interpretative charity'.

4 Wilhelm Dilthey, *Selected Works III: The Formation of the Historical World in the Human Sciences*, ed. with an Introduction by Rudolf A. Makkreel and Frithjof Rodi (Princeton, NJ and Oxford: Princeton University Press, 2002), 54.

5 Sande Cohen, *Historical Culture: On the Recoding of an Academic Discipline* (Berkeley: University of California Press, 1986). Indeed, Hayden White may in this sense be regarded as an anti-narrativist.

6 C. Behan McCullagh, *The Logic of History: Putting Postmodernism in Perspective* (London and New York: Routledge, 2004), 194.

7 Ibid.

8 It is useful to note that when we talk about the nature of history we are also bound to make judgements about its cultural functioning. See, for example, Martin L. Davies, *Historics: Why History Dominates Contemporary Society* (Abingdon and New York: Routledge, 2005). But a history may also examine the nature of that functioning and this inevitably raises the issue of the relationship between story and discourse. See for example Alun Munslow, *Discourse and Culture: The Creation of America, 1870–1920* (London and New York: Routledge, 1992). See also Marie-Laure Ryan, *Possible Worlds, Artificial Intelligence and Narrative Theory* (Bloomington, IN: University of Indiana Press, 1991); Catherine Emmott, *Narrative Comprehension: A Discourse Perspective* (Oxford: Oxford University Press, 1997); David Herman, *Story Logic: Problems and Possibilities of Narrative* (Lincoln, NE: University of Nebraska Press, 2002).

9 David W. Noble, *The Progressive Mind, 1890–1917* (Chicago: Rand McNally, 1970).

10 A recent attempt to rescue 'knowledge' from constructivism is Paul Boghossian, *Fear of Knowledge: Against Relativism and Constructivism* (Oxford: Oxford University Press, 2006).

11 John Patrick Diggins, *The Rise and Fall of the American Left* (New York and London: W.W. Norton, 1992 [1973]).

12 Ibid., 15–16.

13 Christopher Lasch, *The Agony of the American Left* (London: Andre Deutsch, 1970 [1966]).

14 Seymour Chatman, *Story and Discourse: Narrative Structure in Fiction and Film* (Ithaca and London: Cornell University Press, 1978), 96–145.

15 Gérard Genette, *Narrative Discourse*, trans. Jane E. Lewin (Oxford: Basil Blackwell, 1986 [1972]) and *Narrative Discourse Revisited*, trans. Jane E. Lewin

(Ithaca: New York, Cornell University Press, 1990 [1983]); Chatman, *Story and Discourse.*

16   Genette, *Narrative Discourse Revisited*, 13–20.
17   Ibid., 13.
18   Ibid., 14–15.
19   Ibid., 15.
20   Ibid., 15.
21   C. Ginzburg and A. Prosperi, *Giochi di Pazienza: Un Seminario sul 'Beneficio di Cristo'* (Turin: Einaudi, 1975). This book is examined by Jonathan Walker and the nature of the 'research and writing' process in generating history in his 'Let's Get Lost: On the Importance of Itineraries, Detours and Dead Ends', *Rethinking History: The Journal of Theory and Practice* 10, no. 4 (2006): 573–598.
22   Genette, *Narrative Discourse Revisited*, 16–17.
23   Ibid., 15.

▶ 2   History as Content/Story

1   Fredric Jameson, *The Political Unconscious: Narrative as a Socially Symbolic Act* (Ithaca: Cornell University Press, 1981), 35.
2   Frank, R. Ankersmit, *Historical Representation* (Stanford, CA: Stanford University Press, 2001), 81.
3   Ibid., 135–138.
4   This is a position argued for with great skill by Kalle Pihlainen. See his 'The Confines of the Form: Historical Writing and the Desire That It Be What It Is Not', in *Tropes for the Past: Hayden White and the History/Literature Debate*, ed. Kuisma Korhonen, 55–67.
5   Seymour Chatman, *Story and Discourse: Narrative Structure in Fiction and Film* (Ithaca and London: Cornell University Press, 1978), 19.
6   Janice Radway, *Reading the Romance: Women, Patriarchy, and Popular Literature* (Chapel Hill: University of North Carolina Press, 1984).
7   Roman Jakobson, 'Closing Statement: Linguistics and Poetics' in *Style in Language*, ed. Thomas Seboek (Cambridge, MA: Massachusetts of Technology Press, 1960); Roman Jakobson, *Selected Writings* edited in six volumes by Stephen Rudy (The Hague, Paris: Mouton, 1971–1985); Vladimir Propp, *Morphology of the Folk Tale* (Bloomington, IN: Indiana Research centre in Anthropology, 1958); Roland Barthes, 'Introduction to the Structural Analysis of Narratives', in *Barthes: Selected Writings*, ed. Sontag (Oxford: Fontana Collins, 1983), 251–252; Gérard Genette, *Narrative Discourse*, trans. Jane E. Lewin (Oxford: Basil Blackwell, 1986 [1972]) and *Narrative Discourse Revisited*, trans. Jane E. Lewin (Ithaca, NY: Cornell University Press, 1990 [1983]); A.J. Greimas,

Of Gods and Men: Studies in Lithuanian Mythology, trans. Milda Newman (Bloomington, IN: Indiana University Press 1992 [1985]); Tzvetan Todorov, 'La description de la signification en littérature', *Communications*, vol. 4 (1964): 33–39; Mink, 'Narrative Form as a Cognitive Instrument' reprinted in *The History and Narrative Reader*, ed. Roberts (London, New York: Routledge,2001), 211–220; Paul Ricoeur, *Time and Narrative*, trans. Kathleen McLaughlin and David Pellauer, vol. 1 (Chicago: University of Chicago Press, 1984).

8 Compare Eric Hobsbawm, *Industry and Empire: From 1750 to the Present Day* (Harmondsworth: Penguin Books, 1983 [1968]); with Charles More, *Understanding the Industrial Revolution* (London and New York: Routledge, 2000).

9 William Gallie, *Philosophy and the Historical Understanding* (London: Chatto & Windus, 1964), 21.

10 Chatman, *Story and Discourse*, 19.

11 Michael C. Lemon, *The Discipline of History and the History of Thought* (London and New York: Routledge, 1995), 43.

12 Paul Ricoeur, 'The Model of the Text: Meaningful Action Considered as a Text', *Social Research* 38, no. 3 (1971): 529–562.

13 Mary Rogers and Paola Tinagli, *Women in Italy, 1350–1650: Ideals and Realities* (Manchester and New York: Manchester University Press, 2006).

14 Ibid., 2.

15 White, 'An old question raised again: Is historiography art or science?' (Response to Iggers), *Rethinking History: The Journal of Theory and Practice*, 4 (2000): 391–406; White, *Figural Realism: Studies in the Mimesis Effect* (Baltimore: The Johns Hopkins University Press, 1998); White, *The Content of the Form: Narrative Discourse and Historical Representation* (Baltimore, London: The Johns Hopkins University Press, 1987); White, *Tropics of Discourse: Essays in Cultural Criticism*; White, *Metahistory*.

16 W.H. Walsh, *An Introduction to the Philosophy of History* (n.p.: Harvester Press, 1970 [1951]); Leon Goldstein, *Historical Knowing* (Austin: University of Texas Press, 1976); Arthur C. Danto, *Narration and Knowledge* (New York: Columbia University Press, 1985) and *Analytical Philosophy of History*; Dray, *Laws and Explanation in History*; Ricoeur, *Time and Narrative* (vol. 1); White, *Metahistory*; Ankersmit, *History and Tropology: The Rise and Fall of Metaphor* (Berkeley: University of California Press, 1994); and Ankersmit, *Historical Representation*.

17 John Tosh, *Manliness and Masculinities in Nineteenth Century Britain* (Harlow: Pearson Longman, 2005).

18 Ibid., 13.

19 Marwick, *The New Nature of History: Knowledge, Evidence, Language*, pp. 38–50.

20 Ankersmit, *History and Tropology: The Rise and Fall of Metaphor* and Ankersmit, *Sublime Historical Experience* (Stanford, CA: Stanford University Press, 2005).

21 Over the years, many historians have been evaluated in terms of the aesthetic (especially the figurative) character of their writings. A useful example is Maura B. Nolan, 'Metaphoric History: Narrative and New Science in the Work of F.W. Maitland', *Proceedings of the Modern Language Association* 118, no. 3 (2003): 557–572.

22 Saskia Sassen, 'The Global City: New York, London, Tokyo', in *The Global History Reader*, ed. Bruce Mazlish and Akira Iriye (New York and London: Routledge, 2005), 116–124.

23 Eelco Runia, 'Presence', *History and Theory* 45, no. 1 (2006): 1–29.

24 Stephen C. Pepper, *World Hypotheses* (Berkeley, Los Angeles and London: University of California Press, 1942), 84–114.

25 Barbara Melosh, ed., *Gender and American History Since 1890* (London and New York: Routledge, 1993); Jeremy Black, *A History of the British Isles* (Houndmills: Palgrave, 1997).

26 Peter Linebaugh and Marcus Rediker, *The Many-Headed Hydra: The Hidden History of the Revolutionary Atlantic* (London and New York: Verso, 2000); Jane Dailey, Glenda Elizabeth Gilmore and Bryant Simon, eds, *Jumpin' Jim Crow: Southern Politics from Civil War to Civil Rights* (Princeton and Oxford: Princeton University Press, 2000).

27 Melosh, ed., *Gender and American History Since 1890*, 1–13.

28 White, *Metahistory*; N. Frye, *Anatomy of Criticism: Four essays by Northrop Frye* (New York: Atheneum, 1967 [1957]).

29 Ricoeur, *Time and Narrative* (Vol. 1), 1; (Vol. 3), 185.

30 Ibid.

31 Propp, *Morphology of the Folk Tale*; Frye, *Anatomy of Criticism*; Greimas, *Of Gods and Men*; Todorov, *Communications*, 33–39; Gérard Genette, *Narrative Discourse*, trans. Jane E. Lewin (Cornell, Ithaca: Cornell University Press, 1980 [1972]); Mink, *The History and Narrative Reader*; Ricoeur, *Time and Narrative* (Vol. 1); K. Jenkins and A. Munslow, eds, *The Nature of History: A Reader* (London and New York: Routledge, 2004).

32 Ricoeur, *Time and Narrative* (Vol. 1); White, *Metahistory*; Mink, *The History and Narrative Reader*.

33 Mari Jo Buhle, Paul Buhle and Harvey J. Kaye, eds, *The American Radical* (New York and London: Routledge, 1994).

34 Erich Auerbach, *Mimesis: The Representation of Reality in Western Literature* (Princeton, NJ: Princeton University Press, 1953).

35 White, *Metahistory*; Frye, *Anatomy of Criticism*. Godard quote: courtesy of Robert Rosenstone's introduction to Alun Munslow and Robert A. Rosenstone, *Experiments in Rethinking History* (New York and London: Routledge, 2004), 1.

36 White, *Metahistory*, 7.

37 R.H. Tawney, *Religion and the Rise of Capitalism* (Harmondsworth: Penguin Books, 1966 [1926]).

38 Donald R. McCoy, *Coming of Age: The United States During the 1920s and 1930s* (Harmondsworth: Penguin Books, 1973).

39 Bryant Simon, 'Narrating a Southern Tragedy: Historical Facts and Historical Fictions', *Rethinking History: The Journal of Theory and Practice* 1, no. 2 (1997): 165–187.

40 John Y. Simons and Michael Stevens, *New Perspectives on the Civil War: Myths and Realities of the National Conflict* (Lanham, MD: Rowman and Littlefield, 2002 [1998]).

41 Richard Evans, *Telling Lies About Hitler: The Holocaust, History and the David Irving Trial* (London and New York: Verso, 2002), 23.

42 Martin Kreiswirth, 'Merely Telling Stories? Narrative and Knowledge in the Human Sciences', *Poetics Today* 21, no. 2 (2000): 311.

43 Beverley Southgate, ' "A Pair of White Gloves": Historians and Ethics', *Rethinking History: The Journal of Theory and Practice*, 10, no. 1 (2006): 49–62. We should also remember Ricoeur's distinction between ethics and morals. The former aims for the good and the just. Morals, however, concern sticking to rules of behaviour. The former always has priority over the latter.

44 Jeremy D. Popkin, *History, Historians and Autobiography* (Chicago: University of Chicago Press, 2005), 208.

45 Sue Morgan, ed., *The Feminist History Reader* (London and New York: Routledge, 2006).

46 David Henige, *Historical Evidence and Argument* (Madison, WI: University of Wisconsin Press, 2005), 242–243. Another modest historian is Richard Evans whose defence of history is troped in a humble fashion. Though unassuming before the data, he is, like Henige and Arthur Marwick, scrupulous and self-critical. All his conclusions are always less than final. See Evans' *In Defence of History* (London: Granta, 1997).

47 Ernst Breisach, *On the Future of History: The Postmodernist Challenge and Its Aftermath* (Chicago and London: University of Chicago Press, 2003), 74.

48 Ibid., 75.

49 Ibid., 107.

50 Ibid., 75.

51 Arthur Marwick, *The New Nature of History*, 153.

52 Ibid.

53 Arthur Marwick, *Class: Image and Reality in Britain, France and the USA Since 1930* (Glasgow: Fontana/Collins, 1980), 283.

54 Arthur Marwick, *The New Nature of History*, 156.

55 Ibid., 201.

56 Ibid., 195–240.

57 Kevin Passmore, 'Poststructuralism and History', in *Writing History: Theory and Practice*, ed. Stefan Berger, Heiko Feldner and Kevin Passmore (London: Hodder Arnold, 2003), 118–140.

▶ 3 Narrating and Narration

1 Gérard Genette, *Narrative Discourse*, trans. Jane E. Lewin (Oxford: Basil Blackwell, 1986 [1972]) and *Narrative Discourse Revisited*, trans. Jane E. Lewin (Ithaca, NY: Cornell University Press, 1990 [1983]).

2 Roland Barthes, 'The Death of the Author' in *Authorship: From Plato to Postmodernism: A Reader*, ed. Sean Burke (Edinburgh: Edinburgh University Press, 1995), 125–130; Foucault, 'What Is An Author?', in *Textual Strategies: Perspectives in Post-Structuralist Criticism*, ed. Harari (London: Methuen, 1979), 141–160.

3 Bernadine Dodge, 'Re-imag(in)ing the Past', *Rethinking History: The Journal of Theory and Practice* 10, no. 3 (2006): 345–368.

4 Marwick, *The New Nature of History: Knowledge, Evidence, Language*, 41. See also Foucault, *Textual Strategies*. Helpful to those who need a basic grounding in the theory of authorship is Andrew Bennett, *The Author* (New York and Abingdon: Routledge, 2005).

5 Moshe Lewin, *The Soviet Century* (London: Verso, 2005), vii.

6 This is like saying we can tell the truth about our pet cat or our neighbours simply by describing them in excruciating detail.

7 Robert A. Rosenstone, *Mirror in the Shrine: American Encounters with Meiji Japan* (Cambridge MA and London: Harvard University Press, 1988).

8 Richard Price, *Alabi's World* (Baltimore: Johns Hopkins University Press, 1990).

9 Wayne Booth, *The Rhetoric of Fiction* (Chicago: University of Chicago Press, 1961).

10 Ann Laura Stoler, ed., *Haunted By Empire: Geographies of Intimacy in North American History* (Durham and London: Duke University Press, 2006), 1.

11 Ibid., 4.

12 As we shall see, each mode of expression will potentially have a different narratee (sometimes called 'an addressee'). Also, when writing history books historians have to agree the market level for their audience with their publisher.

13 Gerald Prince, *Narratology: The Form and Functioning of Narrative* (Berlin: Mouton, 1982).

14 Foucault, *Textual Strategies*, 153.

15 E. Tonkin, *Narrating Our Pasts: The Social Construction of Oral History* (Cambridge: Cambridge University Press, 1992).

16 Jacquelyn Dowd Hall quoted in Vicki L. Ruiz and Ellen Carol DuBois, *Unequal Sisters: A Multicultural Reader in US Women's History* (New York and London: Routledge, 2000), xiii. All histories are voiced. A recent example of an overt authorial voice is the collection edited by Phillips *Deconstructing Sport History* that was deliberately constructed to explore developments in one particular form of history (sport) from a deconstructionist perspective. The contributors are overt narrators who openly voice their interventions.

17 Mieke Bal, 'Notes on Narrative Embedding', *Poetics Today* 2, no. 2 (1981): 41–59; Mieke Bal, 'The Narrating and the Focalizing: A Theory of the Agents in Narrative', *Style*, trans. Jane E. Lewin, 17 (1983): 234–269; Mieke Bal, *Narratology: Introduction to the Theory of Narrative* (Toronto: Toronto University Press, 1985); Monika Fludernik, 'New Wine in Old Bottles? Voice, Focalisation and New Writing', *New Literary History* 32, no. 3 (2001): 619–638.

18 Hayden White, 'The Structure of Historical Narrative', *Clio* 1 (1972): 5–19 and 'The Historical Text as Literary Artifact', in *Tropics of Discourse*, 81–100; Mink, 'Narrative Form as a Cognitive Instrument', reprinted in *The History and Narrative Reader*, ed. Roberts, 211–220; Chatman, *Story and Discourse*, 147; Paul Ricoeur, *Time and Narrative*, trans. Kathleen McLaughlin and David Pellauer, vol. 2 (Chicago: University of Chicago Press, 1984), 64–65, 88–99. The debate between Berel Lang and Hayden White on the most appropriate voice for the historian to take when talking about the Holocaust is only the most famous example of what is a common activity. See Berel Lang, *Act and Idea in the Nazi Genocide* (Chicago: University of Chicago Press, 1990) and Hayden White, 'Historical Emplotment and the Problem of Truth', in *Probing the Limits of Representation: Nazism and the 'Final Solution'*, ed. Saul Friedlander (Cambridge, MA: Harvard University Press, 1992), 37–53.

19 Hayden White has examined how humanist Marxist historian E.P. Thompson voiced and focalised (though White did not use these specific terms) in the 'Introduction' to his *Tropics of Discourse*, 15–20.

20 Ricoeur, *Time and Narrative* (Vol. 2), 64–65; see also Roland Barthes, 'To Write: An Intransitive Verb?', *The Rustle of Language*, trans. Richard Howard (Berkeley: University of California Press, 1989); Roland Barthes, *Roland Barthes* (New York: Hill & Wang, 1977).

21 Frank R. Ankersmit, *Encounters: Philosophy of History After Postmodernism*, ed. Ewa Domanska (Charlottesville: University of Virginia Press, 1998), 86–87.

22 The historian always has a perspective on the past – an angle from which events are refracted before they can be understood. As I have suggested, every history assumes a narratee – the readership – for whom the text is intended. This text, for example, is substantially driven by my (the narrator's) desire to be 'accessible' and not 'difficult'. I do not wish (partly at my publisher's behest)

to produce a 'monograph' that would be 'student unfriendly'. So I focalise diegetically as an overt narrator intervening within this narrative through my asides and direct speech to you. I am trying to create a mood of authorial interventionism but not omniscience that gives the impression that this is the way 'it is'. But, clearly, I have a point of view.

23 Quoted from Richard J. Carwardine's biography of Abraham Lincoln, *Lincoln* (Harlow and Essex: Pearson Longman, 2003), 83–84.

24 Ibid., p. 311.

25 Suzanne Fleischman, *Tense and Narrativity: From Medieval Performance to Modern Fiction* (London: Routledge, 1990).

26 Ibid., 24.

27 Paul Ricoeur, *Time and Narrative* (Vol. 3) (1987), 181.

28 The question of time is being investigated afresh by historians like Philip J. Ethington, who argues that historians need to acknowledge the relationship between space and time in their work. See Philip J. Ethington, 'Presenting the Past: The Places of History in the Spaces of Time', *Rethinking History: The Journal of Theory and Practice* (forthcoming).

29 Lawrence W. Levine, *Black Culture and Black Consciousness: Afro-American Folk Thought From Slavery to Freedom* (Oxford: Oxford University Press, 1977); Eugene D. Genovese, *Roll Jordan Roll: The World the Slaves Made* (New York, Vintage Books, 1972 [1974]).

30 William Gallie, *History and Religion* (Harlow and New York: Pearson, 2007), forthcoming.

31 Wilhem Dilthey, *Selected Works, Vol. III, The Formation of the Historical World in the Human Sciences*, ed. with an Introduction by Rudolf A. Makkreel and Frithjof Rodi (Princeton, NJ and Oxford: Princeton University Press, 2002), 9.

32 Surprisingly, perhaps, an analysis of the history of time in the work of historians managed to completely ignore the functioning of narrative in the 'timing' of history. See Dan Smail, 'In the Grip of Sacred History', *American Historical Review* 110, no. 5 (December 2005): 1337–1362.

33 Chatman, *Story and Discourse*, 46–47. And it is not good enough for historians to say history is a never-ending story. The movement of the past into the present and future might be the case (for all we know) but the history narrative is an artificial construction that imposes synthetic narrational structures and decisions on the past.

34 Metonymy is most usually associated with history prose because it is the trope that establishes contiguity between things – in this case Lincoln and an '. . . enhanced and ambitious nationalism'. According to the attested data, although Abraham Lincoln was born, lived and died, no historian starts and ends with this. Historians take this temporal reality and turn it into a narrative that can only 'explain' through a contrived and 'fictive' timing process. As Kuisima Korhonen notes, historical time is 'by definition' the time of writing,

'the time of written time and written documents'. See Korhonen, ed., *Tropes for the Past*, 9.

35 Ricoeur, *Time and Narrative* (Vol. 1), 3–86.

36 Ibid., 83–84. Aporia is a figure of speech in which a speaker is in doubt about what to say or decide. It is now increasingly taken to refer to the undecidability of the act or impasse where meaning cannot be resolved.

37 Munslow, *The New History*, 37–38.

38 Ricoeur, *Time and Narrative* (Vol. 2), 6, 100–152.

39 Ibid., 80; Genette, *Narrative Discourse* and *Narrative Discourse Revisited*.

40 Ricoeur, *Time and Narrative* (Vol. 2), 83.

41 Louis M. Hacker, *The Course of American Economic Growth and Development* (New York and London: John Wiley & Sons, 1970), 98.

42 Ricoeur, *Time and Narrative* (Vol. 2), 84.

43 David Hackett Fischer, *Paul Revere's Ride* (Oxford: Oxford University Press, 1994), 138.

44 Fernand Braudel, *A History of Civilizations* (New York: Penguin, 1993 [1987]), 226.

45 Andrew Pettegree, *Europe in the Sixteenth Century* (Oxford: Blackwell Publishers Ltd., 2002), 1–18.

46 F.R. Bridge and Roger Bullen, *The Great Powers and the European States System, 1814—1914*, 2nd ed. (Harlow: Pearson Education, 2005 [1980]).

47 Genette, *Narrative Discourse*, 113–160; Ricoeur, *Time and Narrative* (Vol. 2), 85.

48 The history of everyday life (*Alltagsgeschichte*) and mundane cultural practices might require a use of iteration.

49 Gary Gerstle, *Working Class Americanism: The Politics of Labor in a Textile City, 1914–1960* (Cambridge: Cambridge University Press, 1989).

50 Mikhail Bakhtin, *The Dialogic Imagination: Four Essays*, ed. Michael Holquist, trans. Caryl Emerson and Michael Holquist (Austin, TX: University of Texas Press, 1981), 84–85.

51 Quoted in Munslow, *Discourse and Culture*, 73.

52 Simon Dentith, *Bakhtinian thought: An Introductory Reader* (London and New York: Routledge, 1997).

53 Ricoeur, *Time and Narrative* (Vol. 2), 187.

54 A recent analysis of historian's intentionality deploying the role of newspapers in sport history is provided by Jeffrey Hill 'Re-Reading the Sporting Press', *Rethinking History: The Journal of Theory and Practice* 11 (2007) (forthcoming).

55 Bal, *Style*.

56 Pierre Bourdieu, *An Outline of a Theory of Practice*, trans. Richard Nice (Cambridge: Cambridge University Press, 1972).

57 Mark Bevir, *The Logic of the History of Ideas* (Cambridge: Cambridge University Press, 1999); Ankersmit, *Historical Representation*.

58 Robert Dallek, *Lone Star Rising: Lyndon Johnson and His Times, 1908–1960* (Oxford: Oxford University Press, 1991).

59 Wendell H. Oswalt and Sharlotte Neely, *This Land Was Theirs: A Study of North American Indians* (Mountain View, CA: Mayfield Publishing Company, 1996 [1988]); E.P. Thompson, *The Making of the English Working Class* (Harmondsworth: Penguin, 1968 [1963]), 13.

60 Not be confused with Ricoeur's process of mimesis$_1$, mimesis$_2$ and mimesis$_3$.

61 Robert A. Rosenstone, 'John Reed', in *The American Radical* (New York and London: Routledge, 1994), 143–149; Eric Homberger 'Reed, John, 1887–1920', in *Encyclopedia of the American Left*, ed. Mari Jo Buhle, Paul Buhle and Dan Georgakas (Chicago and London: St. James Press, 1990), 648.

62 See, for example, the characterisation of John Locke and his *Essay Concerning Human Understanding* in the work of Carl. Becker, *The Declaration of Independence* (New York: Alfred A. Knopf, 1922); Arthur M. Schlesinger, *The Birth of the Nation* (New York: Alfred A. Knopf, 1968) and Gordon S. Wood, *The Creation of the American Republic, 1776–1787* (New York and London: W.W. Norton, 1972 [1969]).

63 Alan Palmer, *Fictional Minds* (Lincoln: University of Nebraska Press, 2004); Jonathan Culpeper, *Language and Characterisation* (Harlow: Longman, 2001); James Phelan, *Reading People, Reading Plots* (Chicago: University of Chicago Press, 1989).

▶ 4 History as Expression

1 Barthes, 'Introduction to the Structural Analysis of Narratives', in *Barthes: Selected Writings*, ed. Sontag, 251.

2 The notion of 'realistic portrayal' is a classic realist oxymoron.

3 The fact that I am still using the printed book should not be taken as evidence of the incorrect nature of the argument. E-books are now making inroads and who can predict how soon printed pages will disappear entirely? Of course, as we shall see, digitised books remain locked into an epistemological world-view.

4 Richard J. Evans, 'Prologue: What is History Now?', in *What is History Now?*, ed. Cannadine (Houndmills: Palgrave, 2002), 13.

5 Undoubtedly the leading analyst of the epistemological relationship between film and history, Robert A. Rosenstone has produced an essential body of work. See 'The Future of the Past: Film and the Beginnings of Postmodern History', in *The Persistence of History: Cinema, Television and the Modern Event*, ed. Vivian Sobchack (New York: Routledge, 1996), 201–218; 'Does a Filmic

Writing of History Exist?', *History and Theory* 41, no. 4 (2002): 135–144; *Visions of the Past: The Challenge of Film to Our Idea of History* (Cambridge, MA: Harvard University Press, 1995); *Revisioning History: Film and the Construction of a New Past* (Princeton, NJ: Princeton University Press, 1995) and *History on Film/Film on History* (Harlow: Pearson Longman, 2006).

6 Oliver Daddow, 'Still No Philosophy Please, We're Historians', *Rethinking History: The Journal of Theory and Practice* 9, no. 4 (2005): 491–495.

7 Ibid.; see also Alun Munslow's 'Getting on with History', *Rethinking History: The Journal of Theory and Practice* 9, no. 4 (2005): 497–502.

8 See Rosenstone, 'The Future of the Past'; 'Does a Filmic Writing of History Exist?'; *Visions of the Past*; *Revisioning History*; *History on Film, Film on History*; Marc Ferro, *Cinema and History* (Detroit: Wayne State University Press, 1988) and 'Does and Filmic Writing of History Exist?', *Film and History* 17, no. 4 (1987): 81–89; Richard Allen, *Projecting Illusion: Film Spectatorship and the Impression of Reality* (Cambridge: Cambridge University Press, 1995); see also a series of articles in the 1988 *American Historical Review* Forum on film and history: Robert Brent Toplin 'The Filmmaker as Historian', *American Historical Review* 93, no. 5 (1988): 1210–1221; John E. O'Connor, 'History in Images/Images in History: Reflections on the Importance of Film and tele-vision Study for an Understanding of the Past' *American Historical Review* 93, no. 5 (1988): 1200–1209; Hayden White, 'Historiography and Historio-photy', *American Historical Review* 93, no. 5 (1988): 1193–1199; David Herlihy, 'Am I a Camera? Other reflections on Films and History', *American Histor-ical Review* 93, no. 5 (1988): 1186–1192 and Robert A. Rosenstone, 'History in Images/History in Words: Reflections on the Possibility of Really Putting History onto Film', *American Historical Review* 93, no. 5 (1988): 1173–1185; Pierre Sorlin, *The Film in History: Restaging the Past* (Totowa, NJ: Barnes and Noble Imports, 1980); Mark C. Carnes, ed., *Past Imperfect: History According to the Movies* (New York: Henry Holt & Co., 1995); Tony Barta, *Screening the Past: Film and the Representation of History* (Westport, CT: Praeger, 1998); Roland Barthes, 'The Realist Effect', *Film Reader No. 2* (Wisconsin: North West University Press, 1978), 131–135; Natalie Zemon Davis, ' "Any Resemb-lance to Persons Living or Dead": Film and the Challenge of Authenti-city', *Yale Review* 76 (Summer 1987): 477–502; Chatman, *Story and Discourse: Narrative Structure in Fiction and Film*; Tessa Morris-Suzuki, *The Past Within Us: Media. Memory and History* (London and New York: Verso, 2005); Siegfried Kracauer, *History: The Last things Before The Last* (Princeton: Marcus Wiener Publishers, 1995 [1965]); Susan Sontag, *On Photography* (New York: Farrar, Straus and Giroux, 1973); Robert Brent Toplin, *History By Hollywood: The Use and Abuse of the American Past* (Illinois: Illinois University Press, 1996); Robert A. Rosenstone, ed., 'Film and History' themed issue *of Rethinking History: The*

Journal of Theory and Practice 4, no. 2 (2000): 123–238; Willem Hesling, 'The ○ Past as Story: The Narrative Structure of Historical Films', *European Journal of Cultural Studies* 4, no. 2 (2001): 189–205; Marcia Landy, ed., *The Historical Film: History and Memory in Media* (Piscataway, NJ: Rutgers University Press, 2001). See also Nancy Armstrong, *Fiction in the Age of Photography: The Legacy of British Realism* (Cambridge, MA: Harvard University Press, 1999).

9 Robert A. Rosenstone, 'The Future of the Past'.

10 The literature on the epistemological character of the photographic image is substantial, but not to be missed are Roland Barthes, *Image, Music, Text*, trans. Stephen Heath (New York: Hill and Wang, 1977); J.J. Long, 'History, Narrative and Photography in W.G. Sebald's *Die Ausgewanderten*', *Modern Language Review* 98, no. 1 (2003): 117–137; Marie-Laure Ryan, 'The Modes of Narrativity and Their Visual Metaphors', *Style* 26 (1992): 368–387.

11 Siegfried Kracauer, *History: The Last things Before the Last*, completed by Oskar Christeller (Princeton, NJ: Markus Wiener Publishers, 1995 [1969]), 47.

12 Ibid., 46.

13 Ibid., 46–47.

14 Ibid., 32.

15 Of course shareholder profit remains a fixed point of reference as it does with films and as it does with history books as well.

16 Pierre Nora, *Les Lieux de mémoire/Realms of Memory: The Construction of the French Past*, trans. Arthur Goldhammer (New York: Columbia University Press, 1997).

17 Alison Landsberg, *Prosthetic Memory: The Transformation of American Remembrance in the Age of Mass Culture* (New York: Columbia University Press, 2004).

18 Ibid., 6.

19 TV historians also like to make a style statement – a long black overcoat, or jeans, or duster coat, or ill-conceived multi-coloured clothing.

20 Tuija Virtanen, 'Issues of test-Typology: Narrative – A "Basic" Type of Text?', *Text* 12 (1992): 293–310.

21 In much the same way global publishers today serve the undergraduate market by matching the intellectual demands of the text with a price.

22 A flavour of the range of radio history can be gauged from the description in the *BBC History Magazine* of a programme broadcast on BBC Radio 4 on 22 December 2005, entitled 'The True and Inspirational Life of St. Nicholas' as an attempt to '. . . restore Santa to his original identity – as a fourth century Christian hardliner, battling heretics and toeing a fiercely orthodox line. David and Caroline Stafford's rollicking drama suggests that the ascetic Nicholas would struggle to recognise himself in today's well-padded Father Christmas', *BBC History Magazine* 6, no. 12 (2005): 65.

23 Hugo Frey and Benjamin Noys, 'History in the Graphic Novel', in *Rethinking History: The Journal of Theory and Practice* 6 (2002): 255–260.

24 Ibid., 255.

25 Art Spiegelman, *Maus I: A Survivor's Tale: My father Bleeds History* (New York: Pantheon, 1986); Art Spiegelman, *Maus II: A Survivor's Tale: And Here My Troubles Began* (New York: Pantheon, 1991) and Art Spiegelman, *Comix, Essays, Graphics and Scraps* (New York: A Raw Book, 1998); White, 'Historical Emplotment and the Problem of Truth', in *Probing the Limits of Representation: Nazism and the 'Final Solution'*, ed. Friedlander, 37–53.

26 Will Eisner, *Comics and Sequential Art* (Tamarac: Poorhouse Press, 1990 [1985]).

27 W.J.T. Mitchell, *Picture Theory* (Chicago: University of Chicago Press, 1994).

28 Eli Bartra and John Mraz, 'Las Dos Fridas: History and Transcultural Identities', *Rethinking History: The Journal of Theory and Practice* 9, no. 4 (2005): 449–457.

29 Stuart Hood and Litza Jansz, *Fascism for Beginners* (Cambridge: Icon Books, 1993), 15.

30 *BBC History Magazine*, any issue.

31 Jay Winter, *Sites of Memory, Sites of Mourning: The Great War in European Cultural History* (Cambridge: Cambridge University Press, 1998 [1995]); Nora, *Les Lieux de mémoire/Realms of Memory: The Construction of the French Past*, trans. Arthur Goldhammer (New York: Columbia University Press, 1997); Kerwin Lee Klein, 'On the Emergence of Memory in Historical Discourse', *Representations* 69 (Winter 2000): 127–150; Max Page and Randall Mason, eds, *Giving Preservation a History* (New York and London: Routledge, 2004).

32 Ian Tyrell, *Historians in Public: The Practice of American History, 1890–1970* (Chicago, IL: University of Chicago Press, 2006).

33 Barthes, 'Introduction to the Structural Analysis of Narratives' in *Barthes: Selected Writings*, ed. Sontag, 252.

34 White, 'The Value of Narrativity in the Representation of Reality' in *The Content of the Form*, 1.

35 Hayden White, 'The Public Relevance of Historical Studies: A Reply to Dirk Moses', *History and Theory* 44, no. 3 (2005): 333–338. His claim is, of course, only provocative to those who are provoked.

36 Ibid., 335.

37 Susan Davies, 'History and Heritage', in *Making History: An Introduction to the History and Practices of a Discipline*, ed. Lambert and Schofield, 280–289.

38 Susan Porter Benson, Stephen Briar and Roy Rosenzweig, eds, *Presenting the Past: Essays on History and the Public* (Philadelphia: Temple University Press, 1986); Roy Rosenzweig and David Thelen, *The Presence of the Past* (New York: Columbia University Press, 1998); Randolph Starn, 'A Historian's Brief Guide

to New Museum Studies', *The American Historical Review* 110, no. 1 (2005): 68–98.

39 Ludmilla Jordanova, *History in Practice* (London: Arnold, 2000), 141. See also the special issue of the *Journal of American History* on 'The Practice of American History', 81, no. 3 (1994): 933–1217, which deals at great length with many aspects of public history in the United States.

40 Raphael Samuel, *Theatres of Memory*, 2 vols (London: Verso, 1994, 1998); Starn, *The American Historical Review*, 91.

41 Peter Burke, 'Performing History: The Importance of Occasions', *Rethinking History: The Journal of Theory and Practice* 9, no. 1 (2005), 35–52. See also Alexander Kozin and Katharina Draheim, 'A Standoff with History: At the Site of the "Bad River Gathering"', *Rethinking History: The Journal of Theory and Practice* 12 (forthcoming, 2008), which addresses the making and re-making of history at the site of performance.

42 Deborah Gilbert, 'Sarah Winnemucca Hopkins: Reformer, Activist and Educator: Teaching Western History in the First Person', *Journal of the West* 43 (Fall 2004): 24–31; Stacey F. Roth, *Past into Present: Effective Techniques for First Person Historical Interpretation* (Chapel Hill, NC: University of North Carolina Press, 1999).

43 R.G. Collingwood, *The Idea of History*, rev. ed., ed. Jan van der Dussen (Oxford: Oxford University Press, 1994 [1946]); W.H. Dray, *History As Reenactment: R.G. Collingwood's Idea of History* (Oxford: Clarendon Press, 1995). See also Karsten R. Stueber's argument that reenactment is the primary way to explain the reality of the past, 'The Psychological Basis of Historical Explanation: Reenactment, Simulation, and the Fusion of Horizons', *History and Theory* 41, no. 1 (2002): 25–42.

44 Anthony E. Pattiz, 'The Idea of History Teaching: Using Collingwood's Idea of History to Promote Critical Thinking in the High School Classroom', *The History Teacher* 37, no. 2 (February 2004): 239–250.

45 There is also the not-so-small problem with first-person interpretation of the mock-heroic – an ironic burlesque style on the part of the interpreter – that is amusingly incongruous and ahistorical.

46 David Harlan, 'Editorial', *Rethinking History: The Journal of Theory and Practice* 8, no. 2 (2004): 186.

47 Ibid., 187.

48 The reason David J. Staley thinks history will be radically altered in its thinking as well as its practice by digitisation is that it will make history (again) like science. Briefly, new technological practices will open up new modes of cognition mainly by doing away with conventional notions of storytelling which are linear and artificial. See David J. Staley, *Computers, Visualization, and History: How New Technology Will Transform Our Understanding of the Past* (Armonk, NY: M.E. Sharpe, 2002).

49 Mark Poster, 'Manifesto for a History of the Media', in *Manifestos for Historians*, ed. Keith Jenkins, Sue Morgan and Alun Munslow (London and New York: Routledge, 2007), forthcoming.

50 Lev Manovich, *The Language of New Media* (Cambridge, MA: Massachusetts Institute of Technology Press, 2001); Marie-Laure Ryan, *Possible Worlds, Artificial Intelligence and Narrative Theory* (Bloomington, IN: University of Indiana Press, 1991); Janet H. Murray, *Hamlet on the Holodeck: The Future of Narrative in Cyberspace* (Cambridge, MA: Massachusetts Institute of Technology Press, 1997).

51 Michael J. Guasco, 'Building the Better Textbook: The Promises and Perils of E-Publication', *The Journal of American History* 89, no. 4 (2003), http://www.historycooperative.org/journals/jah/89.4/guasco.html (accessed September 5, 2005).

52 Jerome Bruner, *Acts of Meaning* (Cambridge, MA: Harvard University Press, 1990); White, 'The Value of Narrativity in the Representation of Reality', *The Content of the Form*, 1–25; Monika Fludernik, *Towards a 'Natural' Narratology* (London and New York: Routledge, 1996).

▶ 5 The Past, the Facts and History

1 Frank R. Ankersmit, 'The Dilemma of Contemporary Anglo-Saxon Philosophy of History' in *History and Tropology: The Rise and Fall of Metaphor* (Berkeley: University of California Press, 1994), 44–74.

2 Morgan, ed., *The Feminist History Reader*, 1.

3 Ricoeur, *Time and Narrative*, 3 (1988), 181.

4 Patrick Gardiner, *The Nature of Historical Explanation* (Oxford, Oxford University Press, 1952); C. Behan McCullagh, *The Truth of History* (London and New York: Routledge, 1998) and *The Logic of History: Putting Postmodernism into Perspective*; Martin Bunzl, *Real History* (London and New York: Routledge, 1997); Searle, *The Construction of Social Reality*; Perez Zagorin, 'History, the referent, and narrative. Reflections on Postmodernism now', *History and Theory* 38 (1999); David Carr, 'Narrative and the Real World: An Argument for Continuity', *History and Theory* 25 (1986): 117–131; David Carr, *Time, Narrative and History* (Bloomington: Indiana University Press, 1991 [1986]); David Carr, 'Getting the Story Straight: Narrative and Historical Knowledge', *Historiography Between Modernism and Postmodernism: Contributions to the Methodology of the Historical Research*, ed. Jerzy Topolski (Amsterdam and Atlanta: Rodopi, 1994), 119–134; William H. Dray 'Narrative and Historical Realism' reprinted in Roberts, ed., *The History and Narrative Reader*, 157–180; Dray, *Laws and Explanation in History*; Andrew P. Norman, 'Telling it Like it was: Historical Narratives on their Own Terms' reprinted in Roberts, ed., *The History and Narrative Reader*,

181–196; John Zammito, 'Ankersmit and Historical Representation', *History and Theory*, 44, no. 2 (2005): 164.

5 G.W.F. Hegel, *The Philosophy of History*, trans. J. Sibree (New York: Dover Publications, 1956), 60–61.

6 Searle, *The Construction of Social Reality*, 154–155.

7 Donald Davidson, 'Is Truth a Goal of Inquiry? Discussion with Rorty', *Donald Davidson: Truth, Meaning and Knowledge*, ed. Urszula M. Zeglen (Abingdon and New York, 2006 [1999]), p. 17.

8 Rorty, *Philosophy and the Mirror of Nature*; Ankersmit, *Historical Representation*; Ankersmit, 'The Dilemma of Contemporary Anglo-Saxon Philosophy of History', in *History and Tropology: The Rise and Fall of Metaphor*, 44–74.

9 Mink, 'Narrative Form as a Cognitive Instrument' reprinted in Roberts, ed., *The History and Narrative Reader*, 211–220.

10 Jerome Bruner, 'The Narrative Construction of Reality', *Critical Inquiry* 31 (1991): 1–21; Danto, *Narration and Knowledge*; Mink, 'Narrative Form as a Cognitive Instrument' reprinted in Roberts, ed., *The History and Narrative Reader*, 211–220; Frank R. Ankersmit, 'Six Theses on Narrativist *Philosophy of History*', in *History and Tropology: The Rise and Fall of Metaphor*, 33–43.

11 David Harlan, 'Intellectual History and the Return of Literature' *AHR* Forum, *American Historical Review* 94, no. 3 (1989): 581–609.

12 Claire Norton, 'Fiction or Non-fiction? Ottoman Accounts of the Siege of Nagykanizsa', *Tropes for the Past: Hayden White and the History/Literature Debate*, ed. Korhonen (Amsterdam, New York: Rodophi, 2006), 119–130.

13 Manuscript accounts generated over 200 years of a Habsburg siege of the Ottoman-held castle of Nagykanizsa in present-day Hungary. Ibid.

14 Ibid., 127.

15 Lee Benson, *The Concept of Jacksonian Democracy: New York as a Test Case* (New York: Atheneum, 1964 [1961]), vii. Reconstructionists would say they are testing their 'assumptions'.

16 Note the implicit opposition between 'concept' and 'fiction'.

17 Benson, *The Concept of Jacksonian Democracy: New York as a Test Case*, 335.

18 Ankersmit, *History and Tropology: The Rise and Fall of Metaphor*, 6.

19 A view expressed by David Henige as a 'characteristic of postmodern argument', *Historical Evidence and Argument*, 24.

20 Ibid., 25.

21 William Pencak, 'The American Civil War Did Not Take Place: With Apologies to Baudrillard', *Rethinking History: The Journal of Theory and Practice* 6, no. 2 (2002): 217–221.

22 Elizabeth Deeds Ermarth, 'The Closed Space of Choice: A Manifesto on the Future of History', *Manifestos for Histories*, ed. Jenkins, Morgan and Munslow (London, New York: Routledge, 2007), forthcoming.

23 Barthes, 'Le Discours de l'histoire', *Information sur les Sciences Sociales* (1981 [1967]), 65–75.

24 Ibid.

25 Frederick A. Olafson, *The Dialectic of Action* (Chicago: University of Chicago Press, 1979).

26 Bevir, *The Logic of the History of Ideas* (Cambridge: Cambridge University Press, 1999).

27 Geoffrey Roberts, 'Narrative History as a Way of Life', *Journal of Contemporary History* 31 (1996): 221–228.

28 Arguably the two central myths of nineteenth-century bourgeois society were the knowing subject and, consequently, their agency.

29 Ricoeur, *Time and Narrative* 1 (1984): 49.

30 Ibid., 50.

31 Hans Ulrich Gumbrecht, *In 1926: Living at the Edge of Time* (Cambridge, MA: Harvard University Press, 1997).

32 Hayden White, 'Introduction: Historical Fiction, Fictional History, and Historical Reality', *Rethinking History: The Journal of Theory and Practice* 9 (2005): 147–157.

33 Ankersmit, *History and Tropology: The Rise and Fall of Metaphor*, 113–115.

34 Jean Baudrillard, *The Intelligence of Evil or the Lucidity Pact,* trans. Chris Turner (Oxford and New York: Berg, 2005 [2004]), 39.

35 Ibid.

36 Ibid., 41.

37 An extremely lucid description of and commentary on the concept of narrative substance is provided by Keith Jenkins, *Why History? Ethics and Postmodernity*, 132–160.

38 Howard Zinn, *A People's History of the United States: From 1492 to the Present* (London and New York: Longman); C.M.H. Clark, *A History of Australia*, 6 vols (Melbourne: Melbourne University Press, 1962–1987).

39 Hélène Bowen Raddeker, *Sceptical History: Postmodernism, Feminism and the Practice of History* (New York and London: Routledge, 2007).

▶ 6 Understanding [in] History

1 I have written about this process previously. For a far more detailed treatment see Munslow, *The New History*.

2 Still the best introduction to issue of historical explanation is William Dray's famous account *Laws and Explanation in History*. By far the most accessible, short and lucid recent study of historical explanation from a classic empirical-analytical position is that of the realist philosopher of history

C. Behan McCullagh, *The Logic of History: Putting Postmodernism in Perspective*. See Chapter 8 for his incisive analysis. See also Stephen Davies, *Empiricism and History* (Houndmills: Palgrave, 2003).

3 Carl G. Hempel, *Aspects of Scientific Explanation* (New York: The Free Press, 1965); Karl Popper, *The Logic of Scientific Discovery* (New York: Basic Books, 1959). See also Gardiner, *The Nature of Historical Explanation* for the classic defence of the covering law model.

4 Joel Perlmann, *Ethnic Differences: Schooling and Social Structure Among the Irish, Italians, Jews and Blacks in an American City, 1880–1935* (Cambridge: Cambridge University Press, 1988).

5 Ibid., 219.

6 An excellent introduction to developments in historical thinking and practice is MacRaild and Taylor, *Social Theory and Social History*.

7 Gabrielle M. Spiegel, *Practicing History: New Directions in Historical Writing After the Linguistic Turn* (New York and London: Routledge, 2005), 1–2.

8 Carla Hesse, 'The New Empiricism', *Cultural and Social History* 1 (2004): 201–207.

9 A brief examination of the concept of historicism and what it means to historians can be found in Alun Munslow, 'Historicism' in *The Routledge Companion to Historical Studies*, Second Edition (London and New York: Routledge, 2006), 140–142.

10 White, *Figural Realism*; Markku Lehtimäki, 'History as Crazy House: Norman Mailer, Hayden White, and the Representation of a Modernist Event', *Tropes for the Past: Hayden White and the History/Literature Debate*, ed. Korhonen, 135–150.

11 Dray, *Laws and Explanation in History*, 156–169.

12 Chris Ward, 'Lenin's Death in the British Press', *Rethinking History: The Journal of Theory and Practice* 10, no. 4 (2006): 599–630.

13 Bevir, *The Logic of the History of Ideas*, 31.

14 I.A. Richards, *The Philosophy of Rhetoric* (Oxford: Oxford University Press, 1936), 3.

15 As Wittgenstein argued in the latter part of his career, meaning can only be grasped as part of the larger set of rules that govern its creation. Arguably, only the briefest acquaintance with history as a narrative-making activity confirms the truth of this. This suggests that the variety of turns, linguistic, narrative, aesthetic, cultural and even ethical, are incommensurate with the empirical-analytical unless the latter can be incorporated within them.

16 It is a fundamental error, though one still regularly made by a few classic realist historians, that those colleagues they refer to as 'epistemological sceptics' are saying that it is impossible to understand not just the meaning of the past, but derive any meaning. This is neither a new argument nor any

less spurious because its central assumption is false. This is that there must be two opposite and necessarily hostile approaches to the past – either you know what it means epistemologically or you don't. The Italian historian Benedetto Croce (1866–1952) and the British idealist-influenced philosopher of history R.G. Collingwood (1889–1943) disposed of this odd notion a good while ago. Both agreed it is only because we all share the same constituent of thought and cognition, that is, language, that we can possibly provide a culturally useful (and factually based of course) meaning for the past. See also Antoine Prost, *Republican Identities in War and Peace: Representations of France in the Nineteenth and Twentieth Centuries* (Oxford and New York: Berg, 2002). See also Raddeker, *Sceptical History, op. cit.*

17   The list of potential references here is huge. The following are merely indicative. See, for example, Donald Davidson's collection *Inquiries into Truth and Interpretation*; Bruner, *Acts of Meaning*; Paul Ricoeur, *The Rule of Metaphor: Multidisciplinary Studies of the Creation of Meaning in Language*, trans. Robert Czerny (London and New York: Routledge, 1994 [1978]); Gottlob Frege, *Collected Papers* (Oxford: Oxford University Press, 1984); Rorty, *Philosophy and the Mirror of Nature*; White, 'The Historical Text as a Literary Artifact', *Tropics of Discourse*, 81–100; Perez Zagorin, 'History, the Referent, and Narrative. Reflections on Postmodernism now', *History and Theory*, 38 (1999): 1–24; John E. Toews, 'Intellectual history after the linguistic turn: The autonomy of meaning and the irreducibility of experience', *American Historical Review* 92 (1987): 879–907; Nelson Goodman, *Ways of Worldmaking* (Indianapolis and Cambridge: Hackett, 1978).

18   J.L. Austin, *How to Do Things with Words* (Oxford: Clarendon Press, 1975 [1962]).

19   Paul S. Boyer *et al. The Enduring Vision: A History of the American People* (Boston and New York: Houghton Mifflin, 2005), 205.

20   Science claims to escape this – which leads to the grotesque notion that truth is what science tells us it is.

21   C. Behan McCullagh, *Justifying Historical Descriptions* (Cambridge: Cambridge University Press, 1984), *The Truth of History* and *The Logic of History: Putting Postmodernism in Perspective*, pp. 18–42.

22   Ibid., 19.

23   McCullagh, *The Logic of History: Putting Postmodernism in Perspective*, 18–36.

24   Ankersmit, *Sublime Historical Experience*, 79.

25   Ibid., 96.

26   Terry Eagleton, *Literary Theory: An Introduction* (Oxford: Blackwell, 1983), 68.

27   White, *An Old Question Raised Again: Is Historiography Art or Science* (Response to Iggers), 391–406; White, *Figural Realism: Studies in the Mimesis Effect*; White, *The Content of the Form*; White, *Tropics of Discourse*; White, *Metahistory*.

28   Wolfgang Iser, *The Act of Reading: A Theory of Aesthetic Response* (Baltimore, Johns Hopkins University Press, 1978).
29   David Carr, 'Narrative and the Real World: An Argument for Continuity', *History and Theory*, 131.
30   Ibid., 117–131.
31   Palmer, *Descent into Discourse: The Reification of Language and the Writing of Social History*.
32   Hutcheon, *The Politics of Postmodernism*, 63.
33   Robert H. Zieger, *America's Great War: World War 1 and the American Experience* (Boston and Oxford: Rowman and Littlefield, 2000), 230–232.
34   Edmund Morris, *Dutch: A Memoir of Ronald Reagan* (New York: Random House, 1999).
35   Ankersmit, *Sublime Historical Experience*, 55; Robert A Rosenstone, 'Introduction: Practice and Theory', *Experiments in Rethinking History*, Munslow and Rosenstone (eds), 1.
36   Ibid.
37   Ibid., 2.
38   Ibid.
39   Greg Dening, 'Writing, Re-writing the Beach: An Essay', *Experiments in Rethinking History*, ed. Munslow and Rosenstone (London, New York: Routledge, 2004), 30–55.
40   White, *Figural Realism*.
41   Sumiko Higashi, 'Not a "Kodak Moment": Picturing Asian Americans', *Experiments in Rethinking History*, ed. Munslow and Rosenstone (London, New York: Routledge, 2004), 77–83.
42   Henry Adams, *The Education of Henry Adams* (New York: The Modern Library, 1931 [1918]).
43   Walter Benjamin, *The Arcades Project* (Cambridge, MA: The Belknap Press of Harvard University Press, 1999). See also 'Walter Benjamin: The Arcades Project' in *The Nature of History Reader*, Jenkins and Munslow (eds), 135–141.
44   Gumbrecht, *In 1926: Living at the Edge of Time*, x.
45   Synthia Sydnor, 'A History of Synchronised Swimming', *Journal of Sport History* 25, no. 2 (1998): 252–267.
46   Ibid., 260.
47   Robert A. Rosenstone, *The Man Who Swam into History* (Bloomington, IL, 1st Books, 2002).
48   Sven Lindqvist, *A History of Bombing* (New York: W.W. Norton, 2003 [2001]).
49   Hans-Robert Jauss, *Toward an Aesthetic of Reception*, trans. Timothy Bahti (Minneapolis: University of Minnesota Press, 1982).
50   Ankersmit, *Sublime Historical Experience*.

51 Fauvism was the first major aesthetic movement of the last century founded on a belief in the absolutism and intensity of colour (form) and represented by painters like Matisse and later Dufy and Braque.
52 There can be histories that combine both.

▶ 7 The Oar in Water

1 Resulting from the narrative decisions they make, every historian has his or her own style of course.
2 Tamsin Spargo, ed., *Reading the Past: Literature and History* (Houndmills and New York: Palgrave, 2000).
3 The key articles are collected in Paul Ricoeur, *History and Truth*, trans. and introduced by Charles A. Kelbley (Evanston: Northwestern University Press, 1965 [1955]).
4 Antoinette Burton ed., *Archive Stories: Facts, Fictions and the Writing of History* (Durham and London: Duke University Press, 2005)
5 Deborah A. Symonds, 'Living in the Scottish Record Office', *Reconstructing History*, ed. Elizabeth Fox-Genovese and Elisabeth Lasch-Quinn (New York and London: Routledge, 1999), 164–175; Durba Ghosh, 'National Narratives and the Politics of Miscegenation: Britain and India', *Archive Stories: Facts, Fictions and the Writing of History*, ed. Burton, 27–44.
6 C. Behan McCullagh, 'Bias in Historical Description, Interpretation, and Explanation', *History and Theory*, 39–66.
7 Paul Ricoeur, 'Objectivity and Subjectivity in History', in Ricoeur, *History and Truth*, Kelbley, 21–40.
8 Ibid., 25.
9 Ibid., 31.
10 Ankersmit, *Sublime Historical Experience*, 98–105.
11 Ibid., 197–198.
12 More radically, the French psychoanalyst Jacques Lacan has explored the notion of 'symbolic order' whereby, as he argues, for human beings the world (of things) is created by (the world of) words. See Jacques Lacan, *Ecrits: A Selection*, trans. Alan Sheridan (London: Routledge, 1977).
13 McCullagh, *The Truth of History*, 5, 13–57.
14 John Burnett, *England Eats Out: 1830-Present* (Harlow: Pearson Longman, 2004), 108.
15 Michael Oakeshott, *Experience and Its Modes* (Cambridge: Cambridge University Press, 1990 [1933]); Goldstein, *Historical Knowing*.
16 I have dealt with these theories of truth in more detail elsewhere. See Munslow, *The New History*, 80–98.

17 Lemon, *Philosophy of History: A Guide for Students*, 339.
18 E. Guba, and Y. Lincoln, 'Competing Paradigms in Qualitative Research', *Handbook of Qualitative Research*, ed. N. Denzin and Y. Lincoln (London: Sage, 1994), 105–117.
19 J. Bruner, 'Life as Narrative', *Social Research* 54, no. 1 (1987): 11–32.
20 Glory tells the story of the 54th Massachusetts Volunteer Infantry, an early African American military unit in the American Civil War largely through the documented voice of its abolitionist colonel.
21 Gadamer, *Truth and Method*; Martin Heidegger, *Being and Time*, trans. J. Macquarrie and E. Robinson (Oxford: Basil Blackwell, 1962); Michel Foucault, *Power/Knowledge: Selected Interviews and Other Writings, 1972–1877*, ed. Colin Gordon (Brighton: Harvester Press, 1980); Rorty, *Objectivity, Relativism and Truth: Philosophical Papers Vol. 1*; Bruner, *Actual Minds, Possible Worlds*.
22 Chatman, *Story and Discourse: Narrative Structure in Fiction and Film*, 96–145.
23 Although White's position has been roundly attacked by the realist philosopher Bernard Williams. See Bernard Williams, *Truth and Truthfulness: An Essay in Genealogy* (Princeton: Princeton University Press, 2002).
24 Donald P. Spence, *Narrative Truth and Historical Truth: Meaning and Interpretation in Psychoanalysis* (New York: Norton, 1982).
25 Hilary Putnam, *Realism with a Human Face*, James Conant, ed. (Cambridge, MA, Harvard University Press, 1990), 15.
26 While it should by now not be necessary, I feel obliged once again to reassure reconstructionists and constructionists by reiterating that this does not mean the exclusion of the existence of evidentially justified belief.
27 Marwick, *The New Nature of History: Knowledge, Evidence, Language*, 38–50.

▶ Conclusion

1 Genette, *Narrative Discourse*, 27.
2 Peter Gay, *Style in History: Gibbon, Ranke, Macaulay, Burckhardt* (New York and London: W.W. Norton, 1988 [1974]), 217; Chris Lorenz, 'Can Histories be True? Narrativism, Positivism, and the Metaphorical Turn', *History and Theory* 37 (1998): 309–329.

Further reading

▶ **Introduction**

If there is one fundamental argument in this book, it is that the nature of history depends on the historian's epistemological choice(s). This necessitates some idea about the theory and nature of knowledge itself. This is well provided in three books: Jonathan Dancy, *An Introduction to Contemporary Epistemology* (Oxford, 1985), Robert Audi, *Epistemology: A Contemporary Introduction to the Theory of Knowledge* (New York, 1998), and David Cooper, *Epistemology: The Classic Readings* (Oxford, 1999). Historians do not have to be philosophers but we need a basic understanding of the epistemological connection between past existence and present knowledge. This is why we also need an understanding of the ontology of the history narrative and also the historian's own ontological commitments. I recommend Reinhardt Grossmann, *The Existence of the World: An Introduction to Ontology* (London, 1992), and Chapter 2 in Robert Nozick, *Philosophical Explanations* (Oxford, 1981). A recent examination of epistemological scepticism is to be found in Hélène Bowen Raddeker, *Sceptical History: Postmodernism, Feminism and the Practice of History* (London and New York, 2007).

Several texts provide a good starting point for the understanding of the relationship between narrative and history. These include William Gallie's *Philosophy and the Historical Understanding* (London, 1964), W.H. Walsh, *An Introduction to the Philosophy of History* (Place of publication unknown, 1970 [1951]), Leon Goldstein, *Historical Knowing* (Austin, 1976), Arthur C. Danto, *Narration and Knowledge* (New York, 1985) and *Analytical Philosophy of History* (Cambridge, 1965) and William Dray, *Laws and Explanation in History* (Oxford, 1966 [1957]). Of crucial importance is Paul Ricoeur, 'Narrative Time' in *On Narrative*, edited by W.J.T. Mitchell (Chicago, 1981), pp. 168–186. See, in addition, Paul Ricoeur's essential three volumes *Time and Narrative*, trans. Kathleen McLaughlin and David Pellauer (Vols 1 and 2) and Kathleen Blamey and David Pellauer (Vol. 3) (Chicago, 1983–1985). The classic texts on narrative and history remain Hayden White, *Metahistory: The Historical Imagination in Nineteenth Century Europe* (Baltimore, 1973) and Michel de Certeau, *The Writing of History*, trans. Tom Conley (New York, 1988). See also the more basic introductions (which also assume a broad epistemologically sceptical stance) by Alun Munslow, *The New History* (Harlow, 2003) and *The Routledge Companion to Historical Studies* (London and New York, 2006 [2000]). Although it has omissions, the best-collected introduction to narrative and history is Geoffrey Roberts (ed.), *The History and Narrative Reader* (London and New York, 2001). Also useful is Martin McQuillan (ed.), *The Narrative Reader* (London and New York, 2000). The indispensable survey of narrative thinking and practice is the *Routledge Encyclopedia of Narrative Theory* edited by David Herman, Manfred Jahn and Marie-Laure Ryan (Abingdon and New York, 2005).

On the broader impact of narrative thinking and practice see Jerome Bruner, *Actual Minds, Possible Worlds* (Cambridge, MA, 1986), Martin Kreiswirth, 'Narrative Turn in the Humanities' in the *Routledge Encyclopedia of Narrative Theory* edited by David Herman, Manfred Jahn and Marie-Laure Ryan (Abingdon and New York, 2005), pp. 377–382 and Jürgen Straub (ed.), *Narration, Identity and Historical Consciousness* (New York, 2005). The nature of representation is well addressed in Linda Hutcheon, *The Politics of Postmodernism* (Abingdon and New York, 2005 [1989]).

The work of Gérard Genette and Seymour Chatman are, of course, pivotal to understanding the nature of narrative and history. See Genette's *Figures* (Paris, 1966), *Narrative Discourse*, trans. Jane E. Lewin (Oxford, 1986 [1972]) and *Narrative Discourse Revisited*, trans. Jane E. Lewin (Ithaca, 1990 [1983]) and Seymour Chatman, *Story and Discourse: Narrative Structure in Fiction and Film* (Ithaca and London, 1978). The range of work on history and narrative has grown substantially in the past 10 years. Representative are Dorrit Cohn, *The Distinction of Fiction* (Baltimore and London, 1999), and Sande Cohen, *History Out of Joint: Essays on the Use and Abuse of History* (Baltimore and London, 2005). The major figure working today on narrative and the representational nature of history is undoubtedly Frank R. Ankersmit. His main texts are *Narrative Logic: A Semantic Analysis of the Historian's Language* (The Hague, 1983), *History and Tropology: The Rise and Fall of Metaphor* (Berkeley, 1994), *Historical Representation* (Stanford, 2001) and most recently *Sublime Historical Experience* (Stanford, 2005) and with Hans Kellner (eds) *A New Philosophy of History* (Chicago, 1995).

The conventional understanding of history as an empirical-analytical endeavour is nowhere better examined than in C. Behan McCullagh, *The Logic of History: Putting Postmodernism in Perspective* (London and New York, 2004), and 'Bias in Historical Description, Interpretation, and Explanation', *History and Theory*, 39, 1 (2000), pp. 39–66. The notion of reality is addressed accessibly by John Searle, *The Construction of Social Reality* (London, 1995), and the wide-ranging study of Aviezer Tucker, *Our Knowledge of the Past: A Philosophy of Historiography* (New York, 2004). A substantial application and critical appraisal of the reconstructionist, constructionist and deconstructionist epistemological model can be found in Douglas

Booth, *The Field: Truth and Fiction in Sport History* (London and New York, 2005). See also the collection edited by Murray G. Phillips, *Deconstructing Sport History: A Postmodern Analysis* (Albany, 2006).

▶ Chapter 1 Narrating the past

The nature of history as a representation, as already noted, is well served by Frank R. Ankersmit, but the philosopher Richard Rorty has famously cast doubt on the notion of unproblematic representation in *Truth and Progress: Philosophical Papers Vol. 3* (Cambridge, 1998). See, in addition, his edited *The Linguistic Turn: Recent Essays in Philosophical Method* (Chicago, 1992 [1967]), and his most famous work, *Philosophy and the Mirror of Nature* (Princeton, 1979). For those who wish to pursue the philosophical debates in greater detail see Donald Davidson, *Inquiries into Truth and Interpretation* (Oxford, 1984) and his *Essays on Actions and Events* (Oxford, 1980). On history as a cultural representation see Martin L. Davies, *Historics: Why History Dominates Contemporary Society* (Abingdon and New York, 2005) and Alun Munslow, *Discourse and Culture: The Creation of America, 1870–1920* (London and New York, 1992). Almost alone in the United Kingdom, Keith Jenkins has confronted conventional historical thinking and practice. Essential reading for all historians is his re-issued *Rethinking History* (London, 2002 [1991]), *On 'What is History?'* (London, 1995), *The Postmodern History Reader* (London, 1997), *Why History? Reflections on the Possible End of History and Ethics under the Impact of the Postmodern* (London, 1999) and *Refiguring History* (London and New York, 2003).

▶ Chapter 2 History as content/story

The narrative model of history thinking and practice relies on the work of a variety of thinkers outside history. Among them are Ferdinand de Saussure, *Course in General Linguistics*, trans. Wade Baskin (Glasgow, 1974), Louis Hjelmslev, *Prolegomena to a Theory of Language*, trans. Francis J. Whitfield (Madison, 1963 [1943]) and *Language: An Introduction*, trans. Francis J. Whitfield (Madison, 1970). In addition see A.J. Greimas, *Structural Semantics: An Attempt at a Method*, trans. Danielle McDowell, Ronald Schleifer and Alan Velie (Lincoln, 1983 [1966]), Vladimir Propp, *Morphology of the Folk Tale* (Bloomington, 1958), Roland Barthes, 'Introduction to the Structural Analysis of Narratives' in Susan Sontag (ed.), *Barthes: Selected Writings* (Oxford, 1983), Jacques Derrida, *Writing and Difference* trans. Alan Bass (Chicago, 1978) and *Of Grammatology*, trans. G.C. Spivak (Baltimore, 1976).

Now a classic is Louis O. Mink, 'Narrative Form as a Cognitive Instrument' reprinted in Roberts (ed.) *op. cit.*, pp. 211–220, and Peter Munz, 'The Historical Narrative' in Michael Bentley (ed.) *Companion to Historiography* (New York and London, 1997). In addition to *Metahistory*, Hayden White's major texts include *Figural Realism: Studies in the Mimesis Effect* (Baltimore, 1998), *The Content of the Form: Narrative Discourse and Historical Representation* (Baltimore and London, 1987) and *Tropics of Discourse: Essays in Cultural Criticism* (Baltimore, 1978). Useful in addressing the literary nature of the historical enterprise is Keith Jenkins and Alun Munslow (eds), *The Nature of History: A Reader* (London and New York, 2004). More specialised but invaluable is Northrop Frye, *Anatomy of Criticism: Four Essays by Northrop Frye* (New York, 1967 [1957]).

► Chapter 3   Narrative and narration

The texts already noted by Gérard Genette and Seymour Chatman remain central here but see also Wayne Booth, *The Rhetoric of Fiction* (Chicago, 1961), and Gerald Prince, *Narratology: The Form and Functioning of Narrative* (Berlin, 1982). The work of Mieke Bal is significant. See 'The Narrating and the Focalizing: A Theory of the Agents in Narrative', trans. Jane E. Lewin, *Style*, 17 (1983), pp. 234–269, *Narratology: Introduction to the Theory of Narrative* (Toronto, 1985). Equally important is Monika Fludernik, 'New Wine in Old Bottles? Voice, Focalisation and New Writing', *New Literary History*, 32, 3 (2001), pp. 619–638, and Suzanne Fleischman, *Tense and Narrativity: From Medieval Performance to Modern Fiction* (Routledge, 1990). The work of Roland Barthes on the process of narration is essential. See his 'The Death of the Author' in Sean Burke (ed.) *Authorship: From Plato to Postmodernism: A Reader* (Edinburgh, 1995), pp. 125–130. To be read in tandem is Michel Foucault, 'What Is An Author?' in J.H. Harari (ed.), *Textual Strategies: Perspectives in Post-Structuralist Criticism* (London, 1979), pp. 141–160. Hayden White's analysis of focalisation is usefully introduced in the 'Introduction' to his *Tropics of Discourse: Essays in Cultural Criticism* (Baltimore, Johns Hopkins University Press, 1978), pp. 15–20. Of central importance once again is the Ricoeur trilogy. Still worth the effort is Mikhail Bakhtin, *The Dialogic Imagination: Four Essays*, Michael Holquist (ed.), trans. Caryl Emerson and Michael Holquist (Austin, TX, University of Texas Press, 1981). More generally see Philippe Carrard, *Poetics of the New History: French Historical Discourse from Braudel to Chartier* (Baltimore and London, Johns Hopkins University Press, 1995). A basic introduction to the theory of authorship is available in Andrew Bennett, *The Author* (New York and Abingdon, 2005). For an exemplary application of the theory and practice of the author-historian see Robert A. Rosenstone, *Mirror in the Shrine: American Encounters with Meiji Japan* (Cambridge and London, 1988). For an original and influential analysis of tense/time see Elizabeth Deeds Ermarth *Sequel to History* (Princeton, 1992). Also important is Kuisima Korhonen's edited collection, *Tropes for the Past: Hayden White and the History/Literature Debate* (Amsterdam and New York, Rodopi, 2006), and Alan Palmer, *Fictional Minds* (Lincoln, University of Nebraska Press, 2004). For the technically minded narrative historian see Jonathan Culpeper, *Language and Characterisation* (Harlow, Longman, 2001), and James Phelan, *Reading People, Reading Plots* (Chicago, University of Chicago Press, 1989).

▶ Chapter 4   History as expression

The literature on history modes of expression is growing at what seems to be an exponential rate. The key analyst of the epistemological relationship between film and history remains Robert A. Rosenstone. See his 'The Future of the Past: Film and the Beginnings of Postmodern History' in Vivian Sobchack (ed.), *The Persistence of History: Cinema, Television and the Modern Event* (New York, 1996), pp. 201–218; 'Does a Filmic Writing of History Exist?', *History and Theory*, 41, 4 (2002), pp. 135–144, *Visions of the Past: The Challenge of Film to Our Idea of History* (Cambridge MA, 1995), *Revisioning History: Film and the Construction of a New Past* (Princeton, NJ, 1995), *History on Film, Film on History* (Harlow, 2006). See, in addition, Marc Ferro, *Cinema and History* (Detroit, 1988) and 'Does and Filmic Writing of History Exist?', *Film and History*, 17, 4 (1987), pp. 81–89, and Richard Allen, *Projecting Illusion: Film Spectatorship and the Impression of Reality* (Cambridge, 1995). The series of articles in the 1988 *American Historical Review* Forum, 93, 5 (1988), on film and history is also a landmark. Once again Roland Barthes has made a contribution with 'The Realist Effect', *Film Reader No. 2* (Wisconsin, 1978), pp. 131–135. See also Siegfried Kracauer, *History: The Last things Before The Last* (Princeton, 1995 [1965]). On photography see Susan Sontag, *On Photography* (New York, 1973), and J.J. Long, 'History, Narrative and Photography in W.G. Sebald's *Die Ausgewanderten' Modern Language Review*, 98, 1 (2003), pp. 117–137. Of interest is Marie-Laure Ryan, 'The Modes of Narrativity and Their Visual Metaphors', *Style*, 26 (1992), pp. 368–387. A wide-ranging analysis is offered by Alison Landsberg's *Prosthetic Memory: The Transformation of American Remembrance in the Age of Mass Culture* (New York, 2004).

On the graphic novel see Hugo Frey and Benjamin Noys, 'History in the Graphic Novel', in *Rethinking History: The Journal of Theory and Practice*, 6 (2002), pp. 255–260, and Art Spiegelman, *Maus I: A Survivor's Tale: My father Bleeds History* (New York, 1986), *Maus II: A Survivor's Tale: And Here My Troubles Began* (New York, 1991) and *Comix, Essays, Graphics and Scraps* (New York, 1998). Another contribution by Hayden White is his 'Historical Emplotment and the Problem of Truth' in Saul

Friedlander (ed.), *Probing the Limits of Representation* (Cambridge, 1992), pp. 37–53. On remembrance and memorialisation see Jay Winter, *Sites of Memory, Sites of Mourning: The Great War in European Cultural History* (Cambridge, 1998 [1995]) and Pierre Nora, *Realms of Memory: The Construction of the French Past*, trans. Arthur Goldhammer (New York, 1997), and Susan Davies, 'History and Heritage' in Peter Lambert and Phillipp Schofield (eds) *Making History: An Introduction to the History and Practices of a Discipline* (London and New York, 2004), pp. 280–289. On public history see Susan Porter Benson, Stephen Briar and Roy Rosenzweig (eds) *Presenting the Past: Essays on History and the Public* (Philadelphia, 1986), Ludmilla Jordanova, *History in Practice* (London, 2000), and Raphael Samuel, *Theatres of Memory*, 2 vols (London, 1998).

On digital representation see David J. Staley, *Computers, Visualization, and History: How New Technology Will Transform Our Understanding of the Past* (Armonk, 2002), Marie-Laure Ryan, *Possible Worlds, Artificial Intelligence, and Narrative Theory* (Bloomington, 1991), Janet H. Murray, *Hamlet on the Holodeck: The Future of Narrative in Cyberspace* (Cambridge, 1997), and Mark Poster, 'Manifesto for a History of the Media' in Keith Jenkins, Sue Morgan and Alun Munslow (eds), *Manifestos for Historians* (London and New York, 2007).

▶ Chapter 5   The past, the facts, and history

There are many 'classic' texts in this area. One could do worse than start with Patrick Gardiner, *The Nature of Historical Explanation* (Oxford, 1952), C. Behan McCullagh, *The Truth of History* (London and New York, 1998) and his *The Logic of History: Putting Postmodernism into Perspective* (New York and London, 2004). In addition see Martin Bunzl, *Real History* (London and New York, 1997), Perez Zagorin, 'History, the Referent, and Narrative. Reflections on Postmodernism now', *History and Theory*, 38 (1999), David Carr, 'Narrative and the Real World: An Argument for Continuity', *History and Theory*, 25 (1986), pp. 117–131. See also his *Time, Narrative and History* (Bloomington, Indiana University Press, 1991 [1986]) and 'Getting the Story Straight: Narrative and Historical Knowledge' in Jerzy Topolski (ed.) *Historiography Between Modernism and Postmodernism: Contributions to the Methodology of the Historical Research* (Amsterdam and Atlanta, 1994), pp. 119–134. Another text by William Dray worthy of attention is 'Narrative and Historical Realism' reprinted in Roberts (ed.), *op. cit.*, pp. 157–180, and *Laws and Explanation in History* (Oxford, 1966 [1957]). Andrew P. Norman's 'Telling it Like it Was: Historical Narratives on their Own Terms' reprinted in Roberts (ed.), *op. cit.*, pp. 181–196, and John Zammito, 'Ankersmit and Historical Representation', *History and Theory*, 44, 2 (2005), pp. 155–181.

► **Chapter 6   Understanding [in] history**

An excellent introduction to historical explanation is William Dray's *Laws and Explanation in History* (Oxford, 1966 [1957]). The classic texts remain Carl G. Hempel, *Aspects of Scientific Explanation* (New York, 1965), Karl Popper, *The Logic of Scientific Discovery* (New York, 1959), and Patrick L. Gardiner, *The Nature of Historical Explanation* (Oxford, 1961 [1952]). More recently see Mark Bevir, *The Logic of the History of Ideas* (Cambridge, 1999). A solid introductory survey of historical thinking and practice is Donald M. MacRaild and Avram Taylor, *Social Theory and Social History* (Houndmills and New York, 2004).

On language and explanation see J.L. Austin, *How to do Things with Words* (Oxford, 1975 [1962]), C. Behan McCullagh, *Justifying Historical Descriptions* (Cambridge, 1984), Wolfgang Iser, *The Act of Reading: A Theory of Aesthetic Response* (Baltimore, 1978), Bryan D. Palmer, *Descent into Discourse: The Reification of Language and the Writing of Social History* (Philadelphia, 1990). A book-length example of experimental history is Edmund Morris, *Dutch: A Memoir of Ronald Reagan* (New York, 1999). On experimental history more generally see the 'Introduction: Practice and Theory', *Experiments in Rethinking History*, Alun Munslow and Robert A. Rosenstone (eds) (London and New York, 2004). In that collection are a number of experimental histories but in particular see Greg Dening, *Writing, Re-writing the Beach: An Essay*, pp. 30–55. A further book-length experimental approach is to be found in Hans Ulrich Gumbrecht, *In 1926: Living at the Edge of Time* (Cambridge MA: London, England, 1997).

The-past-*as*-history notion, which acknowledges the postmodern epistemologically sceptical understanding of history, can be approached through two early editorials in the journal *Rethinking History: The Journal of Theory and Practice* 1 (1997), pp. 1–20 and 111–123. See, in addition, Alun Munslow *Deconstructing History* (London and New York, 2006 [1997]), *The Routledge Companion to Historical Studies* (New York and London, 2005 [2000]), and Keith Jenkins and Alun Munslow, *What is History? A Reader* (London and New York, 2004). Also of importance is Hans-Robert Jauss, *Toward an Aesthetic of Reception*, trans. Timothy Bahti (Minneapolis, 1982).

► **Chapter 7   The oar in water**

Historians do not, in the normal course of their activities, read much on objectivity, truth and relativism especially in the context of the narrative-making logic of history. Nevertheless, it becomes necessary to break this habit if we are to more fully understand the nature of history. An essential start is with a comparison between the approaches to history through the polarised perspectives of Hayden White and C. Behan McCullagh (see the texts already noted). But there are a number of other texts which are valuable, not least Michael Oakeshott, *Experience and Its Modes* (Cambridge, 1990 [1933]), Leon Goldstein, *Historical Knowing* (Austin, 1976), and Michael C. Lemon, *Philosophy of History: A Guide for Students* (London and New York, 2003). For those of a more philosophical bent the following are essential: Hans-Georg Gadamer, *Truth and Method* (New York, 1975), Martin Heidegger, *Being and Time* trans. J. Macquarrie and E. Robinson (Oxford, 1962), Michel Foucault, *Power/Knowledge: Selected Interviews and Other Writings, 1972–1977*, edited by Colin Gordon (Harvester Press, 1980), and Richard Rorty, *Objectivity, Relativism and Truth: Philosophical Papers Vol. 1* (Cambridge, 1991). See also Donald Davidson, *Inquiries into Truth and Interpretation* (Oxford, 1984), and Patrick Finney, 'Ethics, historical relativism and Holocaust Denial', *Rethinking History: The Journal of Theory and Practice*, 2 (1997). For one of the most sophisticated recent understandings of relativism in all its manifestations see Robert Eaglestone, *The Holocaust and the Postmodern* (Oxford, 2004).

Index